The English Saints

Trefor Jones was educated at Colfe's School, Cambridge University [Corpus Christi College], London University and the College of St Mark and St John. He holds degrees in Anglo-Saxon, Norse and Celtic Studies and in Economic History.

He is a tutor for the WEA and is at present engaged in research into early English ecclesiastical biography and East Anglian regional history. He is a regular contributor to various regional and national historical and heritage journals.

His other interests include politics [of a reform persuasion] and aspects of the natural sciences – notably evolution, genetics, quantum theory and cosmology.

He has been a clergyman of the Orthodox Church since 1984 and has assisted with church communities in the East Anglian region.

He has lived in East Anglia with his family for twenty-six years and currently resides at Wells-next-the Sea, Norfolk.

The English Saints

East Anglia

Trefor Jones

CANTERBURY
PRESS
Norwich

© Trefor Jones 1999

First published in 1999 by The Canterbury Press Norwich
(a publishing imprint of Hymns Ancient & Modern Limited
a registered charity)
St Mary's Works, St Mary's Plain
Norwich, Norfolk, NR3 3BH

British Library Cataloguing in Publication Data

A catalogue record for this book is available
from the British Library

ISBN 1-85311-258-5

Typeset by Rowland Phototypesetting Ltd
and printed in Great Britain by
Biddles Ltd, Guildford and King's Lynn

'Non Angli, sed Angeli . . .'

'Not Angles, but Angels . . .'
(St Gregory of Rome – the Apostle to the English)

This book is dedicated to Barbara, Rosemary, Christopher
and Antony;
to my parents, late parents-in-law, and my grandparents; to
all of my family and my many friends, past and present.

Deo Gratias

It is also dedicated to the memory of three late friends,
Archimandrite David,
Anna Dimascio
and
Ivan Fletcher.

'Amongst the Saints, give rest, O Lord . . .'

Contents

Maps, Figures and Plates

The English Saints

<caption>xii</caption>

Acknowledgements

I should like to place on record my sincere acknowledgement of the following persons who assisted me, either directly or indirectly, in the preparation of this book and without whom, in one way or another, it would not have been possible.

My indebtedness goes firstly to my long-suffering wife, Barbara, who 'miraculously' combined the demanding exigencies of night-time nursing duties at our local hospital with journeying to the libraries and along the highways and byways of East Anglia, assisting me in the collection of information and frequently amazing me with her own perception. This book is a considerable part of her labour as well as of my own! A word of thanks must also go to my son, Antony, who provided me with the facilities of a quiet refuge for work in the later stages (Norfolk villages are not as tranquil as one might suppose!).

I must also express my sincere gratitude to those who inspired me to pursue this field of study during my recent return to academic life at Cambridge University, either by the inspiration of their lectures and publications, or simply by personal encouragement, notably Dr Simon Keynes (Trinity College) particularly for his assistance with some Anglo-Saxon nomenclature, Professor David Dumville (Girton College), Professor Michael Lapidge (Clare College), Dr Catherine Cubitt (now of Birmingham University), Dr Lesley Abrams (now of the University of Wales), and several former friends, fellow-students and researchers within the University's Department of Anglo-Saxon, Norse and Celtic Studies. My thanks also go to the Master and Fellows of Corpus Christi College,

Cambridge (my own *alma mater*), for having allowed me the continued use of the College Library when required.

I should also like to express my acknowledgement of those who, in an earlier period of my life, gave me an awareness of our own English saints, not a few of them East Anglians, and an appreciation of the early Church, and who were of my own Christian Church communion. Notable amongst these was the late Archimandrite David of Walsingham, who in many ways laid down the present path of restored Church iconography in this field. This help and encouragement has continued into recent years, particularly from Mr Leon Liddament, of the Icon Studio of St Seraphim, Walsingham, who kindly supplied the contemporary icon reproductions depicted in this work (and yet another place of peaceful working refuge!). I am also obligated to his assistant, Ms Beccy Nelson, for her help in rendering the drawings of St Fursey's Monastery and the exemplars of the Sutton Hoo Collection; and also to 'Konica' of Fakenham for last-minute help with reprographic problems.

I should also like to place on record my thanks to the Dean and Chapter of Ely Cathedral for having permitted me to photograph the memorials of St Etheldreda and St Owen there. Mention must also be made of those responsible for the various parish churches in Norfolk and Suffolk who permitted me to photograph in them, particularly the Rector of St Nicholas' Church, East Dereham, for the photography of the panel of St Witburgha in that church and the rood screen of North Tuddenham Church. Special thanks are due to Mr Edwin Rose of the Norfolk Landscape Archaeology Unit, who drew my attention to the possible connections between West Dereham and St Withiburga. The map of Anglo-Saxon England is taken from David Hill's *Atlas of Anglo-Saxon England* and similarly the reference to East Anglian pilgrimage and relic centres. The Travelogue takes into account some of the sites listed in the Revd Andrew Phillips' *The Hallowing of England*.

Finally, and by no means least, my thanks go to the staff of the Cambridge University Library and the British Library for their incalculable help in tracking down elusive works of reference; to the Norfolk Archaeological Society, Norwich, for their facility of the Garsett House Library, and to the staff of Wells-next-the-Sea Library for their helping in 'calling-up' books that at times escaped my capture elsewhere!

I am also extremely grateful to Ms Carol Twinch for having kindly sent me a copy of her work on St Walstan and to my editor, Mrs Christine Smith, for having suffered my interminable delays!

This book does not profess to be definitive or authoritative. I have only sought to introduce the subject to others, whom, I hope, will enjoy exploring the spiritual history of East Anglia, as I have done.

Trefor Jones
Lent 1999

Introduction

This book is in many ways a type of travelogue, one that journeys
not only along the highways and byways of East Anglia, that
attractive and accessible part of England, but also to its former
(and even current) hallowed places. In one sense, it is also a
journey through time. The journey takes us to a seemingly remote
age when religion and warfare were the dominant determinants,
though we might reasonably question to what extent either was
the main preoccupation of the ordinary men and women who
lived through those times. Life during the early centuries dealt
with here was short and brutal for most people, whether due to
the basic struggle for survival in the face of economic and natural
disasters, the ever-present ravages of plagues and diseases, or the
power-seeking caprices of rulers. One might be tempted to say
that little has changed during the succeeding ages, and in a sense
this is true, for large swathes of the human population still live
under precarious circumstances which would not have been
unfamiliar to our early English ancestors. Our Western world has
made stupendous advances in terms of technology, particularly
during the twentieth century, together with remarkable improve-
ments in the length and quality of life, and a degree of protection
against epidemics. Advances in scientific understanding and tech-
nological development have gone hand in hand with a preferred
reliance upon reason and a lesser one upon traditional faith
systems, resulting in a decline in institutionalized forms and
expressions of religion, but it would appear that the basic human
instincts which former religious faith and fervour fulfilled are still
very much there. Karl Marx regarded religion as an 'opium of

the people', i.e. a palliative from the harsh conditions of their lives caused by adverse economic and social circumstances, and he predicted that when the latter improved, the former would disappear.

Marx, it would seem, got it wrong. Religion, even in its most traditional and popular forms, continues to exercise much the same power and influence over human beings as it has done for centuries and millennia – one only needs to visit the popular pilgrimage centres of the great world religions such as Benares, Lourdes and the southern Mediterranean countries, for evidence of this. Even in this country, where it seems that traditional religion has been displaced, ancient Christian venues such as Walsingham, Glastonbury and Canterbury continue to attract thousands of pilgrims and visitors every year; and the last three decades have also witnessed a revival in more fundamentalist and traditionalist forms of Christianity, together with what can only really be described as a type of 'neo-paganism', which purportedly seeks to 'rediscover' the pre-Christian beliefs and customs of our very early ancestors (whilst failing to take account of the fact that we know and understand next to nothing about them!). As Professor Raymond Page has said, 'Our age shows a lamentable tendency to flee from reason, common sense and practicality into the realms of superstition and fantasy.[1] Even the cultist adulation given to secular 'idols' and their associations (as often as not the creations of the mass media) by many who profess not to be religious in any way, mirrors older forms of religious fervour and devotion and can justifiably be regarded as a type of 'secular paganism' (i.e. non-Christian cultism). All in all, it would seem that much of this is not so much a reaction against Western secularism and materialism, but more an expression of basic and deeply-felt instincts and needs found within most human beings.

This book deals with religion as its central theme – the religion of our ancestors and of an earlier era as it was in a particular part of England. It takes as its primary theme those who in that former time were regarded and venerated as its saints, champions and exemplars of the form of Christianity that once prevailed there;

though having stated that, I must utter a few words of reservation and caution. I have approached the subject of our early English saints (starting with those of East Anglia) as an historian and not as a theologian or a regurgitator of medieval mythology. The approach of a serious Church historian must be a scientific and rational one, requiring an objective and critical examination of the available evidence, which must also apply to the study of hagiography (ie the 'Lives' and traditions of the saints); though with regard to the latter serious difficulties arise, given that, as we shall see, hagiography cannot be regarded as history even though it may provide us with some clues to such. What might be termed a 'pseudo-historical' approach to these subjects is often little more than romantic nonsense, presented, as much of it was during the Victorian era and well beyond, often quite authoritatively, notably dealing with the subject of the 'Celtic Church' and its saints, and in its appearance yet again in respect of the early English (ie Anglo-Saxon) saints. The reader, hopefully, will find none of that approach in this study, such as it is. As a Church historian, I have taken the saints and their 'Lives' as my central theme and have endeavoured to study the saints as real people within the context of the times in which they lived, which includes the political and ecclesiastical framework of that age. In this respect and given this approach, pure history – ecclesiastical and political – intertwines with hagiographical tradition and it is impossible to take a realistic approach without reference to all three. The reader will, then, find as much history as saintly matters here, and I have allowed for the fact that for many people the historical and topographical circumstances dealt with may be unfamiliar, given that we live in an age which is perhaps less familiar with saints or concepts of sanctity than previous times. I have tried to familiarize the reader with these topics in what I hope is an explanatory and introductory way, and one which may serve to encourage further exploration, whether the interest be in the saints, the early English Church, or the history of those times. Indeed, the history of this period and the theological background to its saints have already been amply dealt with by others who are far more erudite than myself (though much remains to be done in respect of East Anglia) and I have tried to point the newcomer to these matters to such sources. Having made, as it were, an *apologia* for this book, we now need look at the terms of reference and a few definitions.

East Anglia

Firstly, the reader might well ask. 'Why East Anglia and what is meant by it?'

My answer to the first part of this question is that I have had the pleasure of living, working and studying in East Anglia, which in the modern sense usually means Norfolk, Suffolk and Cambridgeshire, for nearly half of my life. Like many who are acquainted with the region, I have been impressed by the magnificence of its heritage and reminders of its past, which can be seen in the form of church remains, former monasteries, and surviving churches and cathedrals. All these have lingering traditions and evocative pointers to an earlier age which might retrospectively (though romantically, I confess!) be termed a vanished 'Christian age' – an age of faith, kings and warlords, churchmen and saints. Given that during this age and for many subsequent centuries East Anglia was one of the richest and most powerful kingdoms and regions within England, exercising an intermittent political independence until the tenth century, and that it was possessed of a rich and powerful Church which was part of that framework, it merits, in my estimation, a study as an entity in its own right, as do also its saints and their Church. Having said this, I hope to demonstrate in future studies that in most respects the Church and its saints in East Anglia were not noticeably different from those of any other contemporaneous early English kingdom. One slight difference is that for East Anglian saints, unlike the saints of former Wessex and Northumbria, there seems to be something of a paucity of information, and much the same can be said in terms of its Church culture of that time: it appears to have produced no 'super-ecclesiastics' comparable to St Dunstan and St Aethelwold of Wessex, though much of the reason for this seems to have been due to politics rather than to personal or saintly propensities.

East Anglia is also a tantalizingly difficult part of England to deal with, as I have implied, due to lack of primary source material and information, and, for the purposes of this book and for convenience more than anything else I have not adhered strictly to the historical definition of East Anglia. East Anglia proper, and certainly during the times that we are considering here, means the present-day counties of Norfolk and Suffolk, straying into the eastern Fenlands. The Fens themselves do at one time seem to have comprised a part of East Anglia, and the Venerable Bede, one of our main sources for the early period of the East Anglian kingdom and Church, considered them to have been such. For most of the subsequent centuries the Fens were clearly an integral part of the Midlands Kingdom of Mercia, though East Anglian interest in this frontier zone was ever present. Thus I have taken the liberty of including the Fenlands and even the easternmost Midlands in my sweep of study, whilst excluding that other eastern county, and former kingdom, of Essex, so that what we are really examining is East Anglia and much of the eastern region of England.

Saints and Relics

Traditionally, and by definition, the saints are those who literally share in the holiness of God, their lives having borne witness to the authenticity and truth of the Christian gospel which is the sure gift of God's holiness to mankind. The Church classified the saints, in terms of its liturgical commemoration of them, according to the particular aspects of their holiness, i.e. apostles, evangelists, martyrs, confessors and so on,[2] and in the earliest times it seems to have been popular acclaim which led local Christian communities to venerate a person who had suffered death through persecution, or who had been of such outstanding holiness that none could doubt his or her eternal destiny.[3] There was no absolute agreement as to what constituted sanctity in this earlier time that we are to examine, and many types of virtue came to be regarded as meriting acknowledgement or glorification, e.g. great asceticism, the defence of the faith, or the pastoral work and teaching of a good bishop.[4] Formal canonization was not established in the West until 1215 onwards and previously the process often only required the sanction of a local bishop. By the end of the ninth century, the actual 'translation' of the body of a saint was regarded as a formal canonization (whether a bishop had sanctioned it or not, though the bishops often investigated claims and made decisions).[5]

'Lives' of the Saints

The saints were regarded as people who had entered heaven through the God-given exercise of spiritual power in their lives, demonstrated by Christian virtues and miracles, and many influential written accounts of saints' lives recurred which influenced subsequent writings (or hagiographies) and in this respect, for the English Church, Continental sources were of extreme importance. Some hagiography was written to reflect the devotions, attitudes and needs of the age, and the early English placed a great emphasis upon virginity and the renunciation of worldly status, which contrasted with neighbouring *Frankia* (France) where matronhood and widowhood ranked equally in importance. The recorded and acclaimed miracles of a saint, together with a written 'Life', would sustain a veneration (or cult) and the clergy and the monks often encouraged this as certain acclaimed saints seem to have been able to exercise a powerful patronage (e.g. St Etheldreda of Ely and St Edmund the Martyr). Each church had its own saints and relics and it seems that about three hundred saints were culted in Anglo-Saxon England (the period we are mainly dealing with) of which thirty were to be found in East Anglia, i.e. approximately a tenth of the total. The most popular saints seem to have been those who were regarded as 'confessors' and who were generally found amongst the monks and the clergy and who were thus particularly suitable for the latter's purposes; second only to these were the martyrs who were often used as a rallying inspiration against aggressors. Most of the acclaimed saints were, as we shall see, of royal or noble stock and these cults served to promote those interests, and the hagiographies invariably embellished the real circumstances of the saints' lives for a definite purpose.

The purpose of hagiography was to praise the saint and to edify the reader and not to provide a historical biography (which is why we cannot treat hagiography as history), though sometimes clues to such biographical details can be found tucked away in the accounts. In a sense, hagiography was akin to Church iconography, where the depiction of the saint was executed for the expression of the eternal purpose of God Incarnate – Christ – through his saints.[6] Such 'Lives' would record portents relating to the saint's birth, miracles worked, virtues witnessed, and posthumous manifestations of sanctity. Many of the 'Lives' were used liturgically by the Church and were read aloud to assembled congregations during the vigil services on the eves of the feasts of particular saints.

Not a few of the original 'Lives' of the earlier saints, some of which had been written reasonably close to the date of the saint's death, were partly based upon living recollections and oral testimonies, though they were later embellished, and quite often fictionally and erroneously distorted, by Norman churchmen who were seeking to further promote the power and prestige of their monasteries who claimed the patronage of the saint.[7] Even during the earlier period, competition between churches and monasteries led to the introduction of even more cults and the increasing discovery of incorrupt relics. An Anglo-Saxon Church document, the *Secgan*, helpfully indicated who was venerated where, whilst names and accounts of lives and miracles were recorded also in Church litanies, liturgical calendars, martyrologies and passions. The 'Lives' of the English saints started to appear in the eighth century and more appeared in the tenth century, notably those of sainted bishops and powerful Church prelates, as a result of the Monastic Reform Movement, with a further flowering in the eleventh century. Royal saints became quite notable during the later period, reflecting the growing power and prestige of the kings, and from the tenth century onwards we see a development of very localized cults, centred in the deeper and remoter regions of the countryside, some of them semi-Christian (and even non-Christian) in origin, such as the East Anglian cults of St Walstan, St Ives, and the Virgin Mary at Walsingham, which reflect a greater involvement of the laity and the attempt by the Church to fully integrate them.

Relics and Pilgrimages

We will notice, in any serious study of the Church during this period, the importance and centrality attached to the relics of the saints (i.e. their bodily remains) and their significance in terms of prestige for the churches and monasteries that possessed them and as focal points for pilgrimage. The collection of relics at this time was assiduous, based upon the notion that a spiritual charisma resided in the physical relics of saints and that the relics of such, like their earthly associations to which pilgrimage was also made, represented a focus of the saint's virtues – a meeting of heaven and earth. The official teaching of the Church was that the body was sanctified and transfigured together with the soul and was thus deserving of great reverence after death. It was believed that, as the grace of God had been active in the saint's body during life, so it remained active in the relics after death, and that God used those relics as a channel of divine power and, on occasions, as an instrument of healing. It was also believed that in some cases the bodies of the saints were miraculously preserved from corruption, and, even when this had not happened, great veneration continued to be shown. In practice, and at a popular level, the attitude to relics often went far beyond this, and in an age of superstition and credulity a brisk trade was often carried on and fortunes made in the purveying of relics, many of them of doubtful authenticity or even outright fabrication. Even secondary relics, such as handkerchiefs and girdles, and sometimes tertiary relics, such as pieces of stone or earth from holy places, were regarded as instruments of healing power.

The division of the bodily relics of saints (though never officially approved by the Church) usually went hand in hand with the spread of the cult to other parts of the country and even further, and it became a distinction for a church or monastery to possess the relics of distant churches, one rivalling another in their number and quality, the acquisition of which often entailed the spending of vast sums of money.[8] The taking of land from a monastery that possessed the relics of a saint was viewed as theft from the saint (St Etheldreda was regarded as the undying defender of Ely Abbey's lands!), though the theft of the actual relics from one church by another seems to have been interpreted as being 'with the saint's consent' and the following exposition of the relics and any revealed incorruption would be considered and used as a 'seal of approval'.[9] The relics themselves were usually contained in portable reliquaries and even within statues and icons, and were sealed within altars and sometimes the walls of the churches. They were used for oath-taking, trials by ordeal and penitential processions, and the taking of oaths on relics was regarded as solemn and having been undertaken in the presence of the saint – to break the oath was perjury and sacrilege. By the eleventh century, the veneration of relics and the solemnity of oaths taken thereon had become virtually a national institution.

The early English were noted for their love of pilgrimage and many would have visited the shrines of the saints not only within their own regions, but even sometimes venturing elsewhere in the country and as far away as Rome, Jerusalem and Compostella. Wills of the period often refer to prospective pilgrimages and there seems to have been an impulse deeply embedded within early English (and Celtic) society for this, perhaps originating from some of the extreme notions of asceticism and voluntary exile to be found in the early Irish Church. In some ways, pilgrimage itself represented a sort of 'iconographical' representation of the true Christian concept of life, in that life was a pilgrimage to the heavenly kingdom. How far this notion was fully understood, given that many of the pilgrimages to saints' relics were purely for the purpose of obtaining cures and miraculous favours, is difficult to assess retrospectively, and a frequent and simple factor may simply have been that of wanderlust, together with confessors sending penitents on pilgrimage for a form of spiritual cleansing.

The Kings

It is impossible to look at the saints of this time without taking note of the role and influence of the kings and the secular realm of politics in which the former, as real living people, were invariably caught up. East Anglia was a separate kingdom, with varying fortunes, until the tenth century and its earlier kings were noted as having been powerful and influential protectors and patrons of the Church, much of what we can say about them having been applicable to their contemporaries elsewhere in England. They adopted Christianity, in the seventh century, for a variety of reasons including genuine personal conviction, though there was at all times an overriding political determinant. By the seventh century, the Church was *the* great civilizing force in Europe and it was through the Church that earlier Roman tradition had survived and was perpetuated for the education of the new barbarian civilizations that had emerged from the fifth century onwards. It was because it was Roman more than because it was Christian that these barbarian kings embraced the Church, which thus enabled them for centuries to come to acquire and maintain a control over their societies. For most of the kings, the patronage of the Church offered new ways of re-inforcing, or expanding, their political power. Christianity, in the form of the institutionalized Church, offered a hierarchical model in which authority was descending and which legitimatized the king's influence over others; and the baptism of client-kings, with the over-king acting as a sponsor, implied regal superiority. The clergy with their useful skills in literacy also had the power to direct divine favour towards their royal patrons and the authority of bishops offered ambitious kings the means to export priests and subordinate bishops into the courts of their clients, thus placing a check upon any separatist tendencies. This can be seen particularly with the establishment of churches and royal monasteries in borderland and frontier areas.[10]

Having, as it were, established the nature and location of our journey, it is time to venture upon it.

Map 1 *The England of Bede* c. *731. Place names from the* Ecclesiastical History. *Reproduced with permission from David Mill's* Atlas of Anglo-Saxon England, Oxford, 1989, p. 30

I

Darkness before Dawn

Origins

Sixth-century Anglo-Saxon England was a land entrenched in paganism (though we might question whether this was entirely so), having emerged out of the wreckage of late Roman Britain, a province that had been at least nominally Christian by the early fourth century. This emergence had been fairly contiguous with the decline of the Roman presence here in its later stages and was the result of about a hundred and fifty years of transformation, i.e. a process begun by the end of the fourth century AD and fairly complete by the early sixth century, though even this is probably on over-generalization. The transformation had at first been gradual and then it seems to have been heavily re-inforced by 'shock waves' of external barbarian attacks – Celtic from the west and Germanic from the east – the latter eventually taking control of the major part of what would emerge as England, following upon attacks and significant settlements in key areas of the east of the island, such as East Anglia, the north-eastern coast and Kent.

The eclipse of Roman Britain during the fifth century also resulted in the eclipse of the Christian Church, at least as a significant presence in a substantial part of the island, and notably in areas of Germanic settlement and control, which contrasted with similarly affected parts of Western Europe, such as Gaul, though there were probably complex reasons for this. The only reasonable conclusion we can come to is that late Roman Britain may have been subjected to a more concentrated settlement than its Continental neighbours (though this is arguable) and that perhaps, due to its maritime exposure, it was more vulnerable to attack. Also, Britain may have been less Romanized than Gaul and was thus more susceptible to the imposition of another barbarian culture and religion upon that of the Celtic substratum. The Church of the late Roman period in Britain seems to have been mainly town-based, holding the allegiance of the middle classes, e.g. officials and traders, and the towns were smaller and more sparsely populated than their Continental counterparts. They were certainly well into decline and decay by the end of the fourth century and we can only guess as to the extent of the hold of Christianity by the onset of the invasion period, though it seems likely that it was very fragile and probably barely present at all over large swathes of the country, particularly the rural areas.

For East Anglia, set against this general background, it is even more difficult to make any estimation. The only significant town, and a small one at that by wider Roman standards, was *Venta Icenorum* (modern-day Caistor St Edmund in Norfolk), the cantonal capital of the powerful Iceni tribe who dominated Norfolk and much of Suffolk. There were shore forts at *Branodunum* (Brancaster) on the Norfolk coast, together with Caister and Burgh Castle, and Walton in Suffolk, and there may well have been adherents of Christianity at these as well as at *Venta*, though we cannot assume that the members of the garrisons, whose origins lay outside Britain, were any more Christian than the native population in the rural hinterland. In any case, much of the apparent Christianity that there was may well have been purely nominal, for the religion had become officialized by the Empire only from the fourth century onwards and seems to have acculturalized many of the old beliefs and customs – a type of syncretism. As we shall see later, it probably took three hundred years at least to fully Christianize Anglo-Saxon England (arguably seven hundred), so there is no reason to suppose that fourth-century Britain was anything but barely Christianized, and in the case of outlying and quite remote regions such as East Anglia, the situation may still have been fairly bleak for the Church.

The decline of the towns had also gone hand in hand with the introduction into Britain, by Romano-British officials, of Germanic warriors, many from outside the bounds of the ailing Empire, and many also pagan. They seem to have been hired by the native British aristocracy for the purpose of helping to contain and combat other Germanic tribesmen who were freebooting and openly attacking the coastal regions and more accessible parts of eastern Britain, probably in a similar way to the Vikings some centuries later. With the absence, from the early fifth century onwards, of any serious semblance of centralized Roman authority, native British warlords seized absolute power, ruling as regional kings over many of the former tribal units of Roman Britain (in East Anglia this would have corresponded to the territories of the Iceni and Trinovantes – roughly Norfolk and Suffolk). As they struggled against each other and their rival kingdoms for power, they exacted tribute from both the local native population and their imported Germanic allies, no doubt using the external trappings of Christianity and the vestigial remnants of Roman authority and identity in order to confirm their status. The mercenaries were initially given the same status as the native population and were supported from the proceeds of taxation, together with grants of land for settlement, disputes over which would become the excuse for power seizures by the newcomers at the expense of the British population and this may well have been frequent. There is a strong possibility that, at least at the outset, East Anglia was an early focus for quite significant and populous Germanic settlement particularly around its more coastal areas. It was not too easy to approach by land, being surrounded by rivers, swampy fens and forests, but it had a large and vulnerable coastline and it was from the sea that it was the most accessible, the North Sea being, by this time, a principal route for various Germanic peoples.

It does seem that many of these early Germanic settlers (who probably came from fairly diverse areas outside and inside the disintegrating Roman Empire, and whom posterity, rather too conveniently and following the definition of the eighth-century chronicler Bede, would generically describe as Anglo-Saxons) temporarily became allies and land-holding retainers of the native British establishment, numerically in a minority, but even as such appearing to have been more vigorous and determined than their temporary masters whom they would overthrow.[1] By the early fifth century (in the case of East Anglia) they may have completely overthrown the surviving British ruling caste, who then doubtless, together with the servile population, came to adopt the speech, customs and religion of these newcomers. Christianity under these conditions would no longer have been fashionable for those whose primary interest was survival and who might have been trying to hang on to at least some of their dwindling power. For any whose Christian conviction was deep, there remained the option of martyrdom or flight, and it has to be said that though we have no recorded names of any who underwent martyrdom in East Anglia at this time, this does not mean it did not happen. Flight by those who had the means probably did take place, but it could only have been a serious option for the well-to-do and their retainers, and maybe some of the clergy, and, where this did occur, it may well have given rise to the discarded myth of the flight of the Britons westwards into Wales and Cornwall at the hands of the Anglo-Saxons, who were supposed to have repopulated most of the country. What counted ultimately for the native British and officially Christian population, whose descendants remained in increasingly Germanicized East Anglia, as elsewhere, was not religion, but survival and continuity, albeit requiring adapted ways, speech and customs.

Bede, to whom we have referred, would later level bitter accusation against the native British Church and the native Christian British for the reason that they had done nothing to convert the Anglo-Saxons after their arrival in this island (in contrast to the efforts of the later Irish of the seventh century), and he deemed that God had judged and punished them for it.[2] It is usually assumed that Bede was referring to the Welsh, i.e. the British of that territory, but he probably had as much in mind the surviving native population who were supposedly Christian to some degree or other, surviving in large tracts of what was, by the onset of the sixth century, fast becoming Anglo-Saxon England. His acrimony may well tie in with what Gildas, himself a native British Christian and a fiercely polemical Church-writer of the late fifth and early sixth centuries, had to say about his own countrymen and fellow-Christians during the onset of the barbarian troubles. Gildas tells of a rebellion by the barbarians who had been brought in and allowed to settle by the British, during which they devastated town and country (and there is evidence of a fifth-century massacre at *Venta Icenorum*), many of whose inhabitants, leaders and churchmen were slaughtered, the Church leaders (bishops?) and priests having been slain with the people – the church altars congealed with blood and the sanctuaries laid low.[3]

The Germanic settlers, particularly the later waves who were not in the pay or invitation of the British, were out for wholesale conquest and the creation of their own territories, and Bede says that those who took East Anglia were Angles – hence East Anglia's eventual name, originating from Angelus in southern Denmark. The reality, as we have already suggested, was not so certain. Other sources refer to Swabians (Suevi) from southern Germany, Frisians from the Dutch coast and even Goths – clearly a hotch-potch of peoples from various tribes. Although Bede ascribes 'Saxons' to other areas of England, there is archaeological evidence for them also in East Anglia at this turbulent time, and to complicate the picture even further, there seems to be some evidence of Irish settlement in the region, and the Irish themselves would remain pagan until the late fifth century. There also seem to have been two waves of settlement, one in the early fifth century and another in the later part of the century, the first probably having arisen from the semi-controlled and permitted settlement already referred to. The second may have been the uninvited wave, perhaps those referred to by Gildas and who dealt the final shock-blow to what was left of the crumbling Romano-British and Christian culture and structure; and, as we have suggested, this may well have occurred somewhat earlier in East Anglia than in other parts of the island. A rather dubious historical source (a handful of annals preserved from twelfth- and thirteenth-century chronicles) does in fact refer to an invasion of East Anglia from Germany in 527, which could also have been about the time that Gildas was writing, although, as we shall see, there seems to be some evidence for further pagan Germanic invasion of the region with Scandinavian connections towards about the middle or end of the sixth century.

Let us return to the question of how Christian 'proto'-East Anglia had been during the sub-Roman period, and of just how much recognizable Christianity, and its related culture, there had been for the barbarians to wreck and destroy. We have already suggested that the Church was probably a minority following, set amongst the strong native paganism of the rural areas. Any Church administration that there had been, e.g. episcopal organization (there were certainly no monasteries at this stage), would have been wiped out by the barbarians, as Gildas implied. Survivors, such as there were, may not have abandoned their faith overnight, but without bishops and priests, and even churches, what was left undoubtedly went into further decline, with encroaching apostasy and a return to paganism at the end of the road. There does seem to be evidence from visiting Continental churchmen of the fifth century that they expected the British in the areas which still remained under native control to have been pagans,[4] so the situation for the Church in the lost territories, such as East Anglia, must surely have been worse. A further problem for the British Church had been that, even before the Anglo-Saxon invasions, it was poor, and, as well as making little headway amongst the majority of the population, it had, unlike its Continental counterparts, developed no style in Christian art and, by inference, relatively little in terms of wider Christian culture. The fact that there are no surviving churches of the period for East Anglia, and precious few in the parts of England where British control may have persisted for considerably longer, is a bleak indicator of the efficacy and influence of the late and ailing British Church![5]

It does seem, then, that native British paganism was alive and well in East Anglia, as in many parts of the country at the time of the change of control, and that a shift from one form of paganism to another was easier than from Christianity to paganism. The declining and increasingly moribund British Church had also, according to Gildas, another problem with which to contend, and which probably hastened its virtual extinction. Gildas says that the British clergy were decadent and worldly, all of which suggests a decline in standards similar to those that would be seen in the English Church on the eve of the Viking onslaughts (but from which, unlike its British predecessor, it would recover), and there seems to be a suggestion that these clergy were drawn from the town-based establishment of that time. This itself would not have augured well for any fervent and serious missionary work amongst the native people, let alone amongst hostile pagan occupiers with linguistic differences which would have added to the problem. The fall of the native establishment meant the fall of the Church as the two were inextricably interwoven. As far as Bede's castigation was concerned – if the Britons could no longer help themselves, how could they help others? The problem that the shattered British Church had is further illustrated by some sixth-century canons of that Church decreeing severe penalties against native British who betrayed their fellow-countrymen to the invaders, indicating the prevailing hatred for the newcomers.

Missionary activity, when it finally came in a determined and positive way, was primarily of a monastic nature. The monastic movement and its ideals reached what survived of the Christian territories of Britain (and from there to Ireland) which remained Celtic-speaking. This movement had arrived via Gaul by the late fifth century and did much to consolidate the process of the conversion in those regions. The 'lost' regions of Britain, like East Anglia, whatever the degree of Christian survival there, were outside its reach or influence and therefore failed to be renewed by it. Thus, such parts of the country as this would have to wait until the seventh century before any significant missionary outreach would come to them, and when it finally came it arrived from external sources, monastically led, and emanating from Christian Ireland and the Christian Continent.

If there was some little, struggling form of Christian survival by the onset of the seventh century, even as far east as East Anglia, and in ways that cannot be ascertained, it may have served to provide a kind of proto-conversional mould for the recorded, and definite, conversion that would come from the 630s onwards. The only real clues (and they are very flimsy) are to be found in a few place names here and there which seem to have survived from the Anglo-Saxon settlement period. One such name is 'Eccles', of which there are two examples in Norfolk, and which could be an English borrowing from a native British word, itself derived from the Latin '*Ecclesia*' (c.f. Welsh '*Eglwys*'). Also, we have Walton (near Felixstowe) in Suffolk, possibly indicating a settlement or '*tun*' of the Welsh, i.e. British speakers, which, interestingly enough, is situated close to Rendlesham, an eventual base of the ruling Wuffings tribe of the seventh century, the implications of which we shall explore. Wickhampton, Campsey and Camps (all in Norfolk), together with Wickham (Suffolk) denote possible Roman settlements in the area,[6] dating perhaps from 350 to 450. However, even if this equates with possible native survival in the region, it does not necessarily mean the survival of Christianity, other than perhaps in the case of 'Eccles'.

Had there been some form of Christian survival, it could go some way towards explaining the fact that, when the known missions did finally reach East Anglia, a fairly smooth transition to the new faith followed, and without significant resistance. If, prior to the officially recorded conversion of the 630s onwards, there had been any small and active missions, we must seriously doubt whether they had come from the shattered remnant of the native British Church, given Bede's testimony, though there remains the possibility of unrecorded missions from elsewhere, e.g. Frankish Gaul (France).[7] We might reasonably expect Bede to have remained silent about this, given his eagerness to assert pride of place to the mission which originated from Rome in 597. His rather reserved record of the role of the Irish missionaries for the same period, clearly did not do them justice, and we need therefore to treat his record, though admirable in most respects, with some measure of caution. Despite the lack of information from Bede regarding these possibilities (and he still remains our best, and virtually only, source for the conversion of East Anglia, as indeed for the rest of England), there remains a little evidence for the permeation of some active Christian influence prior to the official conversion date. The Sutton Hoo ship burial of Suffolk, which contains Christian baptismal spoons and imported Christian items from elsewhere, seemingly suggests some familiarity with Christianity by the eve of the conversion of East Anglia; and a further clue remains. There is an attested presence of Anglo-Saxon Christians in *Frankia* as early as 560 (thirty-seven years before the arrival of the Christian missionaries from Rome to England) and a record of two Anglo-Saxon monks having been on Christian Iona in Scotland before 597.[8] Thus the possibility of some sort of Christian presence in England, and so in East Anglia also, before the official conversion dates of 597 onwards, should be seriously considered.

The Pagan English

What was the nature of the paganism that the early seventh-century missionaries had to confront in England? The truth is that we have no clear knowledge, save a few hints from surviving fragmentary information. Most of the sparse information that we have regarding our pagan forefathers was derived from Christian writers and chroniclers some time after the eclipse of the old religion, and, naturally, they were hardly eager to give much detail, our further problem being that there is very little archaeological evidence. All we can do is to try to piece together the passing references that remain, and to draw upon analogies with Continental German practices and later Scandinavian ones, a procedure which in itself does not necessarily give us a correct picture.

The Roman writer, Tacitus,[9] referred to a sanctuary of *Nerthus*, the earth-mother goddess, worshipped by the Continental German tribes, to whom the English were closely related, and he names, amongst others, the Angles, from whom the English derived their name, as having been amongst her devotees. He says that they shared her common devotion with other German tribes and that her shrine stood in an open-air sacred grove attended by a priest. Her 'chariot', he tells us, was drawn by cows,[10] and days of rejoicing and merrymaking, together with a cessation of warfare, followed. The sacred chariot, vestments, and the goddess were often cleansed in a lake in which, after the ceremonies, the attendant slaves were also drowned.[11] Bede in his account of the conversion of King Edwin of Northumbria refers to the existence of a chief priest (whom he names as '*Coifi*'), thus indicating that there did seem to be some sort of hierarchical priesthood, though this form of institutionalism could have come about through some contacts with surviving remnants of Christianity. When we read the account of St Wilfred of York's arrival on the shores of the pagan kingdom of Sussex in the seventh century (the last English kingdom to be converted to Christianity), we also hear of a pagan chief priest in the locality, who led a sturdy resistance to the doughty bishop, setting himself up upon a high mound in order to 'bind' the saint and his followers with 'magical incantations'.[12] Such a priesthood we might reasonably expect to have been shamanistic in form; and for all we know, the whole panoply of early English paganism could well have been the result of a fusion of surviving British paganism, Roman pagan traditions, Anglo-Saxon Continental traditions, and some debased and adulterated Christian customs (now devoid of their original meaning), with a diversity of practice in the various regions of the country. Sadly, we have virtually no evidence for East Anglia in these respects, save the remarkable burial ship at Sutton Hoo, which bears all the hallmarks of a pagan burial or cenotaph, but with a few curious and significant Christian items, and which, if the burial was pre-conversion, could be indicative of the religious nature of the kingdom at that time. We should not, however, be too ready to accept this possibility, as the date for the burial continues to remain uncertain and could belong to the time when Christianity was already being reintroduced into East Anglia.

Pope St Gregory the Great, often referred to, justifiably, as the

'Apostle to the English', wrote to Bishop Mellitus, a successor of the missionary St Augustine, early in the conversion period, making a reference to the heathen English practices of sacrificing many cattle to demons (i.e. pagan gods), and instructing that such sacrifices were to be replaced by the festivals of the Christian martyrs, the killing of animals to be permitted only for the purpose of food and the praise of God. He also referred to the permissibility of the construction of boughs and shelters for festal occasions and around churches that were once heathen temples,[13] which seems an indicator of the existence of pagan buildings of worship as well as outdoor sanctuaries. There does seem to have been a preference for outdoor groves, as Tacitus had noted on the part of the Continental Angles, and, as we shall see, many of our later Christian churches came to be built on or close to such sites.

What would these pagan groves have been like? It seems clear that they had some edifices within them and that trees figured importantly. The yew tree traditionally symbolized immortality on account of its potential longevity, and sturdy oaks were clearly worshipped as an emblem of the male generative organ and associated with the principal male fertility god. Interestingly, yew trees were and still are associated with old church sites, suggesting the reconsecration of pagan sites to Christian use, and, as we shall see, we encounter oaks in later association with some of the saints – St Cedd of Essex was supposed to have preached beneath one, and St Edmund was said to have been martyred tied to one. The tree generally may have been of important significance to Germanic peoples, connecting with their myth of Yggdrasil, the 'World Tree', said to be the centre of the world, with its branches stretching out to heaven and earth under the protection of the gods. We may also note with interest that Bishop Wulfstan, as late as the eleventh century, cursed a yew tree in Worcestershire, because the local inhabitants preferred to leave their church unconsecrated rather than have the tree cut down![14] The fascination for tree traditions can also be seen in surviving Anglo-Saxon poems, notably 'The Dream of the Rood' – a Christian epic which deals with the finding of the true cross of Christ by St Helena, supposedly in the fourth century, a fragment of which had been sent to King Alfred the Great in the ninth century and which probably inspired the poem. In it the poet frequently extols the virtues of 'the tree'.[15]

It also seems that many of the pagan sanctuaries referred to were surrounded by ditches or were situated upon either natural or man-made circular mounds. Good examples of these can be found at the church sites of East Lexham, Newton-by-Castle Acre, Titchwell and Holkham (all in Norfolk). Associated with some of these sites, as we have noted, were often wells and springs of water, the future 'holy' wells. Some of these wells and springs were no doubt blessed by the Church in the early stages of conversion for the purpose of baptism, even before a local church came to be built, and if the missionary who used them came in time to be venerated as a saint, the well would then come to be regarded as the well of the saint. Many of the wells persisted in their pagan usage for a much longer time, not becoming incorporated into local Christianity until as late as the eleventh century. Those associated with female deities, as springs and rivers often were, would invariably be reconsecrated to the Virgin Mary (probably a development more of the ninth century onwards) or to a female saint. Some good examples in East Anglia may be found where we have the wells of St Witburgha (East Dereham), the wells of the Virgin Mary at Walsingham (Norfolk) and at Woolpit (Suffolk), three for St Walstan of Taverham associated with cattle and fertility, and doubtless very many more.

The significance of cattle in these pagan rites may perhaps be witnessed by a curious custom that survived until the late Middle Ages in association with the Shrine of St Edmund at Bury St Edmunds. This rite, almost certainly a survival of East Anglian paganism, was performed by women desirous of offspring and was known as the 'oblation of the white bull'. A white bull was annually brought, decked with ribbons and flowers, to the south gate of the abbey, where it was duly blessed, and then led through the streets to the west gate, the women walking at its side and the monks and townspeople following in procession. From the west gate it was then driven back to its pasture, whilst the supplicant women stayed behind at the monastery and prayed at St Edmund's Shrine. The tenant of a field, known as 'Haberdon Field', held the land in perpetuity on the condition that he always kept a white bull there on the land in readiness for this 'sacred' purpose. Foreigners were permitted to participate in this rite by proxy.[16]

Bede, who generally had little to say on the subject, did give us a description of the pagan months of the year. He says that the English year began on 25 December (winter solstice), followed by ceremonies called '*Modra Nect*' (the night of the mothers) which were quite clearly a fertility custom. The last month of the old year and the first of the new, he tells us, were called collectively '*Giuli*' (Yule) which survives as a present-day alternative term for Christmas. The second month was known as '*Solmonath*', when cakes were offered to the gods, the third and fourth months being named after the fertility goddesses, *Hretha* and *Eostre* (hence our word 'Easter'). The fifth was called '*Thrimilci*' – when cows were milked three times a day – and the sixth and seventh months were called after *Litha*, the moon goddess. The eighth month was apparently known as '*Weodmonath*' (month of weeds) and the ninth '*Halegmonath*', (the holy month of offerings and a harvest festival). The tenth month, *Wintirfyllith*, was connected with the appearance of the first winter full moon (i.e. Hallowe'en) and the eleventh was *Bloodmonath* (the sacrifice of cattle to the gods).[17] He also refers to the worship of the earth mother, *Erce*, possibly the *Nerthus* of Tacitus.[18] We must remember, though, that Bede himself was not an East Anglian, but a native Northumbrian, and he may well have been drawing upon surviving memories of pagan custom in his own part of England, which, as we have suggested, may not necessarily have been uniform throughout England. Bede tells us virtually nothing more about the pagan deities whom our ancestors worshipped but if we turn to some further Continental and later parallels, mainly Norse ones, there seems to be a suggestion that there was a main pantheon of gods, particularly *Tiw/Tig* (god of war and battle), *Thunor*, a sky god of thunder and

fertility (c.f. the Norse *Thor*?), *Woten*, the all-father of the pantheon (Norse *Odin*), and *Freya/Frigg*, a fertility goddess.[19]

One thing does seem to become clear, namely the relative resili-
ence of the pagan customs of the English, and well into the Christian era, with not only tree veneration surviving, but much else
also, despite the attempts of the Church to either eradicate or
Christianize them. Numerous examples survive, which include
not only the rededication of wells, trees and so on to saints, but
also the incorporation of pagan mythology into traditions of the
lives and miracles of the saints, and the persistence of some popular
and localized cults which were barely recognizable as Christian at
all! One rather amusing example of this could be found, up to
the time of the sixteenth-century Reformation, at Winfarthing
Church in Norfolk, where was kept its prize 'holy relic', namely
the 'Sword of Winfarthing'. This was apparently efficacious for
ridding men of their unwanted wives, provided candles were
burned before it continually for forty days (Sundays notwithstanding upon pain of curse!). It seems to have parallels with the cult
of St Uncumber (a bearded virgin!), venerated at Worstead in
Norfolk and elsewhere in England, who had the power to rid
wives of unwanted husbands, provided the required bushels of
grain were made to the Church as an offering. It is not improbable
that both these hardy superstitions had deep roots in the pagan
past. The instruction of Pope Gregory that some of the more
resilient aspects of pagan tradition, to which the people were
deeply attached, be assimilated into Christianity was clearly
was carried out with varying degrees of success. Archbishop St
Theodore of Canterbury's *Penitential* of the late seventh century
prohibited certain pagan practices which were obviously rife, such
as:

Women putting daughters on roofs or into ovens for the cure
of fever;
The burning of grain where a man has died as a supplication
for the living and those of the household;
Incantantations, divinations, auguries and omens from birds![20]

This, of course, was less than two hundred years on from the conversion.

Another persistent tradition of East Anglian pagan superstition, and doubtless a survival from pre-Christian times, is that of Black (or Old) 'Shuck', the phantom hound supposed to haunt the Fenlands and coastlines of East Anglia. The word 'Shuck', deriving from the Anglo-Saxon '*Succa*' (a demon), may originate from Norse times as some suggest, but is probably far older, being either the hound of *Woten* or even Romano-British (c.f. the Welsh tradition of '*Cŵn Annwn*' i.e. the dogs of *Annwfn* – 'Lord of the underworld').

The use of magical charms and runic amulets seems to have been an important part of the old religion and would survive long into the Christian period, despite the resistance and protestation of the Church in centuries to come.[21] We find, for example, evidence for runic inscriptions on personal items such as swords and rings well into the Christian period and runic devices even appearing on Christian stone sculptures; for it seems that the runes, though a primitive form of alphabet, were used for some magical purposes as well, though we have absolutely no knowledge as to how.[22] A curious charm also survives from the Christian period, and is probably a good example of the many fertility spells that continued to be used.

> I stand facing the East; I pray for the favour
> I pray to the Great Lord; I pray to the mighty Ruler;
> I pray to the Holy Guardian of Heaven.
> I pray to Earth and High Heaven.

At this point incense, fennel, blessed soap and salt were directed to be rubbed on the wood of the plough, and seed (to be obtained from a beggar-man) also placed upon it. The chant then continues:

> Erce, Erce, Erce, Earth Mother,
> may the Almighty Eternal Lord

> grant you fields to increase and flourish,
> shining harvest of shafts of millet,
> broad harvests of barley . . .
> Hail to thee, Earth, Mother of Men!
> Bring forth now in God's embrace,
> filled with good for the use of men![23]

Finally, place names also give us some further indication of the presence of paganism, though we need to be cautious, as place-name evidence is notoriously unreliable. Curiously, there are very few examples apparent in East Anglia compared to some other parts of the country, which tends to raise again the question of the degree of Christian survival and the realistic appraisal of the strength and nature of paganism. Alternatively, it may simply indicate that there was, when the time came, a fairly smooth and rapid transition to Christianity, by way of comparison to say, Essex, further south, where there were serious reversions to pagan-ism soon after its conversion (suggestive pagan place names are also stronger there). There is a lot of evidence to suggest that most East Anglian place names that survive to the present day were not in place until about the eighth century onwards, and they may well have replaced many earlier pagan-associated ones, Anglo-Saxon and late British. The few survivals that there may be are from the early words for a hill-sanctuary (*Heargh*), a grove (*Lau*), and a temple (*Ealh*).[24] These can be found in Harston (Cambridgeshire), Harleston (Norfolk and Suffolk), Thunreslau, i.e. Thunor's Grove (Suffolk), and Aylmerton, a temple settlement (Norfolk).[25]

By the time that the Christian missionaries reached this part of England, in the early decades of the seventh century, there appears to have been in place a society that was to all intents and purposes pagan, but with a possible and variable substratum of some surviving Christianity. The picture that would emerge some several hundreds of years later would be the reverse – a society apparently Christian, but with a strong undercurrent of resilient paganism. What brought about this transition is to be found in the lives and activities of the missionaries and saints of the intervening centuries, in which they were to be ably assisted by compliant convert kings.

2

A Baptism

The Conversion

In AD 988, to the Principality of Kiev in southern Russia, a handful of Greek missionaries from Byzantium came at the request of the Prince of the kingdom, one Vladimir. They brought the Christian gospel and all that went with it, and began the process of the conversion of a people – a conversion which, despite the vicissitudes of the centuries to come, would prove to be abiding and would establish the foundations of the Christian civilization of Russia. The king and his subjects were converted and a royal edict went out to the effect that the nobles and the king's subjects were likewise to embrace the new faith and to receive baptism at the hands of the foreign missionaries, a command that would be duly enforced with characteristic medieval rigour! Apparently mass baptism followed, the people assembling by royal command at the banks of the River Dnieper and other rivers throughout the principality, stepping into the waters that had been previously hallowed through the prayers and ministrations of the men of God, who duly passed amongst them immersing them under the water three times in the name of the holy and undivided Trinity. Following this and at the appointed time, the people were anointed with the oil of chrism, the confirmation rite, and then, in some form or other, the long and painstaking process of instructing them in the Christian faith began, a process that would take many centuries. We are told that these mass baptisms took place each day until the principality had been 'converted', and since that time the events of 988 have been referred to as the 'Baptism of

Russia', the millennium of which was celebrated with world attention in 1988.

This type of event, described in the somewhat romantic terms
that fail to do justice to the realities of the situation, was not
unique and had taken place in other barbarian lands in northern
Europe in previous centuries. England itself had been no exception, for in 597 a similar handful of missionaries, led by a reluctant
Italian monk possessed of a somewhat 'difficult' personality and
known to posterity as St Augustine of Canterbury, was sent from
Italy by Pope Gregory the Great, arriving at the court of Ethelbert
(*Aethelberht*), King of Kent, preaching the same gospel; the king
and his nobles were duly converted and baptized, and the people
obediently followed the noble example. So rapid was the work of
these missionaries that Pope Gregory wrote to the Eastern Church
Patriarch of Alexandria, Eulogius, reporting that by the Feast of
Christmas, 597, more than ten thousand English had been baptized
(i.e. within the space of a few months!).[1] Soon after the arrival of
Augustine's (or more correctly, Pope Gregory's) mission to Kent,
the enterprise was supplemented by a further forty missionaries,
episcopal sees being set up in Canterbury and Rochester, and it
then fanned out to embrace the Kingdom of Essex, a bishop's
seat being established in the old Roman capital of London. The
process of conversion seemed to go so smoothly, that as far as we
know, there were no recorded martyrdoms for this period. All
the evidence tends to suggest that English paganism, at least in
southernmost England, was already in some decline and that these
parts of the country were predisposed to the reception of Christianity (Essex being an exception), as we have seen, for a variety
of reasons. The major triumph for the Church came ten years on
from the events in 627 with the conversion by Bishop Paulinus,
one of Augustine's missionaries, of the largest tract of England,
Northumbria, and its king, Edwin.[2]

Edwin had in 616 been a refugee and exile at the court of King
Raedwald of East Anglia, following dynastic turbulence within his
own Northumbria, and had fled there on the basis of an existing
alliance between the two kingdoms. This alliance had developed

out of a mutual interest in containing an equally powerful neighbour in central England, the Kingdom of Mercia, and both the allies shared some sort of alliance, or at least an accommodation, with the Kingdom of Kent. Unfortunately for Edwin, Raedwald of East Anglia, a formidable and powerful king in his own right, had, as part of his own 'power game', received a bribe from one of the temporarily successful Northumbrian factions to persuade him to have his refugee guest assassinated. According to Bede, our most reliable and informative chronicler for this period, a friend came to Edwin and promised to deliver him out of East Anglia and into the safety of Kent (Edwin was married to a daughter of the King of Kent),[3] though Edwin refused this offer for reasons that are uncertain. Eventually a 'stranger' came to him and promised to deliver him from all his difficulties and told the exiled king that he would persuade King Raedwald not to harm him. The stranger went on to prophesy to Edwin that he would eventually become a great king who would overcome his enemies; and he further asked of Edwin that, should these prophecies be fulfilled, he would subsequently obey him [the stranger] and follow whatever advice he gave – to which Edwin agreed. Raedwald subsequently underwent a change of heart and Edwin eventually took power in Northumbria, the event being duly followed by the arrival of Bishop Paulinus, presumably from Kent, who, reminding King Edwin of the stranger's promises to him during his exile, urged him, together with his kingdom, to embrace the Christian faith.[4]

Edwin had strong links with the royal, and by now Christian, dynasty of Kent and the reasonable supposition is that the 'stranger' who had rendered him the sound advice had been none other than Bishop Paulinus himself, present in East Anglia during Edwin's own exile. It is quite possible, for East Anglian Raedwald also had strong ties with Kent and a period of twenty-five years is missing in the accounts of St Paulinus' recorded life, which could have put him in East Anglia prior to the recorded beginnings of the East Anglian conversion to Christianity which began in the time of Raedwald's son, Erpwald (616?–628).[5] We might conjecture that Paulinus had been present in East Anglia during this period as part and parcel of some alliance between East Anglia and Kent, involving East Anglian royal marriages to Christian Kentish princesses, which was a usual way of cementing such arrangements. This had happened in Northumbria, where Edwin, whilst still pagan, took a Christian Kentish princess in marriage as part of the alliance, and Paulinus may thus well have been present, in the capacity of negotiator and emissary and with his own missionary agenda, at Raedwald's court. If this was so, we might well ask why Bede made no mention of Paulinus' having been in East Anglia, but there is a possible explanation. Bede could, as we shall see, be highly selective in the use of his information and it does seem that when writing of the conversion of East Anglia he was at pains to stress the foremost role of Bishop Felix in this process, dating from the latter's arrival in the kingdom in 630. Bede, himself a Northumbrian, was clearly keen to designate Paulinus as an apostle to his own territory and may have wished to keep the recorded spheres of activity of the two great missionaries neatly separated.

King Raedwald's conversion turned out to be a half-hearted expediency and one of abject failure, earning him the justifiable title of syncretist, given that he followed up his nominal acceptance of Christianity with the addition, or continuation, of a pagan altar.[6] Raedwald was clearly what we might now describe as a 'hardbitten realist', who based his expediency upon what he perceived to be sound and practical considerations (a perception probably influenced by his royal circle), i.e. the token observance of a religion and new order 'whose time had come', combined with a need to hold on to the old ways and the loyalty of the powerful political interests that supported them. Too much acceptance of the new religion could have meant some submission to Kent, and in this respect Raedwald was probably quite cautious. It is also likely that he was influenced by his wife, who, as well as remaining a full-blooded pagan, seems to have exerted quite a powerful influence upon him. Further to these factors, Raedwald may have had to cope with strong dynastic tensions and conflicts within his kingdom, stemming from deeply conservative factions who may have been extremely hostile towards Christian influence and teaching, associated as these were with the old Romano-British order which had by now been vanquished and superseded. Raedwald also exercised an apparent overlordship outside his own immediate territory as, according to Bede, he was a '*Bretwealda*' (i.e. a king receiving some form of tributary acknowledgement from other kingdoms), and in this role he seems to have overlapped with Ethelbert of Kent, the first recorded Christian English king to also enjoy the title. Even so, his power was clearly declining before his death and would not be exercised to the same extent by his more Christian successors. Bede tells us that Raedwald's son and immediate successor, Erpwald (*Eohrpwald*), embraced the Christian faith under the influence of Edwin of Northumbria, and that he received baptism during his father's lifetime (at whose hands we do not know but Paulinus is a possibility); and at some stage another son, Sigbert, also accepted Christianity, albeit in exile.[7] Sadly for Erpwald, he was, very soon after his accession to the kingship in 627, murdered by a rival royal claimant named Ricberht,[8] who probably acted on behalf of the still-dominant pagan interest, perhaps representing entrenched tribal groups within the East Anglian kingdom. The advance of the Church, tenuous as it had been so far, had clearly suffered a temporary setback, for it seems that following this event, paganism enjoyed a resurgence from top to bottom for three years until Erpwald's half-brother, Sigbert, succeeded to the kingdom. Regrettably, Bede gives us no information on this interregnum.

Proto-Martyr and Martyr-Kings

Erpwald and Sigbert

The pagan interregnum, with Ricberht at its head, meant that Christianity could clearly make no further advance, and the slain King Erpwald, though recorded as having been a Christian, does not seem to have enjoyed any posthumous recognition as a martyr, as would later befall some of his relatives, this probably having been due to the relative weakness of the Church at the time of his demise, together with dynastic factors. However, the setback lasted for only about three years, for in 630 or 631 the succession went to Sigbert (*Sigebeohrt*), the step-son of Raedwald, who had been an exile from the royal court and who would, quite decisively, lay down permanent foundations for Christianity in East Anglia.

Sigbert was, by all accounts, a man of some learning and a devout Christian, who had been an exile for political reasons (reasons which we do not know) during his father's time; his exile was spent in Frankish Gaul (i.e. northern France) where he had been converted to the Christian faith. All the evidence suggests that in his time in exile he had been tutored in the great monastic schools of that region and it seems that after his conversion he felt more inclined to the monastic life than to kingship, an impetus that would dog him after his return to East Anglia, together with a thorough determination, albeit short-lived, to bring about the complete conversion of his realm. Sigbert's exile in Christian Gaul had certainly been formative, and, although we do not know where and by whom he had been instructed and baptized, it is likely to have occurred in the north of the region and in a monastery under the protection of the Frankish King, Charibert, who had probably extended to Sigbert the temporary protection of his own kingdom, no doubt due to Frankish links with both Kent and East Anglia. Not insignificantly, and a generation later, East Anglian royal princesses, and relatives of Sigbert, would also arrive in *Frankia* to take up their places in monasteries under the protection of the Frankish king. Of further significance is the likelihood that several of these monasteries had Irish links and influences,[9] and consequently Sigbert's own conversion may well have owed something to this as much as to Frankish influence, all of which would prove to be of some consequence for Christian East Anglia.

When Sigbert finally returned from *Frankia* in 631 it seems that he was determined to emulate what he had witnessed there and in support of this he duly invited missionaries into his newly-gained kingdom, founding a school for boys where they would be taught sacred scripture, Church teaching and canon law. The most notable missionaries were Bishop Felix of Burgundy, apparently sent to Sigbert at his own request by Archbishop Honorius of Canterbury, a successor of St Augustine, and (Bishop?) Fursey, an Irishman, who arrived in East Anglia a little later with some relatives and companions. This Irish presence would prove to be very significant, for it would show itself to be both highly disciplined and zealous in its purpose, conforming as it did with the strictest traditions of the Desert Fathers, the originators of Church monasticism. It represented, above all, a 'pilgrim' tradition[10] which, because of its zeal and bare simplicity, was ideally suited to evangelism.

We have accounted for the possibility that there were already some Irish Christian communities in East Anglia, together with surviving Romano-British ones,[11] and, if this was so, they would surely have been well disposed towards the missionaries. It certainly seems that St Fursey's mission pre-dated the Irish mission that emanated from Iona to Northumbria, following the overthrow of its king, Edwin, and it is difficult to know what precisely prompted St Fursey and his Irish monks to venture into East Anglia, leaving aside the question of whether King Sigbert actually invited them or had even previously known of them, and upon these matters, given the dearth of evidence, we can only speculate. Whatever the background to the Irish arrival, Sigbert brought in the missionaries, founded his school, and, according to the traditions, went on to found a monastery, becoming (in Bede's words) 'so great a lover of the heavenly kingdom, that quitting the affairs of his crown, he committed the same to his kinsman Ecgric, who before held a part of that kingdom'.[12] This statement of Bede's tells us quite a lot, for it indicates that a form of kingly power-sharing was at work in East Anglia at the time of Sigbert's return, suggesting that his position, and presumably that of the Christian interest, was by no means secure. It would seem that some sort of agreement or accommodation of interests had been reached with the faction that had toppled King Erpwald, an interest that was both pagan and still highly active, and which had succeeded in holding an uninterrupted sway for the three years prior to Sigbert's return from *Frankia*. We cannot assume that this Ecgric, with whom Sigbert had to share power, was pagan (though it remains a distinct possibility), but even if he was a Christian it could have been that he was more amenable to the powerful pagan warlords in the kingdom, of whom account had to be taken.

Sigbert, having renounced his position, perhaps as a combination of genuine 'other-worldly' desire combined with a measure of compulsion, became a monk and retired to a monastery that he had founded, which later traditions would ascribe to *Beodrices-worth* – later, though not certainly, Bury St Edmunds. It is possible that, in view of his Christianity, he was regarded as too weak and compassionate for the prevailing standards of his rivals and opponents and thus not in keeping with the accepted fierce Germanic concepts of kingship,[13] though it would seem that he continued to enjoy some of the prestige attached to the dynasty by virtue of the fact that at least his token leadership would eventually be called upon during supreme crisis. He was certainly not permitted to withdraw for long into his monastic retreat before the call to return came. In a short time, the simmering power struggle between pagan Mercia and the East Anglian/Northumbrian alliance welled up to the surface, and King Penda of Mercia, an expansionist and diehard pagan, invaded, having already slain Northumbria's Christian King Edwin. Sigbert was, Bede tells us, literally dragged from his monastery under protest[14] to lead the East Anglian host in battle against the invader and aggressor. As a monk, Sigbert stubbornly refused to carry weapons, bearing instead a 'wand' as an emblem of his royal status. What exactly this wand was we do not quite know, but there may be a clue from the Sutton Hoo ship burial, where there were found five gold fittings that could have been mounted on a bone or ivory wand. This also links with a rather curious whetstone, apparently a sceptre, which may have embodied royal power inherited from the royal Wuffings tribe to which Sigbert belonged.[15] The final word on the hapless Christian king, who was to be the first of his genre in East Anglia, comes from Bede, who says that, although

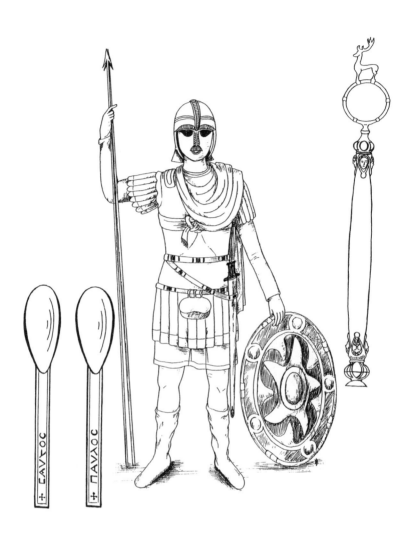

A Wuffings King (Based upon the Sutton Hoo Finds and Showing the Baptismal Spoons and Whetstone)

Sigbert was well defended by his own militia, when the Mercians charged, both he and King Ecgric were killed (637 AD). So died Sigbert, a traditional Christian martyr-king, killed by the pagans, offering no resistance and a professed monk. We are not told where he met his fate nor where he was buried, though it would seem that the monastery founded by him was the likely venue. There is no surviving record of his having been later held to veneration as a martyr-saint, as would be the case with some of his successors, nor of any honouring of his relics, though it would be strange if this had not been so for some time. If this was the case we are only left to assume that such a memory and veneration was later superseded by more potent ones that would be of greater significance to both Church and State. As it turned out, a more generous, though temporary, acknowledgement would befall his successor, King Ana.

Ana

King Ana (*Onna*) was a nephew of the opportunist syncretist, Raedwald, and thus indirectly related to the slain Sigbert,[16] seemingly from a branch of the royal tribe that had formed a rather more committed attachment to Christianity. Bede bestowed paeons of praise upon his memory, as 'a Christian king with devout children',[17] which was not altogether an inappropriate epithet, given that his family included several saints: Hereswitha (his sister-in-law and herself a sister to St Hilda of Whitby, the great Northumbrian abbess), three of his known daughters, and a possible, though somewhat debatable, fourth. It also included one of England's most honoured saints, together with a possible saintly son who would be venerated as a martyr along with his father, though, again, there is some doubt about identity. Ana's connections would also extend to a saintly throng which included granddaughters, a great-granddaughter, and even, though improbably, a saintly bishop of London. Thanks to Ana and his progeny, this would become not only a royal tribe of the Wuffings, but in truth a veritable Christian one.[18] The Christian credentials were in no doubt as far as the Church was concerned, for not only was Ana a Christian king who died defending his people against a pagan, but, as we have already seen, one of Ana's brothers, Aethelric, was married to St Hereswitha and another, Aethelwald, himself a future East Anglian king, sponsored King Swithelm of Essex at his baptism at the royal vill at Rendlesham by Bishop St Cedd (*Ceadda*), an English monk of Irish Church training en route to Essex via the East Angles.[19]

Ana continued to strengthen the links with Christian Northumbria no doubt as part of the grand alliance between the kingdoms, together with Kent (probably exercising some dominance over Essex as well), set against the expanding power of pagan Mercia; and he further strengthened the ties with the north by marrying his daughter, the future St Etheldreda, to King Ecgfrith of Northumbria.[20] We cannot be certain how long it was before Ana took power in East Anglia following the death of Sigbert and it is quite likely that there was another interregnum, this time under Mercian, and thus pagan, domination, perhaps with a puppet king installed (either a pagan or a semi-Christian, even from a rival faction to the Wuffings). We know nothing of the power politics that were at large, or of the factors that enabled Ana to seize back power both for the royal tribe and the Christian interest; but triumph he did, and he went on, throughout what seems to have been a constantly turbulent reign, to build upon the aspirations and foundations of the martyred Sigbert, ensuring the permanence of Christianity in the kingdom, which would survive even the battering of Vikings two centuries later!

To this end, Ana continued to actively support the apostolic work of Bishop Felix and his mission, and also that of Irish Fursey based upon his monastery at *Cnobheresburgh*,[21] the evangelization of the kingdom proceeding apace under royal patronage and the leadership of these two men and their followers. It seems that no part of the kingdom was unreached by these missions and their apparent effectiveness, and the speed of the conversion says much not only for the zeal of the missionaries but also for the power of Ana in his territory and beyond, for it is quite possible that an evangelization of the Fenlands across into the East Midlands (Middle Mercia) began during this period, and thus went hand in hand with revived East Anglian power and expansion under Ana. If this was so, then the beginnings of conversion so far westwards would have pre-dated the acknowledged Irish missions of St Chad and St Diuma in those territories,[22] with the possibility that such an expansion by the Church was checked only because of Ana's reverses at the hands of the Mercians. Such a possibility would further indicate the attested fact of how mutually reliant upon each other Christian missions and royal power interests were.

Ana also gave refuge to another royal victim of Penda, Cenwalh, the exiled King of Wessex, and arranged for him to be baptized by Bishop Felix (though where, we are not told), Ana himself acting as the sponsor. This probably took place at Felix's seat of *Dommoc*, now an unknown site and often, though not definitely, equated with Dunwich on the Suffolk coast – though it could equally have happened at the royal seat of Rendlesham or the monastery said to have been founded by Ana at Blythburgh, if indeed it existed at this stage. It is virtually certain that this expansion of East Anglian power, together with its alliances with Kent and Northumbria, was able to exert some influence and control over Essex and Wessex, in effect isolating and encircling Mercia, and there may have been a resumption of East Anglian expansion into the East Midlands, provoking an inevitable Mercian backlash. Penda, perhaps counting on internal dynastic pagan support still at large in East Anglia, was determined to crush his Christian neighbours and rivals on his eastern flank and thereby to secure his position by reducing them once again to satellite status, this time permanently! The onslaught came during the years from 650 to 652 and Ana was expelled from his kingdom, or simply fled, though to where we cannot be sure. The likeliest places of refuge for him would have been Northumbria (which was accessible by sea), Kent, or even *Frankia*, with which there were close ties and bonds. It has been suggested that he may have sought refuge in the West Midlands/Welsh border area,[23] where there certainly was Christian missionary activity at this time,

though this does seem to be rather unlikely, as there he would
have been in Penda's territory and within his grasp! Wherever he
did go, the Mercians either ruled his subdued kingdom directly
for a period or, and more likely, installed a more co-operative
vassal king in his place, one such possibility having been
Aethelhere,[24] who would eventually succeed Ana and prove
acceptably compliant to the Mercians.

This period of Ana's exile probably saw the final abandonment
of St Fursey's mission, for it appears that (according to Bede)
Fursey had foreseen the endangerment to his fledgling monasteries
by heathen attacks, the use of the plural indicating that the Irish
missionaries had established several of such in the kingdom. It
seems that Fursey himself left in about 645, probably during a
previous period of Mercian invasion and devastation for which
we have no record. This would also suggest that the Irish had
established their monastic centres and missionary bases in remoter
regions of the kingdom and further away from effective royal
protection, thus rendering them more vulnerable to this sort of
attack. A ninth-century source tells us that Fursey left his own
surviving monastery in the care of his brother and companion,
St Foillan, departing for *Frankia* never to return, but the monastery was destroyed and the monks scattered, probably during the
Mercian incursion of 650 to 652. St Foillan, by that time its abbot,
was saved only by 'divine intervention' and the return from exile
of King Ana, the chronicler no doubt regarding the two events
as one and the same thing. The heathen (i.e. Mercians and pagan
collaborators) were expelled only for a while and the monks were
redeemed from slavery, which again tends to suggest that Ana's
position was very precarious if, as the use of the word 'redeemed'
implies, he had to purchase the monks from slavery rather than
exercising an outright liberation. Despite Ana's resumption of
power, and no doubt due to his insecurity, St Foillan and his
other named brother, St Ultan, took repossession of the monastery's relics, altar, and sacred books, and departed also for *Frankia*,
where by now their brother, St Fursey, lay buried. This does not
necessarily mean that all the followers of the Irish mission left

East Anglia for good but the exodus seems to have been significant. Interestingly one known companion of Fursey, St Dicuil, may have found his way to the still pagan Kingdom of Sussex (by what means we do not know), where, if he is identical to a Dicuil named by Bede as having founded a monastery at Bosham (though without much success it would seem), he encountered severe problems.

Ana's respite was to prove only of short duration, for in 654 Penda again invaded East Anglia, no doubt determined this time to finish the business; and this he most certainly did, for Ana met his death, possibly with one of his sons, at Penda's hands and possibly near Bulcamp in Suffolk. His brother, Aethelhere, took the throne, probably with Mercian consent, for there is no evidence that Penda, though pagan, was inimical to Christianity *per se*, nor is there any evidence that his wars were. Bede tells us of Penda: 'He did not obstruct the preaching of the word among his people, the Mercians, if any were willing to hear it; but on the contrary, he hated and despised those whom he perceived not to perform the works of faith, saying, "They were contemptible and wretched who did not obey their God, in whom they believed." '[25] As with all wars, Penda's were to do with power, and the same was certainly true of his adversaries in the Christian kingdoms surrounding him. Indeed, Penda had had no compunction about allying himself with the Christian King of North-West Wales, Cadwallon Gwynedd, in a war against Christian Northumbria, wherein the two leaders and their allied forces had literally hacked to pieces the Christian king, Oswald. Cadwallon had gone one better than his pagan ally, Penda, by attempting to exterminate a sizeable section of the Northumbrian population, for which he earned Bede's stigmatization as a virtual 'apostate'.

Just as Penda and Cadwallon received the posthumous condemnation of the Church, so Ana earned its praise and, certainly within East Anglia, virtual recognition as a martyr-saint, like Sigbert before him. He was deemed not only one who had assisted the Church in the conversion process of his kingdom, but also one who had died for both at the hands of pagans – credentials

enough. He was said to have been buried at the monastery supposedly founded by him at Blythburgh, which may conceivably have
become thereafter the resting place for many of East Anglia's
Christian kings up until the time of another martyr-king,
St Edmund, in the ninth century. As to the extent of Ana's
posthumous recognition as an important East Anglian saint, we
cannot be entirely certain. His relics were said to have been kept
at Blythburgh, together with those of his supposed son, Jurmin,
who had been slain with him, and as such they could have been
a resort for pilgrimage and veneration until the Viking devastation
of the ninth century. In this respect he seems to have gained a
greater recognition than Sigbert, perhaps because he was more
successful, but more probably due to the fact that after his death
the Church was in a more secure position in the kingdom and its
close and well-attested relationship with the successive East
Anglian kings ensured Ana a significant place in the commemorative lists. Whatever the case, there is certainly no evidence for a
significant commemoration of Ana (unlike those of his offspring),
and if there was any, the vestiges of the commemoration may well
have been swept away, together with any commemoration of his
predecessors, Erpwald and Sigbert, during the Viking onslaught
of the ninth century, after which the East Anglian kingdom ceased
to exist. The post-Viking age, and its reconstructed Church, had
a more national outlook with its own martyr-kings, whose later
cults would certainly have pushed the memory of Ana into relative
obscurity. As it happens, the little we know about him has come to
us from surviving Northumbrian sources, i.e. Bede, who, though
favourably disposed to the East Anglians and their Church, was
not preoccupied with them.

Thus this particular line of the Wuffings dynasty came to an
end with the death of Ana, as did also East Anglian independence
for a while; but not so the growing power and influence of the
Church. The work of conversion continued to be pushed forwards
and solid foundations were laid. The first native East Anglian
bishop, Thomas, of the Fenland Gyrwe tribe, succeeded St Felix
upon the latter's death in 652. Penda would soon be dead, his

son, Peada, already exercising kingship in the East Midlands, and a Christian convert at that, and quite possibly some East Anglian missionary output reasserted itself in those territories yet again. The time of conversion and expansion was drawing to a close as a new generation appeared. Consolidation and spiritual achievements would be the next phase of development.

3

Apostles and Evangelists

In order to appreciate how the process of the conversion of East
Anglia unfolded, we need to look at some of the most notable
personalities involved in that task together with the methods that
they used and the measure of their achievements. We also need
to take account of the two main sources, Continental and Irish,
from which those missionary enterprises derived and examine to
what extent they interacted and worked together laying, as they
did, the basis for a unified Church from the late seventh century
onwards. Let us turn to the methods of conversion used by the
pioneer missionaries first.

Until 647 there were no native clergy (as far as we know)
available for the purpose of preaching to the pagan kings or to
their retinues and people, and it is more than probable that in the
early stages the missionaries would have brought trained
interpreters with them, a particular necessity for the Irish missionaries as the Celtic and Germanic languages were unrelated, and
it does seem that in this respect the Irish were quicker off the
mark than their Continental brothers.[1] The deeply entrenched
paganism of the broad mass of the population, which we have
already examined, required a very careful, and at times tactful,
approach in order to accomplish the smooth transition from the
old religion to the new, and this would undoubtedly have involved
a policy of investing pagan sites with a new Christian meaning,[2]
which, as we suggested in the previous chapter, would have
entailed a ceremony of rededication and cleansing prior to the
introduction of the new rituals. This may well have provoked
some hostile reaction and confrontation at local level, though no

records survive of such difficulties – the only recorded incident of violent resistance that we know of having occurred not in East Anglia but on the Isle of Wight at a somewhat later stage. In East Anglia's case, the transition seems to have been quite smooth and peaceful, and violent attacks came from outside the kingdom rather than from within it, having more to do with political power and territorial claims than with religion.[3]

One technique that was used in the teaching and preaching of the first missionaries seems to have been the deployment of the device of depicting the old gods as useless and ineffectual, whilst at the same time placing great emphasis on the superiority of Christ over these deities. Interestingly, the missionaries did not proclaim the non-existence of such gods and goddesses, but rather portrayed them as inferior and moribund (eventually they would be relegated to the status of 'demons' or mythological heroes); and great stress was placed upon the message that adherence to Christ would bring his new followers earthly rewards as well as spiritual ones, which the old gods were incapable of doing – all of which would provide a particular incentive for the kings. A good example of this approach can be seen in an eighth-century letter sent by Bishop Daniel of Winchester to St Boniface, the great English missionary, who at that time was evangelizing pagan German tribes on the Continental mainland. In offering advice, Daniel not only pointed out that the old gods had failed to heap retribution upon the Christians who had scorned them, but (in his own words) 'the Christians possess fertile lands, and provinces fruitful in wine and oil and abounding in other riches'.[4] Thus was Christianity presented as a religion of both advantage and triumph – a victor's religion – which was a powerful message for barbarian chieftains.

In these early stages of evangelization there was probably little emphasis on Church doctrine and we also find few recorded accounts of miracles associated with the early saints of this time. Such events as were perceived to have been miraculous were without a doubt regarded as a potent aid to the process of conversion, particularly amongst a people who had been steeped for centuries in notions of magic and superstition. One of the most important factors in the work of these early missionaries was their lifestyle, in terms of leading by example, and it is significant that Bede makes reference to the 'apostolic' life of St Augustine and his followers as well as to the asceticism of St Fursey, the seventh-century Irish missionary to East Anglia.

Given that the baptism of the mass of ordinary people was carried out on a fairly wholesale scale rather than individual by individual, we might well ask how well it was really understood. The evidence seems to indicate that the missionaries went initially to the kings (this was particularly so in the case of the Continental evangelizers like St Felix) and, if the king underwent baptism, this would then be binding upon the rest of the royal household and its retainers and thence on the local chieftains and the mass of the peasantry. Baptism was the first requirement of conversion and it was compulsory,[5] though we might reasonably expect that many of the newly-baptized would continue for a time with the old pagan customs and observances (King Raedwald, as we have seen, was a prime example of this even at royal level) until proper instruction could follow. The Church may thus have had to exercise some temporary degree of tolerance during this time of transition. The second wave of conversion, catechizing, or instructing, may well have been the task and accomplishment of St Fursey and his companions (most sources, other than Bede, do say that he was a bishop, and if this was so he could have been in a position to administer confirmation) who could have acted in an auxiliary capacity to Bishop Felix, the latter's task having been primarily directed to initial conversion and baptism. Whatever the case, it certainly seems that the East Anglian kings received the missionaries well but we should examine the motivation of the kings, given their fairly favourable and quick response to the new teachings.

Allowing for genuine and unconditional personal conviction, there do seem to have been several intertwining factors at work which allowed for rapid royal response to the Christian missions. As we have noted, conversion was offered as a bargain for earthly reward and it was impressed upon the kings that Christianity would strengthen, rather than weaken, their earthly power, replacing, as it did, the elective tradition of kingship with a theocratic one, with anointing and crowning now being uppermost, thus conferring upon the kings a 'divinely sanctioned' omnipotence.[6] Furthermore, the Church brought a more sophisticated mode of government to the kingdom together with the benefits of literacy,[7] along with the whole organizational skill of the Continental Church. Church dioceses were probably established to mirror the territorial boundaries of the kingdom and would thus provide for a greater cohesion within the latter, again with 'divine sanction',[8] the bishop's seat usually having been close to the centre of royal power.[9] The remaining benefit for the convert kings was that the Church provided for a more peaceful cohesion within the kingdom, with reference to the king's laws and adjudication. The replacement of the traditional blood feud with the *weregild* system[10] was a good example of this, receiving, as it did, enforcement across the country at large at the insistence of Archbishop St Theodore of Canterbury towards the end of the seventh century. The exchange benefit for the Church was that the kings extended their protection to the missionaries and churchmen, which enabled them to expand their missionary work, with the consequential founding of churches and monasteries. There seems to be good evidence that this royal favour and protection was generously given to both St Felix and St Fursey by Kings Sigbert and Ana, and by all the succeeding East Anglian kings for whom we have any detail, though this relationship between royal and Church interests would not be without problems and temptations for the Church in the future.

Monasticism, with its ostensibly high standards of discipline and ascetical ideals, was particularly suited for mission work and was almost certainly one of the key factors in the notable successes and achievements of the Irish missionaries over much of the country, East Anglia included.[11] Once the king had been converted, he would provide a church within the precincts of the royal vill, or close to it, and a church for the bishop and his clergy, all of whom would be monks. When a monastic enclosure was

established, there would be a further expansion of churches following in the wake of the missionaries, with their own clergy to serve
them. These churches, as we have seen, in many cases would be
on, or close to, former pagan sites, and we must also take account
of the possibility of the repair and reuse of abandoned earlier
British churches.[12] Such churches would primarily have been monastic in their organization and orientation and were likely to have
been dependent upon the first foundations. Oratories, or small
chapels, that were founded by magnates in the more outlying
areas, were similarly served from the larger establishments, though
regrettably we know precious little of these very early foundations.
From the established monastic foundations proceeded pastoral
work, the clergy travelling into the surrounding countryside under
the control and supervision of the bishop, all of which allowed
for further baptisms, instruction, and the ministration of the sacraments. In the absence of parish churches and local churches, which
would not appear until many centuries later, specially erected
wooden and stone crosses were set up, serving as temporary places
for preaching and the sacraments,[13] and, as we have seen, nearby
springs and wells, often of previous pagan veneration, sometimes
served for the purposes of baptism and other ecclesiastical
requirements.[14]

Irishmen and Continentals

The missionary advent, when it reached East Anglia, derived then
from two sources, both separate and complementary – Irish and
Continental – and East Anglia was one of several kingdoms that
would be host to both, though it seems without some of the
resultant problems that other kingdoms (notably Northumbria)
would experience; and it is important to understand the nature and
differences of both the missionary sources and their characteristics.

The Continental mission in East Anglia, represented by St Felix
of Burgundy, like the Irish missions, was certainly monastic in its
structure but probably placed a greater emphasis on the status
and role of the bishops and upon Roman diocesan organization

and structure.[15] This structure was particularly attractive to the kings for the reasons we have suggested, and it deliberately directed its appeal to them with great success. The Irish missions, represented in East Anglia by St Fursey, had their own and more primitively ascetical style of monasticism, and the structure of the native Irish Church itself, whose origins principally lay in the earlier British Church, had, like the latter in the regions in which it still prevailed, been transformed during the course of the sixth century by this form of monasticism. The origins of primitive monasticism lay in the Middle East, and as an ideal and movement it had reached the western British Isles via Gaul from the late fifth century onwards. Such a form of monasticism blended in well with the intensely tribal societies of Celtic-speaking Ireland and Wales, and differences between the Church in those lands and the Church on the Continent had become quite noticeable by the seventh century (though not so significant as Victorian and contemporary 'Celtic Church' romancers would have us believe!). Evidence does show that in the Irish Church at least, the abbots and *not* the bishops exercised the greater influence and authority in the territories in which they were situated, the former, as often as not, being themselves of royal standing within the tribal territory and invariably bequeathing the abbatial office to members of their own kindred-group. We see this particularly in the case of St Fursey and his monastery in East Anglia, where he was assisted by at least two of his brothers in the flesh,[16] and it is quite likely that his other monastic companions who are named could also have been related or at least from the same tribal grouping.[17] The Irish monastery was in many ways a spiritual extension of the tribe, just as later and royal foundations in East Anglia and the other kingdoms would become spiritual extensions of the royal dynasty. Other differences between the Irish and the Continentals are better termed as having been 'canonical' rather than organizational,[18] and they lay more in the realm of inherited isolation, archaism and idiosyncrasy.

The Irish Church, like its British/Welsh neighbour, had become relatively isolated from the Church on the Continent[19] during the sixth century and had remained highly conservative and individualistic, its customs often reflecting practices that had since been discarded or modified by the rest of the Church in the West. The most significant development of diversity was over the correct date for the celebration of Easter, known as the '*paschalion*', always difficult to calculate and, for the Church, vital in terms of accuracy! Controversy over the calculation of the correct and proper date had reached its height by the early seventh century and the issue had been virtually settled, though uniformity did take a while to accomplish, the issue ultimately becoming one of authority within the Church. The problem lay in the fact that Easter was (as it still is) a moveable feast and the majority of the Church had decided by the fourth century that it must *never* fall on the same date as the Jewish Passover.[20] A new system of calculation had been accepted by Rome in the early seventh century (in line with the observance of the Eastern Church Patriarchates of Constantinople, Alexandria, Antioch and Jerusalem), and soon afterwards[21] the churches and monasteries of the southern part of Ireland fell into line, a likely indicator of their better lines of communication with the Continent, as compared with neighbouring Celtic-speaking territories. However, Iona, an Irish monastery on the Scottish coast, which wielded great influence in the north of Ireland and in English Northumbria, in concert with the surviving British Church in Wales and Cornwall, held out for the old reckoning and adamantly refused to conform to the new, and by now universal, calculation (the Welsh and Cornish would hold out well into the eighth century!). All in all, this resulted in a twenty-eight-day difference for Lent and Easter observances between the Ionan/Irish missions and the Continental missions, both busily at work in England.

It would appear that there were other, though lesser, differences between the two traditions but for these we have only hints rather than certain information, e.g. the method of tonsuring the clergy and the monks,[22] the requirements for consecrating bishops,[23] and even the baptismal rite,[24] all of which probably point to the survival of more archaic Church customs amongst the Irish, customs which had by now become virtually obsolete in the West. These would by the middle of the seventh century be used as 'ammunition' against the Irish and their English followers, though ultimately the issue would not be about correctness of practice but, as we have said, the question of authority in the Church; and part of that problem would arise from the presence and role of exiled Irish bishops, like St Fursey, who were at large and busy in England, missionizing alongside their Continental counterparts and usually without any clearly defined territorial jurisdictions. Ultimately the Continental-orientated bishops were answerable to the Pope and less likely, at least in the early stages of the mission, to fall under the control of local kings and chieftains, a situation that seems to have prevailed much more noticeably at that time in *Frankia* and Ireland, and which it seems the Continental missionaries were anxious to avoid at all costs.[25]

Having examined the background and nature of the two missions, we now turn to the lives and contributions of the two major personalities who bestrode the conversion stage of East Anglia – despite the sparse and confusing nature of the sources. Of their legacy, as we shall see, there can be no doubt.

St Felix of Burgundy

The earliest and most reliable source of information for St Felix, East Anglia's 'Apostle', is Bede,[26] who, regrettably, was not over-provident in this respect, due to the fact that most of his sources were Northumbrian and Kentish and he does not seem to have been overpossessed of East Anglian information for this period. Any local East Anglian information that there was probably perished during the sack of the monasteries there in the later period, and the only other source we have for Felix, which is much later and probably far less reliable than Bede, is the twelfth-century *Book of Ely*, which has some fragmentary information undoubtedly drawn from surviving East Anglian monastic traditions. If there ever was a formal and full 'Life' of the saint, we no longer have

St Felix of Burgundy (Contemporary Church Icon)

it, though it would seem remarkable if none had ever existed, given Felix's important and seminal position in East Anglia's saintly hierarchy! It is to Bede then that we must turn for help.

Bede tells us that when King Sigbert began his reign he 'made it his business to cause all his province to partake of the faith' and that his exertions were much promoted by the Bishop Felix.[27] He goes on to say that Felix had initially come to Archbishop Honorius at Canterbury[28] and (directly or indirectly – we are not told) from Burgundy in Frankish Gaul.[29] Bede's account is highly significant, for it hints that Sigbert had either known Felix, or had at least known of his reputation, during his own exile in *Frankia* and it is quite feasible, therefore, that Felix had been active either as priest-monk or bishop in that region at some stage, coinciding with Sigbert's own exile there. As a Burgundian, Felix originated from a region where the great Irish missionary-saint and monk, St Columbanus, had been present and active with his followers. It is quite possible, therefore, that Felix was reasonably well disposed to Irish monks and clerics, idiosyncrasies and all, and he may have learned to live with the Irish Easter preference, which could have recommended him to Archbishop Honorius at Canterbury, given that the Irish were considerably ahead, in missionary terms, in many parts of the country. Another point in Felix's favour could well have been that, as a Burgundian, he spoke a Germanic tongue, which was not so vastly removed from Early English and which would have overcome to some extent the need for interpreters.

Information about Felix is sparse and we are told nothing of his career in his Continental homeland. Nor are we told much regarding his arrival in England (there is no date given) and Bede's account leaves us to assume that he went directly from Canterbury to Sigbert. But did he? Had he been in England prior to his being requested by Sigbert and was Bede simply telescoping information due to his lack of it? There is a curious tradition,[30] generally regarded as unfounded, that a ruined church existed in the Fenlands (at that time a swampy and watery wasteland – a 'buffer zone' between East Anglia and Mercia) on the Isle of Ely at a site identified as '*Cratendune*' and said to have been built by St Felix.[31] If there is anything in this tradition, and we must exercise caution, it could point to an unrecorded phase of Felix's activities which could be an earlier rather than later part of a Canterbury and Kentish missionary thrust upwards into that region.[32] If this was so, and we can only speculate, it may well have brought Felix to the attention of East Anglian kings who also had an interest in the Fenlands, though for more worldly reasons and as part of their attested expansion westwards. We do not even know when and by whom Felix was consecrated bishop, and it could just as well have been by Archbishop Honorius as by anyone else in *Frankia*, but we can be certain that he arrived in that capacity in East Anglia in 630 or 631. Bede tells us that 'he brought with him teachers and masters for the King's people, and according to the custom of Canterbury', a clear emphasis that this party was not of Irish Church background.[33]

Felix established his episcopal base, together with a school for the training and instruction of future native clergy and monks in which young native English boys would be taught to read and write in Latin. They would have then been instructed in the Bible and biblical commentaries, together with liturgical music, preaching, and the computation necessary for the calculation of the date of Easter. They would have been taught Church music by a specialist chanter, for it does seem that the Canterbury missionaries were highly proficient in this field (Bede says that by 669 in all the churches of the English they began to learn Church music, which until then had only been known in Kent).[34] Further instruction would have been given in the memorization of the psalms and the daily readings and details from the 'Lives' of the saints. Felix's school was established at his base of *Dommoc* and, as we have noted, the location of this place remains uncertain. Since the fifteenth century (and only since that time, as far as we can tell) *Dommoc* has been identified with Dunwich, the sunken and former city and now a disappearing village, on the Suffolk coast.[35] This somewhat contentious claim has largely been based upon an apparent similarity between the two names. Against this supposition can be set the fact that place names change over many centuries and that, just to complicate matters, another medieval source[36] designates Felixstowe, further down the coast, as having been *Dommoc*. Felixstowe is, of course, an old name meaning 'Felix's Place' or 'Church' and as such could quite easily have replaced the earlier name of *Dommoc*. The arguments for Dunwich and Felixstowe continue amongst present-day researchers and none of them have been conclusive, but there is one serious factor that should not be overlooked. Bede's description of *Dommoc*, in his brief account of Felix, indicates a *civitas*, i.e. a royal power base, as having been close to Felix's episcopal seat, which we would expect. Felixstowe, or whatever it was called at that time, was very close to the known royal base of the East Anglian Wuffings kings near Rendlesham (and the royal burial ground of Sutton Hoo) and as such was also very close to Walton, an abandoned Roman shore fort.[37] The name 'Walton' indicates the possibility of British survivors in the locality and, perhaps, some surviving remnants of Christianity, all of which may well have predisposed Felix to such a site. Regrettably any archaeological evidence for Felixstowe/Walton is now probably lost beneath the encroaching waves of the sea – but then, so is that for Dunwich![38]

Whether from Felixstowe or Dunwich (and the former does seem to have been the likelier) we may possibly be able to detect various phases of Felix's missionary thrusts, spreading from his East Suffolk base[39] upwards into Norfolk, and finally pushing westwards into the direction of the Fenlands (if he had not been there before). The East Suffolk phase of activity might well have coincided with King Sigbert's somewhat limited exercise of power, and thus have been closely associated with the Wuffings royal centre at Rendlesham *civitas*. We may conjecture that the two succeeding phases belonged to King Ana's time, the bishop moving across the territory and westwards in the train of the king's initial expansion and consolidation of power. Later traditions would claim that Felix baptized Ana's daughter, the future St Etheldreda (*Aethelthryth*) of Ely, at Exning in West Suffolk, close by the Fenlands, and, if this was true, it might indicate that by the 640s a royal tribute base had been consolidated in that area which enabled Felix to push on westwards into the Fenland edges themselves. Further to this possibility, another late tradition does say that Felix also set up a school and monastery, as we would expect him to have done, at Soham on the edge of the Fens, though some dispute this location and place it at Saham Toney in Norfolk. When Felix died and was buried at *Dommoc* in 647, his body was moved to his foundation at Soham (Saham)[40] where it was venerated, reputed miracles accompanying it, until the Danish destruction of the ninth century.[41] Other places that claim St Felix's presence and which, if true, could be a clue to his movements can also be found in Norfolk, perhaps the second stage of his mission. These include Babingley, Shernborne and Flitcham, all in the north-west of the county, and a tradition has it that Felix actually sailed up round the coast (which, if true, suggests that his base was further down on the coast) and that he was obligingly led into the estuary of the River Babingley, where he founded churches in the surrounding area, the chancel of the present Babingley Church being supposed to stand on the site of a wooden church built by St Felix. Current archaeological investigative work at Sedgeford in Norfolk, quite close to this area, has revealed the possible foundations of a church dating from the seventh century, which would certainly indicate a fairly rapid transition to Christianity. Though such a foundation can be no earlier than several generations after Felix,[42] it may well be an indicator of his former presence in the area, or that of his associates.

Later Church iconographical depiction would show Felix resting upon a bed of seashells, an angel bearing him a crown, which suggests that he was remembered as a seafaring saint, as the Babingley tradition would have us believe. It is more than likely that he did reach East Anglia by sea, arriving at King Sigbert's base down the Deben estuary. He would hardly have travelled by land,[43] given that the land approach was perilous due to hostilities with Mercia, and the inescapable fact that East Anglia was, and always has been, most accessible from the sea. The evidence of Sutton

Hoo indicates that the Wuffings, Felix's royal hosts, were a seafaring tribe and we might thus reasonably suppose that Felix, under their protection, did much of his gospel-inspired journeying by sea also. If this is true, he had something in common with the Irish saints and missionaries who shared a similar tradition of seafaring,[44] and it is to one of their number that we shall now turn.

St Fursey

There are several sources for St Fursey (*Feársa*),[45] and most of them are of Irish origin. They deal mainly with his earlier life in Ireland and the later period of his activities in *Frankia*, but Bede also gives us some valuable information about his time in East Anglia, together with a shortened version of his visions, remarkable by themselves as part of the tradition of Christian visionary and apocalyptic material.

Bede tells us that during King Sigbert's reign 'there came out of Ireland a holy man, Fursey, renowned for his words and actions and remarkable for his virtues. Fursey's purpose was to live as a stranger for the Lord, wherever an opportunity should offer.[46] He was honourably received by the king and, performing his usual employment of preaching the gospel, converted many unbelievers to Christ, and confirmed in His faith and love those that already believed' (a reference which is surely one to the existence of surviving Christianity in East Anglia).[47] Bede also goes on to say that Fursey built a monastery on ground given to him by King Sigbert, and that it was pleasantly situated in the woods, with the sea not far off; it was built within the area of a fortress, called in the English language *Cnobheresburgh* (and which some like to believe was Burgh Castle on the River Yare estuary,[48] near Great Yarmouth). Bede further says that Fursey was accompanied by his brothers, Foillan and Ultan, and two priests, Gobhan (*Govan*) and Dicuil (*Deicola*), though there is a suggestion that Fursey's other brother, Ultan, was not with them in these early stages. Bede also says that before having come to East Anglia, Fursey

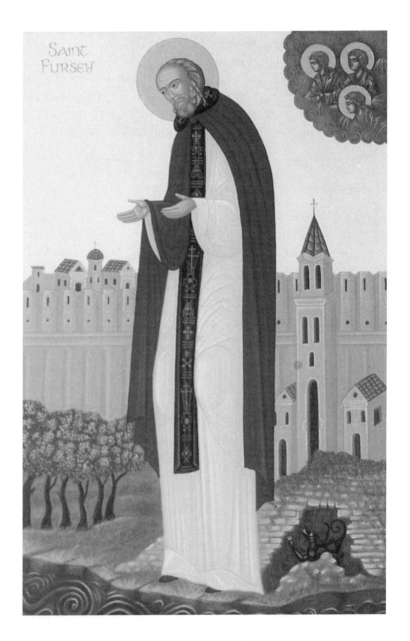

St Fursey (Contemporary Church Icon)

had preached amongst the Irish for many years and that 'leaving his native island, he came with a few brothers through the Britons into the province of the English'.[49] Fursey was, he says, 'of noble Irish blood and from boyhood he had applied himself to reading sacred books, and following monastic discipline'.[50]

The Irish sources for Fursey's life contain much more detail than Bede's account and they also describe miracles attributed to him, together with a fuller description of his remarkable visions and some detail on his brothers and companions. These sources are found in ancient Irish and Latin texts that date back to the twelfth century, though they quite clearly derive from much earlier texts, and it is considered that they reflect those early sources quite accurately. Bede's account was based upon one of these early texts and he simply extracted detail from it. Modern research has come to the opinion that, due to the closeness of Bede's recension compared to the twelfth-century texts, there was clearly an early 'Life' of St Fursey, probably written in Latin, which had itself been written down or narrated by one of the saint's disciples within a generation of Fursey's death, which occurred during the late 640s.[51] According to these sources, Fursey came from the Lough Corrib area of the west of Ireland, maybe the Island of Inisquin, and from within the kingdom of the Connachta, possibly of the Conmaicne tribe. Accounts of his parentage are conflicting, but all the sources agree that he was of noble status, though they are at pains to emphasize that he was more noble by reason of his virtue. He was said to have been the son of a royal chieftain, Fintan, a grandson of Finlugh, King of Munster,[52] and his mother is named as Gelges, a daughter of Aedh, King of Connachta,[53] and, if any of this is true, then Fursey was born in about the 580s. According to the legend, his father, Fintan, was a pagan, though Gelges, his mother, was a Christian;[54] and apparently the sweetness and grace of Gelges won over Fintan to Christianity, much to the fury of Gelges' father, King Aedh, who sent the pair packing and into exile in the neighbouring Connachta tribal area.[55] Fintan's uncle was said to have been St Brendan, the Abbot of Inisquin,[56] and it was there that Fintan took his pregnant wife who duly gave

birth to Fursey, St Brendan baptizing him under that name as it
meant 'virtue'.

It would seem that Fursey was given to the monastery as a boy
to be trained as a monk[57] and that this took place under the
supervision of St Brendan, who at his death was succeeded in this
task by another holy abbot, St Meldhan.[58] When of age, Fursey
left the monastery and retired to become a hermit near the shores
of Lough Corrib, the ruins of which still stand today at Bally
Magibbon near the village of Cross. From there Fursey eventually
went on to establish his own monastery, the site of which is
nowadays called Killarsagh,[59] and its ruins can be seen at Owen
near the River Owenduff. At this monastery Fursey was thronged
by recruits from all over Ireland and those who were drawn to
him were affected by the power of his preaching and the strength
of his personal example. Three of his disciples were brothers,
Algise, Gobhan[60] and Etto, all of whom he would later ordain to
the priesthood and who would be his eventual companions in
faraway East Anglia and *Frankia*. Whilst at this monastery Fursey
fell seriously ill and into some sort of cataleptic trance, experienc-
ing his famous visions.[61] The full account of these can be found
in the Irish 'Life' of St Fursey, of which Bede gives a shorter
version. The main theme of these visions is the effort of the power
of evil to claim the Christian soul as it quits the body on its
passage to the life to come. A fierce struggle is depicted in which
angels engage in conflict with demons, refuting their arguments
and rescuing the soul from the flames of perdition threatening it.
During his final vision Fursey received a visible reminder of the
flames that await unrepentant sinners, which was said to have
remained with him for the duration of his life in the form of scars
on his jaw and shoulder. Bede, independently of the other sources,
goes on to say that an old man in his own monastery and still
alive at the time of Bede's writing (the 730s) had testified to him
that he in turn had known a truthful and devout man in East
Anglia who had heard of Fursey's visions from the saint's own
mouth. He recalled how on a frosty and bitter winter's day, though
Fursey was wearing only a thin garment, the saint would sweat

as he recounted the visions due to the terror of his recollections!

It is quite evident from the Irish sources that Fursey experienced these visions prior to his journey to East Anglia as they contain references to his parents and relatives having gathered around him at the time, fearing that he was dead. In one of the visions Fursey received a command from his former master St Meldhan, instructing him to go and preach a message of repentance to the chieftains and people of Ireland. This instruction he carried out for twelve years, accompanied by eight companions,[62] though in the end he sought a return to solitude and the embracement of exile from his native land.[63] It is possible that he travelled up to the Kingdom of *Uladh* (Ulster), where the Scottish Abbey of Iona held many dependencies and under whose obedience he may have been for a while. Accounts of his life refer to the good that he and his companions brought to the island of Britain and above all to the 'Picts and the Saxons', which tends to suggest a period of activity in southern Scotland and Northumbria before journeying southwards to East Anglia.[64]

Fursey arrived in East Anglia at some time between 633 and 635 and it is quite possible that he had been sent to King Sigbert by the latter's Northumbrian ally, King Oswald, who during his own time of exile had been in Ireland and, as far as we are aware, may have known, or known of, Fursey. How the Irish monks reached East Anglia is uncertain, but it is likely that some of their journey could have been undertaken by sea from a point on the Northumbrian-controlled coast down to where King Sigbert was based, presumably the East Suffolk Sandlings area.[65] Sigbert, as we have already noted, gave Fursey a suitable site for a monastery at a place now unknown unto us, though possibly Burgh Castle in Norfolk, the former Roman shore fort of *Garriannonum* (this suggestion, based on precious little evidence, dates back only as far as the sixteenth century),[66] nearby Caister-on-Sea being another possibility, as it was also a former Roman shore fort.[67] However, nowhere does Bede say that the fortification given to Fursey was an abandoned Roman one, and there are other more plausible possibilities further south, and closer to where the king's power base was likely to have been and exactly where we might expect Fursey to have established himself. A feasible case has been made out recently for the site of the fortification, and thus Fursey's monastery, as having been down on the Orwell peninsula not too far from the royal base of Rendlesham, and close by Felix's *Dommoc* (most probably Felixstowe/Walton).[68] The site is at Shotley, just south of lpswich,[69] and the name 'Shotley' could derive from the Old English meaning 'the wood of the Scots' (i.e. Irish). It certainly is by a river estuary and close to the sea, and this possibility has been strengthened by the revelation through aerial photography of earthworks of considerable proportions having once been there.

Wherever Fursey's monastery was set up (and it seems pointless to speculate until the discovery of stronger evidence), it was most certainly established along traditional Irish lines and became a base for missionary activity in the region under the protection of King Sigbert and the overall supervision of Bishop St Felix. The monastery, like most Irish ones, probably resembled a tribal

St Fursey's Monastery (An Imaginary Representation of Burgh Castle)

enclosure and was likely to have been oval or circular in layout[70] with the church in the centre and perhaps an additional church outside the perimeter for the laity. Such settlements often consisted of three inner circles or enclosures,[71] the inner, as we have seen, containing the church and the huts of the strictest monastic brethren. The second enclosure might have contained wider and more semi-monastic groupings, and in the outer perimeter were the huts of the retainers and those who tended the monastery's land and cattle and so forth.[72] The Irish built their structures mainly of wood, by way of contrast to the Continental preference for stone and mortar. The actual church was probably constructed of wattle, daub and thatch – rectangular and small in dimension, with one door at the west end[73] and a screen dividing the altar area from the main church. Recent research has also indicated that Irish monasteries were often deliberately sited at the boundaries of kingdoms or tribal enclaves, which not only carried inherited pagan associations but also the Christian symbolism of the boundary between this world and the next. Such boundary sites were also the traditional locations for forts and assembly gatherings, which could add a little support to the Burgh Castle claim, as the latter may have been on a former tribal boundary of the North Folk and South Folk.[74]

The accounts of Fursey's life give us little detail about his actual missionary work in East Anglia, work which seems to have endured for about ten years or so, and it has been suggested that the activities of these Irish missionary saints may have been concentrated in the Waveney Valley area of Suffolk (which again assumes that the monastery was in fact at Burgh or Caister). Two miracles are attributed to St Fursey for his East Anglian sojourn.[75] The first was said to have occurred just after the saint had completed the construction of his monastery at *Cnobheresburgh*. Apparently, the only thing the monastery lacked was a bell, and, as Fursey pondered the problem, a widow's only son died and the body was carried to the church for burial. As Fursey met the funeral procession, an angel descended from the sky and gave him a bell. At the first sound of the bell the boy returned to life and went on to live as a monk in the monastery! The second miracle concerned a great famine that had afflicted East Anglia. Fursey, together with his friend and travelling companion, Lactan, went into a field adjoining the monastery. They both began to till the ground with a spade and rake, Fursey then sowing the field with seed. In three days the seed germinated and sprang into maturity, the corn being ripe for the sickle and ready for gathering into the monastery's granary![76]

Fursey's influence was probably quite profound, though no churches in the region bear his dedication, and, if there were any, they have not survived. In his work he was no doubt assisted by the rest of his companions of whom, again, there seems to be no lasting remembrance in East Anglia, other than perhaps Dicuil. It seems likely that Fursey established several smaller monastic dependencies throughout the region but whether or not they had any permanence after his departure in the mid-640s, it is impossible to tell. The urge to further exile and solitude was ever within Fursey, the classic Irish pilgrim and wanderer, and for a time he handed the running of the monastery to his brother, Foillan, and the priests, Gobhan and Dicuil, going off for a while to join his other brother, Ultan (who was living somewhere in the region as a hermit), and to share with him a life of austerity, prayer and labour. By about 645, Fursey left for ever, having entrusted the care of the monastery once more to Foillan, his reason having been, according to Bede, the danger of attacks from the heathen, a clear reference to Mercian invasions during the troubles of King Ana's reign. If he intended to return he failed to do so, which may have had something to do with the insecurity of East Anglia, his continuing proclivity for wandering and the exile notion, and perhaps the death of Bishop Felix in 647. Whatever the case, he went to *Frankia* (with its strong Irish connections), was hospitably received by its king, Clovis II, and built a monastery at Lagny in northern France, being joined there soon after by some of his former companions from Ireland and East Anglia. These included Lactan and Aemilian (others – Radolgus, Algise and Corbican – had already arrived there before him). Shortly after founding his new monastery, Fursey died, probably in about 648 or so. His relics were transferred to Péronne to a church which had been built by a former friend, Erchenwald the Mayor, and soon his relics were declared to be miraculously incorrupt. The relics of Fursey's former teachers, Meldhan and Beoan, were also interred with him, having been brought there by Fursey himself. There the relics of the three would remain until the Franco-Prussian War of 1870 when the church was destroyed. Only Fursey's skull was saved from amongst the debris and it was restored to a new church and reliquary where it remains today as an object of veneration for passing pilgrims, together with a 'holy' well dedicated to the saint.

Back in East Anglia, it would seem that Fursey's two brothers, Foillan and Ultan, remained for a little while, the monastery having probably been the victim of Mercian attack within a year or so of Fursey's departure. Soon afterwards, they followed their brother's footsteps to *Frankia* (though after Fursey was dead), where they also were well received by King Clovis, who gave them some land at Fosses where they built a monastery and hospice for strangers. Following Fursey's example, they set about missionary work in the region and left a strong influence upon its later monasticism, St Foillan going on to become one of the best-loved Irish missionary monks on the Continent. In 655, on the eve of the Feast of St Quentinius (31 October), Foillan served Mass for his community and set out upon a journey with three of his companions. Whilst passing through a forest they were set upon by outlaws who robbed and murdered them, leaving their bodies lying there until they were discovered on the following 16 January. St Ultan, the surviving brother, had prophesied the death of Foillan and arranged for the victims to be buried at the monastery founded by Foillan, where he came to be venerated as a martyr. Ultan succeeded as abbot of Fosses and of Péronne where, after his death, his relics were taken back to join those of his brother, Foillan, at Fosses.[77]

Of the rest who may have been with Fursey in East Anglia, we know very little, save that Algise, Corbican and Radolgus finally settled at Laon where they would long be remembered in the region. Gobhan, who may have left with Fursey, also settled as a hermit in Laon, where he eventually suffered martyrdom at the hands of German heathens. Etto, who may also have left with Fursey, eventually finished up in the Liège area, where he founded an oratory and monastery, dying at an advanced age in 670, his relics being preserved in the church of Dampierre. Mauguille had apparently considered a return to England after Fursey's death, but decided to settle nearer at hand, and saw out his days as a hermit near the monastery of St Riquier, where his relics were preserved until as late as the sixteenth century. Of Aemilian, we know little, other than that he succeeded Fursey in the abbatial office (as did Lactan) at Lagny. Dicuil, as we have seen, may be the same Dicuil to whom Bede referred as having founded a small and unsuccessful monastery at Bosham in Sussex. If he was one and the same, we cannot be certain as to how or why he reached there. One possibility is that he made his way directly there, though probably not by land. The other (and it is more likely) is that he may have accompanied Fursey and the others to *Frankia* and eventually fulfilled an aspiration, shared by Mauguille, to return to England, though this time, whether by design or circumstance, reaching the still pagan Kingdom of Sussex. Whether or not St Dicuil went directly to Sussex after the abandonment of Fursey's monastery, or after a sojourn with his master, Fursey, in *Frankia*, Sussex may have been an attractive proposition as a fresh missionary target. Not only was it still pagan, but it had not yet, it seems, attracted the presence of the Canterbury-based Continental mission, thus enabling the Irish to be first on the scene. There also seems to be a little evidence that King Oswiu of Northumbria, who patronized and favoured the Irish Church and Ionan missions in his own territories (at least until the Synod of Whitby), exercised a temporary overlordship there. If that was so, he may well have encouraged the Irish to get there first as an enablement of the extension of his own *imperium*.

To all intents and purposes, the Irish mission in East Anglia does not seem to have been as effective as its Continental counterpart and it may have failed for several reasons. It depended upon the goodwill of Bishop Felix, whose own mission's organizational structure it lacked, together with the protection of the king. Both of these requirements were uncertain after 647. To assess the Irish achievement in East Anglia is virtually impossible, but the least that can be said is that its presence probably rendered temporary valuable assistance to the Continental mission, particularly in the area of supplementary pastoral support for widespread communities which had either been pre-existent to or established by St Felix. Its influence may have been particularly present in the evolution of a certain, and localized, type of monasticism that could have been in place and quite widespread until the ninth century, and it is perhaps to there that we should look for the legacy of Fursey and his Irish monks. The legacy of Felix can perhaps be summed up in Bede's own words: 'This pious husbandman reaped a large harvest of believers, delivering all of the province (in accordance with his name) from long wickedness and infelicity, bringing it to the faith and works of righteousness, and the gifts of everlasting happiness.'[78] After the departure of Fursey and his companions and the death of Felix, even stronger foundations would be put in place, and it is to those that we now turn.

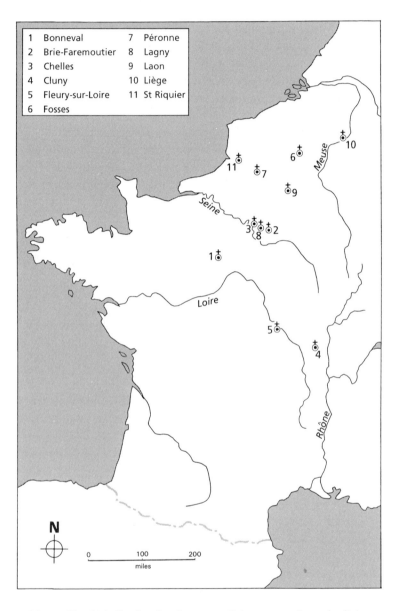

1	Bonneval	7	Péronne
2	Brie-Faremoutier	8	Lagny
3	Chelles	9	Laon
4	Cluny	10	Liège
5	Fleury-sur-Loire	11	St Riquier
6	Fosses		

Map 2 *Frankish Gaul – showing some of the monasteries and religious sites mentioned in the text*

4

An Abbot and a Missionary

St Botolph

The *Anglo-Saxon Chronicle* in its entry for the year 654 records: 'In this year King Ana was killed; and Botwulf began to timber his monastery at *Icanhoe*.'[1] *Botwulf* (or as he is more generally known – Botolph) may have been one of the most significant and important personalities in the foundation of East Anglian Christianity, and particularly in terms of its consolidation in the generation that followed St Felix and St Fursey, i.e. the third quarter of the seventh century. Regrettably we know even less about him than of his predecessors, and even Bede, our best informant for these times, remains totally silent regarding him and his influence, which may well have extended beyond the boundaries of East Anglia. The principal written source that we have for St Botolph is a 'Life' written no earlier than the eleventh century, during the time of King Edward the Confessor (400 years after Botolph's time!), by Abbot Folcard of Thorney,[2] and if there were any earlier written records they do not seem to have survived. Allowing for the possibility of Folcard having drawn upon some contemporary written accounts in East Anglian monasteries (and we should seriously doubt this possibility because of the fairly wholesale destruction of the monasteries that had occurred during the time of the Viking invasions) and the availability of surviving and garbled oral traditions, the 'Life', as it appears, seems to be very fictitious and to have been composed for the purpose of the enhancement of Thorney in the monastic 'pecking order'. This was based upon its possession of what were claimed to be some of the relics of St Botolph, and the possession of a 'Life' was regarded as essential. However, there may still have been a few scraps of facts mixed in with pious invention and fiction. It certainly seems that Botolph was remembered as an important and much revered saint, so can we discern anything about him at all?

According to Folcard's eleventh-century account, he was of 'Saxon' race (i.e. English), but much loved by the Scots (Irish) because he matched word with example. Another source, earlier in origin than Folcard, the *Sleswig Breviary*,[3] refers to him as a 'Scot' (Irishman) of royal descent. The name '*Botwulf*', as it stands, would appear to be Early English, though we must allow for the possibility of its having been an Anglicized form of an Irish name, and similarly with regard to the name of his brother, referred to and rendered in the texts as '*Adwulf*' (Adolph). Interestingly, Botolph did enjoy a liturgical veneration in areas traditionally associated with Irish missionary activity, his name appearing in the *York Calendar*, the *Aberdeen Martyrology*, the *Arbuthnot Missal* and the *Ferne Calendar*, the first of these books having belonged to Northumbria,[4] with its strong Ionan and Irish Church connections, and the rest to Scotland. The *Sleswig Breviary* contains material going back to the eighth century, much of it deriving from the great English missionary, St Willibrord,[5] who went to the Sleswig area of Germany only a few years after St Botolph's death.[6] There remains the possibility that Botolph and his brother were of the first generation of English converts and trained in monasticism by Irish missionaries of the like of St Fursey and for use as interpreters.[7] The fact that the 'Life' refers to Botolph as a 'Saxon' (rather than as an 'Angle'[8] is also curious as this was a term that was used by Bede to describe, amongst others, the inhabitants of Sussex and, as we have seen, there is a possibility that one of Fursey's monks, Dicuil,[9] may have set up a monastery there, presumably from the late 640s onwards, accompanied by five other monks.[10] There are also three known church dedications to St Botolph in Sussex and if all these clues amount to anything, they could indicate that Botolph was directly or indirectly linked to the earlier mission of St Fursey in East Anglia, either as a very young convert brought southwards by Fursey, or as one of Dicuil's followers possibly of East Anglian origin as well.[11]

Saxonia, however, was also a name given to northern France (i.e. *Frankia*), and the 'Life' says that Botolph and his brother were *sent* there to complete their education and monastic training (which suggests that it had already begun elsewhere and that they were quite young when sent there).[12] Depending on when Botolph was born, this opens up three possibilities. Firstly, that he was indeed of Scotto-Irish background (but presumably with a command of English) and went directly from somewhere under Iona's influence to *Frankia* (this seems unlikely as there is no later evidence that he had any preference for Ionan ways, e.g. the calendar). The second is that he was an East Anglian noble youth and sent by Fursey to *Frankia*, or went with him when the Irish mission was abandoned in the mid-640s. The third possibility is that he was a Sussex youth, converted and partly trained by Dicuil from the late 640s onwards. The two latter possibilities seem to be the stronger and fit in with the likely age of Botolph at his time of death. The accounts of his life indicate that he was of an advanced age when he died (probably in about the 680s) and from that we might guess that he was born in the 620s. By the time of Fursey's activities in East Anglia this would have put him in his early teens to early twenties and it would fit in with the possibility of an exit to *Frankia* with the mission, allowing for his eventual ordination and a return to East Anglia. This, as we have seen, may have been in Fursey's mind, if not for himself, then at least for some of his companions and disciples. Whether or not he spent time with Dicuil in Sussex before returning to East Anglia, remains a serious consideration.

Whatever the case, Adolph was in time elevated to the status of bishop either for Utrecht or Maastricht[13] and Botolph returned to England where he was favourably received by a king of the Southern Angles, named as 'Aethelmund', of whom we have no historical trace, and whose kingdom is therefore described in vague and unspecific terms. The 'Life' also says that at the monastery in *Frankia* where Botolph had been prior to his return, there were two sisters of this 'King Aethelmund' who furnished Botolph with letters of recommendation to their brother, as well as to their mother who at the time was regent for the king (apparently still a minor), and they entreated that Botolph be provided with a place to found a monastery. Apparently, Botolph was graciously received not only by the young king but also by Aethelhere, King of the East Angles, and his son who happened to be there at the time (King Aethelhere most certainly *did* exist!). Permission was duly given to Botolph to choose any unoccupied land and eventually he selected a spot called '*Icanhoe*'. Can any of this be reconciled with the few known facts, together with Bede's silence and the terse entry in the *Anglo-Saxon Chronicle*? Possibly.

Firstly the *Chronicle* simply tells us that Botolph came into East Anglia in the year of King Ana's death (whether before or after the event we do not know), which at least gives us the date of 654. Secondly, there certainly were royal sisters in *Frankia* before Botolph's return to England, namely Ethelburgha and Saethryth, a daughter and stepdaughter of King Ana respectively. Thirdly, Ana, after his death, was succeeded by a King Aethelhere, his brother, who reigned for a year only (being succeeded in turn by another brother, Aethelwald, and not the son referred to in the 'Life' – this Aethelhere was killed in battle fighting as an ally of the Mercians against Ana's former Christian Northumbrian allies and his son could have been killed along with him).[14] It is quite possible that Ana, after his death at the hands of the Mercians, left a son and successor (another late source records that a son of Ana, Jaruman (*Eohreman*), died in battle along with his father)[15] who was too young to rule other than under some sort of regency of Ana's widow. We have no name for such a son or indeed his mother, but the 'Life', as we have seen, gives record of an 'Aethelmund' and says that the queen was 'Siwara'. Maybe the kingdom fell apart after Ana's demise or there was a return to power-sharing, and perhaps such a youthful and direct descendant of Ana was allowed a limited and temporary exercise of notional rule due to the former prestige of Ana. If this was so, the real power rested with Aethelhere under Mercian control, and the exercise of power by what was left of Ana's direct descendants had been restricted to the Sandlings area. It may have been there that Botolph went for permission to build his monastery, close to the royal base, on a suitable site.

Whatever really happened, it would seem that Botolph selected a new and previously unused location, which raises the question of where exactly it was.[16] There now seems to be general agreement that *Icanhoe* can be identified with the present-day hamlet of 'Iken', to this day a remote spot on the estuary of the River Alde in East Suffolk. In earlier times it was a peninsula surrounded by the river and its marshes on one side, and by heathland and forest on the remaining sides.[17] There Botolph laid the foundations for his monastery in what was an ideal location (no doubt following the influence of previous Irish tradition), notwithstanding attacks from 'evil spirits' who apparently infested the place.[18] It seems that these 'evil spirits' spoke to Botolph, advising him that they were inhabiting a place where Christians had once resided, all of which bears a noticeable similarity to an account of a later hermit (St Guthlac) who encountered something similar in the Fens, and whose 'evil spirits' on that occasion manifested the ability to speak Welsh,[19] though we are not told anything of the linguistic skills of Botolph's demons! It is tempting to dismiss such accounts of demonic encounter as being the standard stuff of hagiography, depicting the triumphant holy man wrestling with the forces of evil, and the 'Lives' of ascetical saints are replete with them. However, there could be a more tangible explanation underlying this reference. It could be a pointer to some sort of residual and surviving British population, albeit sparse and in a fairly remote area.[20] The element 'Ic' in *Icanhoe* may well relate to the name 'Iceni' – the former British tribe of a large swathe of East Anglia – and nearby names in the same area are suggestive of this, e.g. Campsey Ash – possibly a former Roman-British site. If this is so, the reference to a former Christianity may indicate previous abandonment of the same and a reversion to paganism.

Excavations at Iken Church, carried out in 1977,[21] not only indicated an older early English religious site, with a timber-framed building dating back to the right period, having been there, but also uncovered Roman and British pottery. There is also in the church a ninth-century cross shaft which seems to be commemorative, and it has been suggested that Botolph may have founded the monastery as a memorial to King Ana.[22] Descriptions of *Icanhoe* in Folcard's 'Life' of Botolph do tally with the contemporary topography of Iken, as in the description of 'dismal swamps' together with the wintry aspects and summer beauty, all of which still apply, although the river estuary is now narrower. The clinching factor would appear to be a fourteenth-century rent roll of nearby Butley Priory which refers to Iken as 'Ycano'.

Let us return to Botolph in his monastery as it was. The 'Life' informs us that in a short time Botolph gathered around him a community of monks (from where, we are not told) whom he trained according to the rule of St Benedict, and that he came to be venerated for holiness and miracles and good example amongst his disciples.[23] Amongst the several visitors who spent time with him was Ceolfrith, the eventual Abbot of Monkwearmouth/Jarrow and Bede's future master,[24] who spent several years at the monastery as its baker, until recalled northwards by Benedict Biscop.[25] A further intriguing reference in the *Sleswig Breviary* also says that it was seven years from the time of Botolph's introduction to the king (we are not told which king) until he was given his grant of land, and Folcard's account is also somewhat suggestive of prolonged negotiations having taken place before the building of the monastery could begin. This could mean, of course, that Botolph only began his building work in 654 and that for some reason there were delays. Another possibility is that he had arrived back in England seven years prior to this, i.e. in about 647, and within a year or two of Fursey's death in *Frankia* (if we are correct about his age at that time, he would have been very young – but we need not assume he was in his sixties when he died: he could just as well have been ten years or more older). We might well ask what Botolph was doing in those seven years. Again, there may be a few clues.

If he did return in 647, either as a result of encouragement

from St Fursey or his disciples or on his own initiative, he may
have had to abandon any earlier attempts at refounding former
Irish monastic centres, owing to the precarious nature of the last
years of Ana's reign. As an interim measure, then, he may have
returned to *Frankia* or joined Dicuil in Sussex until more favourable circumstances prevailed. Another possibility is that he may
have set up only a temporary foundation and that for an unknown
period of time he was engaged in missionary work elsewhere until
the permanent establishment of his own monastery (assuming that
he returned to England in 654). The Sleswig source does indicate
that Botolph undertook two important journeys (out of several),
all of which occurred during a space of twenty years and which
were perhaps between 647 and 667 or between 654 and 674,
though the earlier dates do seem to be the more likely. If this is
correct, where could Botolph have been missionizing?

It has been suggested that Botolph was present at the baptism
of King Swithelm of Essex during the latter's exile in East Anglia,
which occurred whilst an apostate king ruled over the Essex kingdom (another Sigbert), and this may have been in about 653.
St Cedd, another Irish-trained English churchman, was present
and undertook the baptism. If both Botolph and Cedd were present in East Anglia at that time, it would tend to suggest that
they were active in the area as missionaries and under East Anglian
control or in territories in which East Anglia had a controlling
interest.[26] These areas, which bordered on to East Anglia, were
obviously Essex to the south and the Fenlands to the west. It
seems that Cedd had been busy as an evangelist in East Mercia
when Peada, Penda of Mercia's son, ruled that territory during his
father's lifetime as a sub-king, and Cedd also had Northumbrian
protection. Botolph could have been with Cedd in that part of
Mercia during his unaccounted-for seven years as part of an initiative jointly exercised by Northumbria and East Anglia, and perhaps
as part of a policy of detaching this part of Mercia. The 'Life' of
Botolph does say that he passed through 'swamps' to reach his
eventual East Anglian destination at *Icanhoe*, and this could be a
reference to a journey through the Fens.[27] There are certainly

church dedications to him close to the edge of the Fenlands,[28] and Thorney later made much of its claim for the saint's relics. Essex also has a high proportion of church dedications to Botolph, notably along the Thames-estuary side, which may tell us something.

As we have seen, King Swithelm of Essex had been driven out of his kingdom by one Sigbert, an apostate who in time repented of his errors and who was prevailed upon by the Northumbrians, perhaps with East Anglian help, to return to Christianity. The reason was no doubt to circumvent or reclaim Essex from encircling Mercian domination, always of particular concern for East Anglia, and Bede tells us that the same Sigbert asked for missionary help in the reconversion process, and no doubt for the continuing purpose of the conversion of his kingdom.[29] The response was the sending of Cedd, who had been in East Mercia, and one other priest, whose name we are not given. We can only speculate as to whether or not this was Botolph, who, if it was, perhaps represented the East Anglian interest in this undertaking. We do not know precisely when St Cedd left Essex[30] but he seems to have been there for no more than a year or two, and thus Botolph's return to the East Anglian kingdom may have been in about 655.[31] The other journeys referred to in Folcard's account may have been connected to return visits to Essex or the Fenland area, and the second journey, perhaps in the early 670s,[32] may simply have been due to a need for change and rest after a snake bite incident recorded in the 'Life' (there still are snakes on Iken Heath).[33] This journey may also have been the occasion for further missionary work and consolidation in East Anglia itself. We are told that on this occasion Botolph founded two churches dedicated to St Peter and St Paul, though their locations are uncertain, the only information being that they were 'remote from the sea, in great solitude, and with a river flowing through a valley accessible through forests'. The grant for these two foundations, according to the 'Life', came from the same king who granted the monastery, though this seems rather unlikely,[34] and the location could have been anywhere in Norfolk or Suffolk. Given that there are nearly three times as many church dedications to Botolph in Norfolk as in Suffolk, some of which may preserve a memory of his presence and activity in the area, perhaps Norfolk remains the likelier place for this phase of Botolph's missionary activity.[35]

Botolph was certainly back at *Icanhoe* by the early 670s, when Ceolfrith, whom we have already mentioned, visited him, and it would seem that at some later stage he was also joined by his brother, Adolph, though whether or not the latter actually was a bishop we cannot tell. One Bury St Edmunds' tradition also claimed that Botolph himself had been a bishop,[36] and if this was true he might have acted in some auxiliary capacity to the bishops of East Anglia,[37] as Fursey had done before him.[38] If this was the case, it might strengthen the possibility of Botolph having been much more orientated towards the Irish mission and its background than we generally assume. However, it seems more likely that this claim had something to do more with Bury's later claims for freedom from episcopal control on the grounds that it had once been an episcopal seat itself since early times, a (spurious) claim which was to be enhanced by the later possession of a major relic of St Botolph (an arm) – thus posthumous episcopal status was duly claimed!

We do need to address the thorny question of Bede's total silence about Botolph, which does raise serious questions.[39] One possibility may be that Botolph's Irish background and practices were indeed more significant than his biographer, Folcard, indicates, and the *Sleswig Breviary* tends to suggest this. We also raised the possibility of earlier connections with, and training by, the Irish mission in East Anglia, and of this Bede would have disapproved. The possibility of Botolph's strong Irish orientation seems to be hinted at from another direction. Traditionally, Botolph had an association with bridges and boundaries: in fact four ancient church dedications to him in the City of London are all at the old gates of the City. If these foundations reflect the presence of the saint there, and during a time when he was in Essex with St Cedd[40] (London was the capital of the Kingdom of Essex),[41] they could be indicators of a strong Irish character to Botolph's work, given the known Irish preference for boundaries, though this could have some connection with St Cedd also.[42] Bede must have known something of Botolph from Ceolfrith and we cannot take seriously the suggestion that Ceolfrith simply forgot to tell Bede about him. We must assume that Bede knew something of Botolph, even if only from Ceolfrith, given that Bede's own sources seem to have been mainly Northumbrian and Kentish with little, if any, from East Anglia. Botolph's Irishness, together with a relative lack of much information about him, may have conditioned Bede's silence.

Despite Bede's lack of testimony and the sparse information for Botolph generally, he probably ranks alongside St Felix and St Fursey in terms of importance for the foundations of Christianity in East Anglia, and his legacy was undoubtedly more durable than that of Fursey, the visionary and Irish 'wanderer'. In a sense Botolph combined Irish 'other-worldliness' with the practical approach of the Continental mission and perhaps represents a fusion of the two. The comparative lack of information for Botolph, measured against the better-known details on Felix and Fursey, may have done his memory a serious injustice.

St Jaruman

Very little is known of this saint,[43] who belongs to the same period, other than that he was a bishop of Mercia. Bede named him as the second English bishop there, who followed in a line of Irish bishops in that kingdom (his predecessor had also been English).[44] Our interest in him is that he may have been East Anglian and had some links with St Botolph. There appear to be place names associated with him in East Anglia, notably at Wiggenhall St German's in Norfolk, where it is likely that the St German of the name is a corruption of Jaruman (the name was probably *Eohreman* or *Irmin*). Wiggenhall is on the edge of the Norfolk Fens and his associations there might have had something to do with the earlier missionary activities of St Botolph, and possibly St Cedd, in that region.[45] Wiggenhall St German's is also close to Stow Bardolph, the name having an association with St Botolph

(Stow Bardolph meaning 'Botolph's Place' or 'Church'), and nearby Wiggenhall St Mary Magdalene also carried a dedication to St Botolph in the Middle Ages, thus suggesting some possible connection between the two saints.

We know nothing of Jaruman's activities during the 650s, though Bede draws attention to him for the 660s onwards, by which time he was Bishop of the Mercians. Bede tells us that, following the death of Swithelm, King of Essex, whom we met undergoing baptism at Rendlesham at the hands of St Cedd, two co-rulers had succeeded in Essex under the overlordship of King Wulfhere of Mercia (by now Penda and his Christian son, Peada, were dead) to which East Anglia was also by now subject. These two rulers, Sighere and Sebbi, together with their subjects, experienced an outbreak of bubonic plague in their kingdom which seems to have been of pandemic proportions. This prompted Sighere to abandon Christianity for the old religion of his forefathers, though Sebbi remained a Christian. All this seems to have been a repetition of what had happened previously under King Sigbert of Essex, who, as we have seen,[46] was prevailed upon to return to the Christian fold by the labours of St Cedd and possibly the assistance of St Botolph. The sending of Jaruman to Essex must be seen as a Mercian attempt to re-establish its control there, the patronage of clerics being a favoured instrument for such purposes, and on this occasion East Anglian assistance, owing to East Anglia's own subjection to Mercia at this time, was at hand.[47] However, in this instance only a portion of the kingdom had lapsed, two factors having possibly been at work. The Kingdom of Essex, at that time, was larger than the present-day county of that name, comprising not only Essex as we now know it, but also taking in the now vanished county of Middlesex, with its capital of London, and possibly some parts of south-eastern Hertfordshire stretching across the Thames into Surrey. The joint exercise of rule of the two kings may have resulted in a roughly east–west division of the kingdom[48] and, given that the eastern part bears evidence for much heavier early English settlement, due to its maritime situation, and probably a more entrenched pagan tradition, it was likely to have been Sighere's domain where pagan-ism reasserted itself. (Its coastal accessibility may also have meant that, due to trading links with *Frankia*, the plague had taken a stronger foothold there.) Bede says that 'Jaruman was sent to Essex to reclaim the lost portion for Christianity, accompanied by a priest [Botolph?]', and that he was 'discreet and devoted to his task – a religious and good man, who travelled through all the country [Essex], far and near, reducing the king and his people to the way of righteousness, so that, either forsaking or destroying the temples and altars which they had erected, they opened the churches, and rejoiced in confessing the name of Christ'.[49] The task being completed, Jaruman and his priests and teachers returned home, where it is recorded that he died in 668 or 669.

Was Jaruman East Anglian? Possibly. A St Jaruman was vener-ated at Blythburgh, but later traditions say that this was a son of King Ana, (though more likely a nephew). It has been suggested also that St Adolph, who was venerated with his alleged brother, Botolph, in East Anglia, their relics having later been mixed up together, was in fact St Jaruman the missionary bishop. It is impossible to tell. The name Jaruman (*Jurmin/Eohrmen/Irmin*) was a rare name in England at this time but it was very common in Continental personal names, especially amongst the Franks. So far, the only known Anglo-Saxons whose names resembled this were invariably from Kent, with its well-known Frankish connec-tions, but we cannot ignore the close East Anglian ties with *Frankia* and Kent and the possibility of dynastic marriages between them. We must allow for at least a possibility of St Jurmin the bishop having been East Anglian, particularly as he had the same name as King Ana's alleged son, and that, if not royal, he was highly placed and eminently suitable as a royal and episcopal instrument in the web of East Anglian, Mercian and Essex politics.

Bede says, when writing of one Anglo-Irish missionary at work in England, that 'he applied himself to ecclesiastical truth and to chastity; to humility, continence and study; travelling about, not on horseback, but after the manner of the apostles, on foot, to preach the Gospel in towns, the open country, cottages, villages, and fortresses'.[50] We may well regard such as description as having been applicable to others of that ilk, such as Botolph and Jaruman, and such a description would be tribute in itself.

5

Sisters, Nieces, and Aunts

In Ely Cathedral, in front of the present high altar, a visitor will see a black memorial slab, around which burn eternal lights and which bears the inscription – 'St Etheldreda'. It marks the former resting place of a daughter of King Ana. Close by were the shrines of two of her holy sisters and a veritable tribe of women ascetics, several of whom had associations with this western hinterland of East Anglia, the Fens.

The Fens at this time, and until quite late in history, were a dank and dismal territory,[1] comprising the largest stretch of inland water in Western Europe, stretching from King's Lynn in the east to Cambridge and Peterborough in the west, from Boston and the Wash in the north, down to Bedford in the south. The northernmost stretch consisted mainly of salt marshes which would flood at high tide, and the central and southern section was made up of freshwater swamps and lagoons interspersed with small islands, nowadays represented by places such as Crowland and Thorney, and the larger former island of Ely. The Fens were the result of prehistoric land subsidence and the consequent flooding by meandering rivers which had no natural outlet to the sea. The Romans may have drained some of the peripheral areas of the Fens, but such drainage as there had been seems to have fallen into neglect and abandonment by the post-Roman period.[2] The Fens had also been a natural entry route for seafaring Germanic settlers and marauders during the invasion period, and had served as a point of entry into the Midlands and western East Anglia, remaining very sparsely populated thereafter, and could even have harboured some protracted native British survival for

The Site of St Etheldreda's Shrine (Ely Cathedral)

a while.[3] By the seventh century the region had become the territory of a tribe named as the 'Gyrwe',[4] who seem to have represented a small sub-kingdom, initially under the dominance of
the East Angles, but in time taken over by the Mercians, though
the control of this territory was probably a continual issue for the
two larger kingdoms.[5] In effect the Fens constituted a frontier
zone, though Bede, when referring to Ely, says that it was in the
province of the East Angles.[6] During the eighth century the Fens
were still described by the chronicler of St Guthlac (writing in
the same century, and whom we shall meet in the next chapter)
as 'a wide wilderness and devoid of habitation', and 'infested with
devils',[7] thus indicating the dread in which the region was held.
As well as being possessed of 'demonic' inhabitants, they seem to
have been a natural hideaway for brigands and outlaws (no doubt
amongst the company of 'devils' that the chronicler had in mind!)[8]
and were noted for their fogs, mists, fevers and ague. All in all,
they would become a natural place of retreat for hermits, monks
and ascetics who wished to flee the world and to follow the traditional 'desert' tradition.[9]

To return to the holy sisters, St Etheldreda (*Aethelthryth*) and
her female kin represented the next stage of Christianity in East
Anglia following on from the conversion period, and, as such, a
flowering of the seeds sown by the like of St Felix and St Fursey,
and probably St Botolph. They represent the spread not only of
monasticism, but also of a royal monasticism, with the first appearance of women in the only ecclesiastical role that was open to
them. An Anglo–Norman chronicler, Roger of Wendover, aptly
described this era of native Christianity as a time 'when religion
shone with so bright a light that kings and queens, princes and
dukes, earls, barons, and churchmen alike, inflamed with the desire
of the heavenly kingdom, became monks, recluses, and voluntary
exiles, forsaking all to follow their Lord'.[10] Previously, it seems
that there had been no monastic outlets for women, certainly not
in East Anglia. A royal widow, St Hereswitha, had had to go to
Chelles in northern *Frankia* in pursuit of her ambition in this
direction,[11] and we might reasonably suppose that a part of the

problem had been the frequent pagan Mercian incursions into the kingdom, which, judging by St Fursey's problems, did not bode well for the permanence of monastic foundations, at least not until the political problem was later resolved. Royal women who sought a monastic vocation would need, for a while, to go to the safer and well-established houses of northern *Frankia* with which East Anglia undoubtedly had strong ties,[12] and where they were less potentially available for capture as hostages by Mercian neighbours, with all the remunerative and political potential that such a situation offered![13] Two of King Ana's daughters, Ethelburgha (*Aethelburh*) and Saethryth (*Sethrytha*)[14] were, as we have already seen, sent to *Frankia* for a monastic vocation during their father's lifetime. Later traditions claimed that a third (and youngest) daughter, Witburgha (*Wihtburh*),[15] did actually succeed in establishing her own monastery in Norfolk,[16] though, as we shall see, this is a somewhat tenuous and probably doubtful claim. The most outstanding of the known daughters would prove to be Etheldreda,[17] who would finish up in the Fens after her father's death during more settled conditions and found what was to become the great Abbey of Ely.

St Saethryth and St Ethelburgha

St Saethryth (*Sethrytha*) was a stepdaughter of King Ana and thus a daughter of a wife of whom we know nothing, probably by a previous marriage. The fact that this female child, possibly the eldest of the saintly progeny,[18] was sent to *Frankia*[19] and one of its monasteries raises the possibility that Ana's unknown wife had herself been a Frankish princess (the name *Sethrytha* is suggestive of Frankish connections). Bede tells us that she was sent there for 'her education and to be betrothed to the Heavenly Bridegroom',[20] and that she was received by St Burgundofara at Faremoutier Abbey in the great forest of Brie.[21] This in fact was quite close to Chelles where St Hereswitha, to whom she was connected very loosely by ties of dynastic marriage, had embraced her own vocation. Bede goes on to tell us that girls of noble family were sent there for either education or the monastic life,[22] and the Frankish monasteries certainly enjoyed a reputation as centres of learning, all of which tends to suggest that such places were regarded as suitable 'finishing schools' for princesses, either in preparation for royal interdynastic marriages or for permanent monasticism with a very definite role to play in the spiritual extension of royal power.

Monasteries such as Faremoutier and Chelles were under the protection of the Frankish King Clovis II and his wife Bathildis (*Bathild*), who herself became a nun during her eventual widowhood, as well as having been a great protectress and benefactress of monasteries in the region.[23] Bathildis was said to have been English and to have been taken in her youth to *Frankia* as a slave. She married in 649 (which might place the time of her capture in the early 640s) and we are left wondering whether she herself might have had East Anglian origins, having perhaps been a victim of one of Penda's attacks around the time of the demise of the Irish mission, though this is but speculation.[24] As to when Saethryth arrived at Chelles we cannot be certain, though it may be that she and St Ethelburgha, her younger half-sister, were sent together and perhaps again during the troubled times of the early 640s though it is equally possible that Ethelburgha, having been younger, was sent there a little later and perhaps around the time of Fursey's own departure.[25] The significance of the fact that St Fursey and his companions also arrived in the same region at some time in the 640s cannot be overlooked, for Irish monastic influence in the region was strong.[26] Burgundofara (known to the French as '*St Fare*'), who received the two East Anglian princesses, had herself been a disciple of the great Irish missionary monk, St Columbanus,[27] whom she had met and had been blessed by when small, and the rule of St Columbanus was said to have been practised at the monastery. The presence of the two royal sisters there[28] would certainly have helped to strengthen the East Anglian/Irish/Frankish Church connection and was no coincidence.

The monastery at Chelles was a double monastery – in effect

two adjacent ones for men and women under one head. Such monasteries had been known in the earlier days of the monastic movement (particularly in the Christian East) and in time they became common in the West, becoming a feature in Ireland as well as *Frankia*, and, before the Viking destructions of the ninth century, in England also[29] despite their condemnation by Archbishop St Theodore in the late seventh century who failed to suppress them.[30] Such monasteries were invariably ruled by women who had no separate monasteries of their own and a prime English example would be Ely under the rule of St Etheldreda. The men of these monasteries were required for the serving of the sacraments and for heavy field labour, whilst the women contributed to the production of Church vestments and embroidery, in turn laying the foundations of early English art which in time developed to enjoy a Continental reputation. The abbesses seem to have exercised considerable power over the communities, in fact wielding as much power and influence as their male counterparts. St Burgundofara was said to have heard the confessions of both men and women in church[31] and even to have had the power of excommunication (both these practices were also condemned by Archbishop Theodore as uncanonical!).[32] It is a possibility that such power, in one form or another, was exercised by Saethryth, Ethelburgha and Etheldreda when they eventually became abbesses.

Saethryth succeeded Burgundofara as abbess when the latter died, and ruled her monastery until her own death in 664, having enjoyed a considerable reputation, both in her lifetime and posthumously, for sanctity and personal austerity. Her half-sister Ethelburgha duly succeeded her as abbess, the hereditary principle being well at work, a distinct feature of these royal monasteries. Of Ethelburgha, Bede said that 'she preserved the glory, so pleasing to God, of perpetual virginity'[33] and he goes on to tell us that she began to build (or rebuild) in her monastery a church in honour of all the Apostles, wherein she desired her body might be buried, though she was prevented by death from finishing it.[34] She died in about 669 and after her death the community discontinued her church-building project for seven years – Bede says 'they were preoccupied with other matters',[35] probably a cryptic way of saying that they ran out of money perhaps due to a temporary withdrawal of royal interest. Another and more modest church was eventually built and the community decided to exhume ('translate' is the usual term) Ethelburgha's body into a new tomb in the new church. Apparently, when they opened the tomb, the body was found to be incorrupt,[36] which was regarded as the confirmation of virginity and sanctity,[37] whereupon it was duly washed, reclothed, and reinterred in the new church of St Stephen the Martyr.

We must now return again to East Anglia with its lack of female monastic houses.[38] As we have said, part of the problem in respect of the founding of monasteries of any permanence in the 640s and 650s was the insecurity prevailing in the kingdom due to the struggles with Mercia. It seems that earlier foundations had collapsed, or had been temporarily abandoned to await the more settled conditions that would enable the likes of St Botolph to set up his monastery at *Icanhoe* and St Etheldreda hers at Ely, and it is to Etheldreda and Ely that we shall now turn.[39]

St Etheldreda

Etheldreda, the most notable and well-known of King Ana's saintly daughters, became the foremost of all Englishwomen to be venerated as a saint, linking, as she does, with other great saints of her age, such as Chad of Lichfield and Wilfred of York.[40] She was likely to have been a great-niece of King Sigbert the Martyr and she links with the times of St Felix and St Fursey – St Felix, according to later traditions, baptized her[41] and such influences must have been of significance for her. The main sources for her life are Bede and the *Book of Ely*,[42] both of which probably incorporate earlier and sometimes independent traditions, some of which may well have come from those who had known her and who had been in association with her, such as St Wilfred of York. According to the sources, from her earliest years Etheldreda

St Etheldreda (Depicted as an Abbess; From the Rood Screen of North Tuddenham Church, Norfolk)

devoted herself to virginity and God (i.e. monastic aspiration) and she was encouraged in this by her parents, having indicated her wishes and intentions to them from the outset. Possibly she had been intended for the same monastery as her two sisters, whom we have already encountered, but if this was so her intentions were forestalled by her father's death in 654, when she may have been no more than about fifteen or sixteen. She may have been permitted a sort of private semi-monastic existence under King Ana's brothers, who succeeded him, whilst they decided upon her usefulness, and it is likely that her future was not in her own hands. Princesses were a useful commodity for kings on a political and 'spiritual' level,[43] and it would be in the political arena that Etheldreda, despite her monastic preference and whatever her parents had originally planned, would be used for what was to be the unhappiest part of her life. One tradition, if it was true, claimed that in her youth she was of dazzling beauty and sought by many, and this may have decided her initial fate.

Etheldreda was given in marriage, probably in 657, by her uncle, King Aethelwald, to a certain Tondberht, King of the Southern Gyrwe in the Fens, no doubt for the purpose of trying to secure, or re-establish, some sort of East Anglian influence there,[44] particularly as East Anglia itself was by now under Mercian domination. Tondberht apparently died within two years of the marriage, but he had respected Etheldreda's preference for virginity and had never consummated their marriage, leaving her at his death, as her dowry, the Isle of Ely. After her husband's death, the widowed Etheldreda prepared for a life of 'meditation', obviously hoping to realize her monastic purpose, and she entrusted her estate to her faithful steward, Owen (*Owini*).[45] Her hopes were to be confounded yet again, for in about 661 she was then married off to Ecgfrith of Northumbria[46] (an ally of East Anglia) no doubt due to her Uncle Aethelwald's[47] continuing perception of her usefulness in the political pawn game! She had probably been given to Ecgfrith, who was in fact no more than about fifteen or sixteen (she was by now in her early to mid-twenties) for the purpose of reviving the alliance between the two kingdoms and of capitalizing upon the prevailing situation in Mercia following Penda's death. Part of the ploy was to detach the border province of Lindsey[48] from Mercia, whose power was starting to revive again under its new king, Wulfhere, following the murder of Penda's son, Peada. Having entrusted her Ely estates to the care of faithful Owen,[49] including *Cratendune* on the island,[50] to which we, like Etheldreda, will eventually return, she joined her new husband, Ecgfrith, son of King Oswiu of Northumbria, who was ruling as a sub-king together with his brother, Alchfrith. (Oswiu did not die, nor did Ecgfrith become king in his own right for another nine years.) Bede says that there Etheldreda remained married to him for twelve years.[51]

Unlike Tondberht, Ecgfrith was less happy about Etheldreda's preferences and tried to prevail upon her to renounce her monastic pretensions and her insistence upon virginity, though he did still hold her in great esteem and affection. Regardless, she remained constant in her purpose, retiring in due course from the royal household to place herself under the spiritual guidance of St Chad, which no doubt caused her further difficulties with Ecgfrith and his retainers. We can only speculate upon the other difficulties that may have beset the hapless Etheldreda in her Northumbrian exile. Possibly the continuing difference over the date of Easter may have been one, for King Oswiu and his sons certainly clung to the Irish customs until 664 and even St Chad's episcopal orders would be regarded as uncanonical when he journeyed southwards to exercise eventual authority. For Etheldreda, arrived from East Anglia where it seems that the correct observances prevailed, there may have been persistent cross-currents of tension in which she found herself caught up.[52]

By 670, Ecgfrith had become King of Northumbria and from that point onwards may well have expected Etheldreda to act as a full consort and to provide him with children and successors – if he did, he was to be bitterly disappointed! St Wilfred, the new (and canonical) Bishop of York, had replaced St Chad and, like Chad, proved to be a valuable friend to Etheldreda. Ecgfrith begged Wilfred to persuade his non-compliant wife to abandon her monastic proclivities but, although Wilfred appeared to comply with the king's wish (and Wilfred was a masterly statesman of the Continental Church mould!), he actually secretly encouraged Etheldreda and went as far as tonsuring her as a nun.[53] Wilfred then advised Ecgfrith to release his wife, which he did, and she was permitted to go to a monastery at Coldingham in Berwickshire,[54] ruled over by the king's aunt, the Abbess Ebba.[55] Wilfred's scheming so enraged the king that the latter vindictively deprived the bishop of the greater part of his diocese, thus laying up a future store of trouble for Wilfred, the king, and the Church, which would drag on bitterly for a long period.

It must have proved apparent to Etheldreda that Abbess Ebba was in no position to protect her from King Ecgfrith's wrath, so with two attendants, who are named as 'Siwenna' and 'Siwara',[56] she wandered away and hid in lonely places, whilst Ecgfrith reneged on his agreement with Wilfred and spent a year tracking her down with a view to forcing her back to her marital position. It is said that when she fled to Coldingham Monastery she initially sought refuge on a promontory, now called Colbert's Head, the sea sweeping up in unusual tides, guarding her there until the baffled Ecgfrith, who was in hot pursuit, left her be. After a week of prayer and fasting the sea receded and Etheldreda was able to commence her long journey homewards. She promptly headed southwards and probably towards the Fenland fastness from which she had earlier come. One tradition records how when she was sleeping on her journey home, her staff struck root in the ground and grew into a great tree, where it came in time to be known as 'Etheldreda's Stowe' (i.e. 'Etheldreda's Place' or 'Church') – probably Stow some ten miles north-west of Lincoln.[57] She is also said, at some stage of her flight, to have crossed the River Humber, passing in due course through Winteringham and Alftham,[58] where she founded churches,[59] and these legends may well preserve ancient recollections of her actual journey, following, as it seems it did, the old Roman road of Ermine Street.[60]

Finally, Etheldreda reached the safety of her Fenland territory in about 672, where by now Mercian power had re-established itself; and, fortunately for her, the Mercian king, Wulfhere, was a patron of monasteries and willing to afford her protection from Ecgfrith. Bishop Chad was also now in Mercia as its bishop,[61] which was no doubt an added support, and he was accompanied by Owen, the faithful steward from Etheldreda's former Ely days.[62] So, at last, in Ely, she was finally permitted to settle down on the island to resume the life that she had left and still craved.[63] It would seem that Bishop Wilfred had remained in contact with Etheldreda upon her return and that he positively encouraged her to establish a regular monastery on Ely (he would himself become an exile in Mercian territory between 690 and 702). It also seems that she set about to build, or rebuild, as a monastic foundation the semi-ruined church of *Cratendune*, which according to the *Book of Ely* was originally built in honour of the Virgin Mary at the instance of St Augustine himself.[64] But she was unhappy with the site, for reasons we are are not told, and chose instead the present-day site of Ely Cathedral. Etheldreda managed to obtain money and resources from her relatives and, according to the Ely source, from her 'brother' who is named as 'Ealdwulf'.[65] Very providentially, St Wilfred planned the design for the monastery, though this seems a little unlikely as Wilfred was still back in Northumbria, but it could be a reference to some involvement that he had, when later himself an exile in Mercia. It is also said that many of Etheldreda's old servants and household members (presumably from East Anglia and Ely) followed her into the monastic community, placing themselves under her direction and guidance. The faithful Owen seems to have been one of their number and probably joined the community after St Chad's death from the plague[66] in Mercia, for he had been with Chad and, according to Bede, was privileged to have experienced a vision of angels singing in Chad's oratory, signifying the impending death of the saintly bishop.[67] Owen also practised great austerity and simplicity of life and seems to have become a hermit under Etheldreda's direction. At Haddenham, only five miles south-west of Ely, where he was said to have had his hermitage, there used to stand a seventh-century memorial cross to him (which can still

be seen in Ely Cathedral[68] to which it was later moved), bearing
the inscription:

LUCEM TUAM OVINO DA DEUS ET REQUIE[M]
AMEN
(*O God, grant Thy light and rest unto Owen, Amen.*)

The original monastery building at Ely was probably constructed
of materials such as wood, mud and reeds, with some stone probably brought across the Fens for the actual church, and around
the monastic huts would have been simple buildings for those
who worked as servants, supplying the monastery with food and
necessities.[69] In the summer the dry fenland could be used for
grazing cattle and on the higher ground fruit and vegetables would
have been grown. Fish and birds were an important source of
food and the common drink would have been ale and mead, the
surrounding water being invariably too stagnant and impure for
drinking.[70] All in all, the arrangements were probably not too
dissimilar from Fursey's earlier monastery in East Anglia, and the
fact that the monastery was clearly a 'double' one meant that
Etheldreda was following a type of monastic organization with
which she would have been familiar at Coldingham and similar
to that used by her relative, St Hilda, at Whitby, during her
Northumbrian sojourn.[71]

For the remainder of her life, Etheldreda struggled in great
austerity and ascetical discipline, particularly with regard to food
and clothing, even, we are told, in respect of washing (she would
only bathe at Easter, Pentecost and Epiphany and then only after
washing the feet of the community first – a gesture of humility).
She wore only woollen garments and apparently ate only one meal
a day,[72] spending time in prayer in the church from Lauds
(2 a.m.)[73] until Prime (daybreak).[74] She seems to have had the gift
of precognition and even prophesied her own death, together with
the deaths of several of the community, from the plague.[75] Prior
to this, she had been in great personal pain, suffering from what
seems to have been a malignant tumour on her throat and lower

St Owen's Cross (Ely Cathedral)

jaw, which she regarded as a penance for her vanity and love of adornments during her early youth.[76] She died in about 679, the day being traditionally regarded as 23 June, having been abbess at Ely for about six years; at the time of her death she had probably reached her early forties. The community buried her in the nuns' cemetery at Ely in a plain wooden coffin as she had requested, and there she was permitted to rest for a further sixteen years, being followed in her abbatial office by her sister, St Sexburgha (*Seaxburh*). In about 695, Abbess Sexburgha resolved to have her dead sister's body exhumed for its translation and reburial in a fine marble sarcophagus which had been discovered by the monks near Grantchester, or Cambridge, indicating that the elevation of Etheldreda to the rank of sainthood was clearly under way, a process no doubt ably assisted by St Wilfred who was by now not far away in Mercia. Wilfred, who was probably the ultimate source of the information, was present at the exhumation together with Etheldreda's former physician, Cynewulf. According to their testimonies, the body appeared to be incorrupt, as though just asleep, the burial clothes still fresh and, remarkably, where the tumour wound had once been there was now only a slender scar.[77] The sisterhood reverently washed and reclothed the body of their late abbess and placed it in its new tomb which was set up near the altar of the church, the old burial clothes being distributed amongst the faithful, as they were held to be a source of miracles through touch.

Later, as we shall see, the monastery was destroyed by the Vikings in the ninth century, but not, it was claimed, the tomb and relics of St Etheldreda[78] which would remain there as a focus of pilgrimage and veneration until the Reformation. In 1541, King Henry VIII's Commissioners scattered Etheldreda's relics with the exception, it was later claimed, of one of her hands, which was rediscovered in 1811 in a priest's hiding-hole at Arundel in Sussex. (The popular assumption was that this surviving relic was rescued and hidden away by an Ely monk at the Reformation who had anticipated and pre-empted the arrival of the King's Commissioners.)[79] This surviving relic was in due course returned to Ely where it remains to this day in the custodianship of the Roman Catholic Parish Church of St Etheldreda. The hand is fitted on a silver spike, on a circular silver dish bearing the inscription:

MANUS SCAE ETHELDREDAE – 679
(The Hand of St Etheldreda – 679)

It was said that, at the time of the rediscovery of the hand, it was still beautifully white, but through exposure to the air it has subsequently become black and mummified-looking.[80]

As we have suggested, the posthumous veneration of Etheldreda as a great saint owes a lot not only to her royal status, but also to the influence of St Wilfred, the most powerful churchman of this period, and he no doubt passed on many personal recollections of the saint, some of which may well have been written down at Ely within the time of her living memory (i.e. by the early eighth century). Bede certainly stated that he had obtained his own account of Etheldreda from Wilfred and we may suppose that at least some of the source material relating to her in the *Book of Ely* came from the same place. Another source for Etheldreda may also have been her close personal associate and priest, Huna (who bore the same name as her late father): he would have been familiar with her outer and inner personal struggles, doubtless having also been present at her death. We know little else of St Huna, other than what is in the *Book of Ely* and a few local traditions, which testify to his austerity and asceticism. He had been instructed by Etheldreda to arrange her burial and he afterwards retired as a hermit to a small island on the Fens, which was eventually named after him '*Huneya*' (Huna's Isle); there is also a 'Honeywell Farm' near Ely which is supposed to have some connection with his name.[81] Bede's greatest tribute to her may be found in a well-known acrostical hymn that he composed for her memory; and he certainly ensured for her an enduring place as the only native female English saint to be included in the *Lives of the Roman Virgin Martyrs*, which was translated into Anglo-

Saxon (i.e. Early English) by the great homilist Aelfric in the tenth century.[82] Above all, Etheldreda came to be portrayed as *the* model of female sanctity, so dear to the tradition of the Church, a virgin who had spurned marriage and the world beset with suffering caused by men, and had sought and found a heavenly bridegroom against all the odds. It is as such that she deserves to be remembered, and the great Cathedral of Ely, the 'Jewel of the Fens', which still stands today in striking magnificence, is a fitting tribute to the memory and influence of this 'jewel' amongst the saints of East Anglia and England!

Bede's Acrostical Hymn to St Etheldreda

Rejoice, Triune Power, who rulest every age.
Assist the numbers which my pen engage.
Let Maro wars in loftier numbers sing.
I sound the praises of our heavenly King.
Pure is my verse, nor of Helen's rape I write;
Light tales like these, but prove the mind as light.
See! from on high God descends, confined
In Mary's womb, to rescue lost mankind.
Behold! a spotless maid our God brings forth,
For God is born, who gave even nature birth!
The virgin-choir the mother-maid resound,
And pure themselves, her praises shout around.
Her bright example numerous votaries raise,
Tread spotless paths, and imitate her ways.
The blessed Agatha and Eulalia trust
Sooner to flames, than far more dangerous lust.
Tekla and chaste Euphemia overcame
The fear of beasts to save a virgin name.
Agnes and sweet Cecilia, joyful maids,
Smile whilst the pointed sword their breasts invades.
Triumphant joy attends the peaceful soul,
Where heat, nor rain, nor wishes mean control.
Thus Etheldreda, pure from sensual crime,

Bright shining star! arose to bless our time.
Born of a royal race, daughter of a king,
More noble honour to her lord shall she bring.
A queen her name, her hand a sceptre rears,
But greater glories wait above the spheres.
What man wouldst thou desire? See Christ is made
Her spouse, her blessed Redeemer weds the maid.
Whilst you attend the heavenly mother's train,
Thou shalt be mother of a heavenly reign.
The holy maid who twelve years sat as queen,
A cloistered nun devout to God was seen.
Noted for pious deeds, her spotless soul
Left the vile world, and soared above the Pole.
Sixteen Novembers since was the blessed maid
Entombed, whose flesh no gnawing worms invade.
Thy grace, O Christ! for in the coffin's found
No tainted drapes wrapping the corpse around.
The swelling dropsy, and dire atrophy,
A pale disease from the blessed vestments fly.
Rage fires the demon, who wilesome Eve betrayed,
Whilst shouting angels greet the glorious maid.
See! wedded to her God, what joy remains,
On earth, in heaven, see! with her God she reigns!
Behold! the spouse, the festive torches shine,
He comes! behold! what joyful gifts are thine!
Thou a new song on the sweet harp shalt sing,
A hymn of praise to thy heavenly King.
None from the flock of the throned Lamb shall move,
Whom grateful passion bind, and heavenly love.

(*HE* 4, ch. 20)

St Sexburgha and St Ermenhilda

Etheldreda's sister, St Sexburgha, who had succeeded her in a
hereditary role as abbess at Ely, seems to have been the oldest of
the natural daughters of King Ana and like her dead sister had

also been used in the royal marriage strategy (though without preserving her virginity); and she, too, probably had monastic preferences from an early age. She was given in marriage to King Eorcenberht of Kent in 640, probably at the time of her father's difficulties with Mercia and for the purpose of strengthening the alliance. Bede says that her husband died in 664[83] and he also says of her that she was 'of wise counsel and example', noted by all her subjects for her humility and devotion along with her goodness and charity.[84] When her husband died, it appears that she ruled as regent in Kent for her son, Ecgberht, who himself reigned for nine years until his death in 673. She founded a monastery there at Minster, on the Isle of Sheppey, but was unable to complete its building until after her husband's death. One source tells that she bought the Sheppey lands from her second son, Hlothere, after she had resigned the regency of the Kentish kingdom.[85] The same source also tells that she foresaw the arrival of an army of pagan invaders and, realizing the need for an effective leader, gave the kingdom over to her son. The only recorded event that might confirm this claim is an entry in Bede who says that in 676 'King Aethelraed of Mercia ravaged Kent with a powerful army, and profaned churches and monasteries, without regard to religion, or the fear of God.'[86]

Sexburgha had gathered around her at Sheppey seventy-four nuns and she entrusted the monastery to her daughter, Ermenhilda (*Eormenhild*), who herself had been previously married to Aethelraed of Mercia's dead brother, Wulfhere (whom we have already met); this suggests that Ermenhilda had fled to the safety of Kent to rejoin her mother. We do not know precisely when Sexburgha left Sheppey for Ely, but if, as seems likely, she succeeded Etheldreda fairly immediately as abbess, it must have been soon after 679, or even a year or two before. This would certainly have coincided with Aethelraed's attack on Kent, and could well have meant that her placement at Ely was less than voluntary! (Such a move would certainly have given the Mercian king control over her, and the arrival of her daughter, Ermenhilda, at Ely from Kent, a few years later, would have suited his same purpose.)

We have already seen how Sexburgha took over Ely and in time supervised the translation of her sister's relics, and there she continued to rule until she died of old age, which probably occurred in the 690s. Following the hereditary principle, her daughter, Ermenhilda, succeeded her. After their deaths, both mother and daughter would come to be regarded as saints, their resting places becoming, like Etheldreda's, attractions for pious devotion for centuries to come.

St Wereburgha

Ermenhilda was, as we have noted, like her mother, a royal widow, not only a granddaughter of King Ana, but also the mother of a future Mercian king, Coenred.[87] She may have left Sheppey in about 680 to join her mother at Ely, voluntarily or involuntarily we cannot tell, and it seems that her own daughter, St Wereburgha (*Waerburh*), according to her 'Life',[88] was already a nun there. Wereburgha had been pressurized by her late father, King Wulfhere of Mercia, to marry a Mercian nobleman, a prospect which she resolutely resisted, and in which resistance she was encouraged by her two young brothers.[89] The three of them also went further by enlisting the assistance and intervention of St Chad, who was currently Bishop of Mercia; and the story goes on to say that the king had been persuaded to revert to paganism by the thwarted nobleman (named as Werebod) and consequently executed the two princes. (If there is any truth in this tale, which is highly unlikely, it might account for Ermenhilda's flight to Kent which would have occurred earlier than we first suggested.) Wulfhere eventually repented of his dreadful deed and took Wereburgha to Ely, where she was received into the community by her great-aunt, Etheldreda, and where in time she became the fourth abbess, succeeding her mother, Ermenhilda, who was its third.

The whole story seems to be largely fictitious and there seems to be no evidence that Wereburgha ever became Abbess of Ely (though her mother probably did). The legend probably arose at a later period in Ely's history when, as we shall see, the abbey was anxious to acquire either the relics or associations of King Ana's saintly descendants – and for reasons that were not altogether to do with piety! There may, though, be elements of truth lurking in the legend. If there is anything in the purported apostasy of King Wulfhere it would indicate how fragile the position of Christianity in Mercia was by the end of the seventh century, and the church-despoiling activities of Wulfhere's successor, Aethelraed, of which Bede tells us (together with Sexburgha's prophecy of a pagan invasion of Kent – if the two references are one and the same), could point in this direction, giving the impression that the professed Christianity of the kings, particularly in Mercia, was more to do with political expediency than pious conviction. It is possible that Wereburgha may have sought temporary refuge at Ely and could have gone there (or have been forcibly placed there) at the same time as her mother, Ermenhilda, particularly if a semi-pagan faction had taken over in Mercia, represented by Aethelraed. Whatever the true realities of what happened, she was later said to have been persuaded by the same King Aethelraed to oversee monastic communities of women in Mercia (in Mid-Anglian territory),[90] and she seems to have died there in the early 700s at Hanbury, where she was buried.[91]

St Wendreda and St Ercongota

Another saintly, and supposed, daughter of Ermenhilda also receives a brief mention in the Ely record, but we know virtually nothing about her and cannot be certain that she was even the person she was claimed to be. This is St Wendreda (*Wenthryth*) who is traditionally associated with the Fenland town of March and who also seems to have had some connection with Exning, near Newmarket, where she may have become confused with an even more elusive St Mindred (*Minthryth*).[92] She was said to have been a thaumaturge, i.e. a saint possessed of great healing powers and possessed of adroit medicinal skill through herbal applications.

We might assume that if she really was the person whom the legends claim her to have been, her presence in and near to the Fens could have had something to do with the flight of the princesses linked to East Anglia referred to above.

Another, and historically attested, daughter of St Sexburgha does merit examination though, and that is St Ercongota (*Eorceng-ota*),[93] who Bede tells us joined her aunts Saethryth and Ethelburgha at the Frankish monastery Brie Faremoutier. Unlike her sister, St Ermenhilda,[94] she was not required for royal marriage purposes, but rather for the alternative route of royal princesses, the Frankish monastery, and for the purpose, no doubt, of continuing the links between the two kingdoms. She is described as having displayed the same religious zeal as her female kin[95] and Bede refers to her in the context of the lack of suitable female monasteries in the kingdom, which tends to suggest that she was sent to Chelles in the early 660s.[96] Bede, who is our only source for her, says that her deeds and miracles were widely known throughout the region; and the only other information he provides us with is an account of her vision of her impending death, which may have occurred in the late 690s or early 700s.[97] He says that she visited the aged and infirm nuns of the monastery, revealing to them prophetically the approach of her death. She had previously seen a company of men in white robes enter the monastery, who told her that they had come 'to take away the gold coin brought from Kent'. The monks of the community also reported that they had heard angelic singing in the monastery and had seen a light coming down to carry away the soul of Ercongota.[98] When she died, her body was laid to rest in the monastery church of St Stephen, where, after three days, it was exhumed for reburial at a greater depth. When this was carried out, those present were greeted with a perfume of incredible fragrance, taken to be a sign of incorruption – the reward of her virginity and holiness.

St Witburgha

We now return to King Ana's daughters and to the most enigmatic of them all in terms of her actual identity. This is St Witburgha (*Wihtburh*), said to have been Ana's youngest daughter and traditionally associated with both Holkham and East Dereham in Norfolk. If indeed she was Ana's youngest daughter, and there is no certainty for this at all, she would have been born in the late 640s or early 650s. She is said in the Ely sources (all of which are very late – Bede says nothing about her)[99] to have professed a monastic aspiration very early in life, perhaps even as a child, and, if there is anything in this, such an influence may have come from her older sisters. She is supposed to have practised personal austerity and seclusion as a hermit on her father's summer estate at Holkham on the north Norfolk coast, where a church would eventually be erected on the site of her former hermitage, a church which still carries her dedication (a rare one); and she was further said to have been born and 'educated' at Holkham. As it stands, none of this is impossible. All but very minor kings were on the move all the time and certainly did have halls in key parts of their kingdoms where they would receive tribute and hospitality from local chieftains and sub-rulers on a regular basis. This was particularly important for keeping a grasp on the peripheral and less secure parts of the kingdom, as this part of Norfolk might well have been.[100] The *Anglo-Saxon Chronicle* then goes on to say that after her father's death (654), she moved further south to Dereham where she gathered round her some female companions, laying the foundations of a church and monastery, though she never lived to complete the work.[101] If this was so, then we might reasonably suppose her to have died at a fairly young age, perhaps during the late 660s.

Little else is told of her, other than one or two hagiographical legends, which bear, as we might expect, affinities to legends in other 'Lives' of early saints. One popular story (still depicted on a frieze in East Dereham's high street) is that at one stage the community was so poor that by the prayers of St Witburgha, two

St Witburgha (Showing the Doe; St Nicholas' Church, East Dereham)

St Witburgha's Well (East Dereham)

does constantly came to the monastery to be milked at a regular
time and place. The town reeve envied the pious sisters this supply
(it is more than likely, though, that such a monastery, if it existed,
would have been a 'double' one) and wickedly hunted the does
with a pack of hounds. As a 'just judgement' the reeve later broke
his neck whilst hunting (here we see an affinity with the tales of
the vindictiveness of early Welsh saints when monastic possessions
were threatened). At Witburgha's death, her body was interred
in the monastic churchyard at Dereham, and then exhumed fifty
years later for translation into the church and, as we might expect,
it was found and declared to be incorrupt. At the original site of
her burial, according to local tradition, a 'holy well' obligingly
sprang up to mark the spot, thenceforth to be venerated, as it
continues to be today, as 'St Witburgha's Well'.[102] In 974, Abbot
Byrhtnoth of Ely resolved to stake his abbey's claims to
St Witburgha's relics in order to place them alongside her two
illustrious and alleged sisters, Etheldreda and Sexburgha. To this
end he and a party of doughty and determined Ely monks

descended upon Dereham and, having plied the townsmen there with copious supplies of alcoholic beverage and food, made away with the saint's body to Brandon, on the Norfolk/Suffolk border, and thence across the Fens to Ely, the enraged townsfolk of Dereham in hot pursuit! The relics were placed alongside those of Etheldreda, Sexburgha and Ermenhilda[103] and remained there undisturbed until 1106, when they were moved into the new church that had been built and to a place near the present high altar. The caskets of all the holy women were opened, and the bodies of Sexburgha and Ermenhilda were found by this time to be only bones. Etheldreda's body was still entire and that of Witburgha was not only sound, but her limbs were still flexible! We can imagine the surprise of those assembled when a monk of Westminster who was present, obligingly demonstrated this by lifting up and moving in several directions Witburgha's hands, arms and feet, the extraordinary event being attested by a bishop who also happened to be conveniently present.

St Cyneburgha, St Cyneswitha and St Tibba

We shall make one final return to the Fens, this time to its western edge and to some more venerable women with indirect East Anglian connections.

Firstly we encounter St Cyneburgha (*Cyneburh*), a daughter of Penda, sister to sub-King Peada (Penda's Christian son) and a sister of King Wulfhere and thus a sister-in-law to St Ermenhilda.[104] She had been married to Alchfrith, son of King Oswiu of Northumbria, who was a brother-in-law to St Etheldreda, and, upon her own husband's death (he had rebelled against his father), she found herself free to return to her own territories, probably in the late 660s. She is said to have founded a monastery on a piece of fenland known as '*Cyneburge-cester*' (now Castor, Northants) and, if this is so, she may well have been influenced by St Etheldreda, with whom she had not a few things in common. At her monastery, she gathered together a band of women and outshone them all in holiness and wisdom, being eventually joined by her sister, St Cyneswitha (*Cyneswit*), who had also dedicated herself to monasticism since her earliest years. King Wulfhere had betrothed her to Offa, King of the East Saxons (Essex), a dependant of Mercia like the East Anglians, but Offa had released her from her pledge at her own request. She was said to have spent many years in solitude and devotion and eventually succeeded her sister as abbess at Castor. Yet another relative, St Tibba (*Tibb*), who had also been a hermitess, joined them at some stage, though it is not quite clear whether or not she lived with them in community or just nearby.

Interestingly, Cyneburgha and Cyneswitha are actually named in the list of those who took part in the assembly which sanctioned the foundation of the Abbey of Peterborough, then known as '*Medeshampstede*', and they are therefore counted as having been amongst its patrons. The *Peterborough Chronicle* says that the abbey was founded by Peada in 655, together with the Northumbrian King, Oswiu, for the furtherance of the Christianization of the region,[105] which makes it unlikely that these saintly females were involved in the original patronage. However, the *Chronicle* goes on to say that in King Wulfhere's time the abbey grew rich and that the king intended to honour and exalt it, aided by his two sisters and others. The *Chronicle* also says that the charter of the abbey for 640 was granted in the seventh year of Wulfhere's reign and that his two sisters were present at the consecration.[106] When the three holy women died their relics were interred at Peterborough and were later moved to Thorney Abbey, on the Fens, following further Danish attacks in the early eleventh century, making a final return to Peterborough in the time of King Henry I. At about the time that Peterborough Abbey was endowed, its abbot, Seaxawulf, asked King Wulfhere if some of his monks might be permitted to settle as hermits on a Fenland island, *Ancarrig* (now known as 'Thorney'), and there to build a church to the glory of St Mary the Virgin. The king agreed and the grant was again testified to by Sts Cyneswitha and Cyneburgha. If the date for the foundation of Peterborough was 657 or 658, then Thorney was founded at some time in the mid-660s.[107]

After a considerable journey around the Fens and beyond, we must remain there for what may be regarded as the final stage in the monastic colonization of the 'watery desert'.

6

Hermits and a Martyr

St Guthlac

The Fens were, as we have seen, a magnet for men and women possessed of an inclination to live out the Christian 'desert' ideal, and it is within that environment and concept that we shall look at the legacy of yet another struggler who would leave an abiding memory in the tradition of Christian spirituality. The swampland now became the location for one of its greatest saints, who would

St Guthlac (A Frieze at Crowland Abbey)

take his place alongside Etheldreda, being like her of royal stock, but coming this time from Mercia – St Guthlac.

St Guthlac was probably born in Mercia in about the late 670s and the main source we have for him was written by an East Anglian churchman, Felix, of whom nothing is known[1] (there are also some later sources for Guthlac but none of them very trustworthy). Felix wrote at the request of an East Anglian King, Aelfwald, about whom quite a bit *is* known, and who reigned from about 713 to 749.[2] The King's request indicates a continuing East Anglian interest and involvement in the Fenlands and the work must have been composed before the king's death in 749, and probably during the 730s, i.e. within a generation of the saint's actual lifetime. Thus it seems reasonable to suppose that some of the material in the 'Life', particularly that which appears to have been based upon personal reminiscences, came from the oral and eyewitness accounts of those who had known Guthlac, notably his surviving disciples, and that these can, therefore, be regarded as quite reliable.[3] To this material Felix added borrowings from other hagiographical tales, particularly those of saints who resembled St Guthlac in his mode of spiritual struggle, which served to embellish and enhance the little that was actually available for the saint himself. Thus we see in the 'Life of St Guthlac' striking similarities to the 'Life of St Anthony of Egypt', the prototype monk and Desert Father of the third century, and this should not surprise us as Felix clearly regarded Guthlac as a worthy successor of Anthony. We can also see some similarities to Bede's accounts of English ascetical saints, particularly St Cuthbert of Lindisfarne; and even the influence of Early English epic poetry and sagas, notably *Beowulf*,[4] can be discerned in the account, wherein the writer portrays Guthlac as a spiritual warrior, the heroic soldier of Christ. Thus an alternative type of sanctity came to be portrayed in Guthlac's 'Life', and it was one that kings and nobles could admire, having been clearly written for them rather than for monks. All this indicates the strong survival in early English society of the old warrior-caste attitudes with its lingering and deeply-rooted pagan associations.[5]

According to Felix's account,[6] St Guthlac was the son of Penwalh, himself descended from a Mercian noble, Icel, and Guthlac
was supposed to have been named after his father's tribe of the
Guthlacings.[7] Penwalh was said to have traced his line of descent
from a long line of warriors and to have lived in the territory of
the Middle Angles,[8] and we need not be too dismissive of these
claims as they may point to some historical reality. There was an
Icel who was named as the legendary founder of the Mercian royal
dynasty, and he was said to have been an ancestor of the formidable
Penda whom we have already encountered.[9] An argument has
been put forward to the effect that the origins of the dynasty and
kingdom did lie in fact in Norfolk, dating back to the late fifth
or early sixth century. Icel was named as the father of Cnebba
(possibly of *Cnobheresburgh*)[10] and it has been suggested that this
Icklings tribe was ousted in the late sixth century by the invading
and expanding Wuffings dynasty of East Anglia, who perhaps
pushed them westwards into the Fens and into Middle Anglia.[11]
It has even been suggested that the name 'Icel' denotes a significant
surviving British element amongst this group, and interestingly,
Felix does claim that Guthlac knew the British (Welsh) tongue.
The names of both Guthlac's parents, if they are correct, might
also suggest a possible British origin. Felix goes on to tell us that
Guthlac was born in the time of King Penda's son, King Aethelbald, and that Guthlac was the only son of his parents and, together
with his sister, Pega, was brought up piously. When of age (probably fifteen), he chose to emulate the exploits of his ancestors,
spending nine years as a soldier, though we are given very little
information about this period of his life. It has generally been
assumed that he was employed in warfare against the Welsh in
the West Midlands and along the Welsh border, and that for a
time he was in exile amongst them, which is where he became
familiar with their language.[12] Could any of this be true? His
period of soldiering would, it seems, have been in the early 690s
and there is no record of any significant English/Welsh conflict
during that time, though incessant border raiding and skirmishing
were ever present.[13] If he did become an exile in Wales, it is

likely to have been due to a voluntary flight on his part, perhaps connected with his royal status and the fact that he was feared as a potential rival by the ruling branch of the Mercian line. Whatever the case, he indicated during this period a propensity for sanctity, being moved by the sufferings of the people he now found himself amongst, and he was said to have returned a third of the pillaged spoils to them. He also spent time reflecting upon the miserable end of his ancestors and upon his own unpreparedness for death, together with the vainglories of this world.[14]

If Guthlac was indeed a political exile, this no doubt occurred during the time of King Aethelraed of Mercia (i.e. the Aethelraed of Kentish church and monastery-burning tendencies whom we met in the previous chapter!) who himself was also to experience some severe reversals of personal fortune. These started for Aethelraed in 697 when his wife was murdered (Bede says by the Mercian chieftains),[15] and five years later Aethelraed was forced to power-share for a further two years, before being totally ousted and packed off to become a monk (in 704). All of this suggests a waning of power from 697 onwards, no doubt making it safer for Guthlac to return from exile (his own relatives could well have been implicated in the power struggles and coups). We can suppose that King Aethelraed's embrace of monasticism was not voluntary, and that supposition is re-inforced by his earlier track record regarding his church violations, unless we are to assume the unlikelihood of a rather convenient change of heart! In fact, forcing unwanted and deposed kings into monasteries became an alternative, and less bloody, way of disposing of them. Aethelraed's nephew, Coenred, succeeded him[16] and this seems to have ushered in a period when it was safe for Guthlac to return from his own exile.[17] Guthlac did this immediately, and at the age of about twenty-four took monastic vows at the Monastery of Repton in Derbyshire, a double monastery presided over by the Abbess Aelfthryth, who was probably related to him in some way. His choice of monastery was significant in terms of his likely pedigree as, from the seventh century onwards, Repton had been a major dynastic spiritual centre and a favoured royal burial place, where royal women tended the cults of the noble Mercian dead.[18] From now on Guthlac could become the 'warrior of Christ' and soon an exile again (the theme, as we have seen, of earlier ascetics, particularly the Irish),[19] all of which would strike a chord with the early English heroic tradition. It is notable in the epic poetry of the time, as we can see in the poem 'The Wanderer', where the exiled warrior laments the loss of his lord's protection and the comforts of the mead hall, taking his comfort in the mercy of God.[20]

It was at Repton that Guthlac indicated his anxiousness to atone for his past neglect of things spiritual and to practise great personal austerity, renouncing strong drink amongst other things, which earned him the personal dislike of his monastic companions! He also succeeded in learning the psalms by heart, together with the scriptures, the 'Lives' of the saints, and the sayings of the Desert Fathers (which indicates, as we might expect, that he may have been illiterate);[21] and he went on to indicate his wish for a more solitary life and struggle, the theme of the exiled warrior showing itself again. For this he was given permission, and he proceeded to make enquiries about the Fens, perhaps having already had some knowledge and familiarity with them. He travelled southwards down along the old Roman road to Cambridge, eventually reaching the very edge of the region,[22] and on his arrival at Cambridge met a fellow-monk named Tatwine, who may have had some connections with Thorney Monastery and who told him of the existence of an island in the more remote recesses of the Fens, feared and avoided by most people and inhabited by 'monsters' and terrors.[23] Tatwine obligingly took Guthlac across to the island by boat and, having inspected it, Guthlac decided that it was highly suitable for his purpose.

After a return to Repton lasting about three months, Guthlac returned again to his chosen island, then known as '*Cru-land*' (and now, as 'Crowland'), accompanied yet again by the eager Tatwine, and by another monk, who we are told was named Bettelin (*Berhthelm*) and probably also from Thorney. The three pilgrims arrived on Crowland on St Bartholomew's Day (i.e. 24 August), probably

The Site of St Guthlac's Cell (Crowland Abbey)

in 699, and Guthlac proceeded to construct for himself a cell within the remains of a prehistoric tomb[24] with Bettelin and Tatwine setting up huts nearby so that they could visit their master and join him in worship from time to time. At a very early stage it seems that Guthlac was severely tempted to abandon his enterprise but, according to his 'Life', was dissuaded from doing so by a vision of St Bartholomew himself, who persuaded him to persevere in his struggles.[25] This Guthlac did, aided by prayer and contemplation, his clothing consisting only of sheepskins and goatskins, his diet made up of barley-bread which he ate but once a day and only after sunset.[26] Guthlac's 'Life' goes on to tell us how the saint's struggles were further enhanced by temptations that he received from what are described as 'two devils' who goaded him with vainglorious thoughts, urging him to match the achievements of Moses and the Prophet Elijah, which sounds suspiciously like temptations arising from words of praise from his two companions who were seeking to emulate his ascetical example. There are also references in the 'Life' to actual physical attacks from 'demons', attacks which are supposed to have occurred during his nocturnal vigils and during which they beat him up and dragged him into the nearby fen. On one particular night, he was even set about by evil spirits who spoke 'Welsh', though he was able to drive them off by chanting the psalms, and on some occasions St Bartholomew himself came to his aid, driving the assailants away.

It is difficult to know what to make of such experiences, given that the account of them probably derived from Guthlac's closest companions who heard of them from the saint himself, other than taking them as they literally stand (which is difficult for most of us!), or seeking a plausible explanation. They could, of course, indicate a disturbance of Guthlac's mind (a common condition amongst some of the more extreme ascetics) brought about by his mode of existence and personal privations and enhanced by the fearsome environment in which he was dwelling, and this must be considered as a serious possibility. Another explanation might be found in a very human situation. The physical attacks upon his person, which the 'Life' recounts, could have been connected with visitations from neighbouring Fenland dwellers, for though habitation of the surrounding islands was sparse, some habitation there most certainly was. Can we take seriously the possibility that some of these Fensmen of that time actually spoke Welsh (not allowing for Welsh-speaking demons!)? The possibility of the survival of the old Romano-British tongue, even in the remote Fens, and at such a late stage in history and so far east, does not seem to be strong, though perhaps it should not be totally ruled out.[27] Another explanation for Guthlac's 'demons' is possible for other similar recorded events. His disciple Bettelin was, according to the 'Life', on one occasion tempted to kill his master. Apparently Guthlac only washed every twenty days and this was when Bettelin would shave him. On such an occasion Bettelin was tempted to cut his master's throat, but Guthlac recognized the temptation and urged Bettelin to drive out the devil from within him, prompting Bettelin to confess his sin. Guthlac duly forgave

Bettelin and promised to assist him in his struggles.[28] A source later than the 'Life' also tells of Guthlac's sister, St Pega, having lived on the island with him in his early days there.[29] Apparently the Devil 'assumed her form' and tried to persuade Guthlac to break his rule by taking food before sunset (maybe on this occasion the saint was ill), but Guthlac recognized the 'source' of the trick and in order to prevent such further 'attacks', he promptly banished Pega from the island, never to see her again!

By 709, King Coenred had 'retired' from the Mercian throne (probably a euphemistic way of stating that he had been deposed!) and left the territory to undertake a personal pilgrimage to Rome. Though Coenred himself is on record as having also been a somewhat enthusiastic despoiler of churches and monasteries (on self-interested occasions), it seems likely that he afforded some measure of protection to St Guthlac on his remote Fenland habitation though this, as we have suggested, was probably more to do with reasons of kin than of piety. Coenred was in turn succeeded by his cousin, Coelred, a son of Coenred's deposed predecessor Aethelraed (and the probable cause of Guthlac's earlier wanderings and exile),[30] and it is likely that the son, like the father, was not too well disposed towards Guthlac, who, though now a different type of exile, had become once again vulnerable, his monasticism notwithstanding. Guthlac's problems may also have been further augmented by the situation of a serious contender for the Mercian throne, Aethelbald, who was of a line of descent outside the immediate succession (perhaps rather like Guthlac's earlier situation – it is possible that the two men were closely related). This Aethelbald would in time take the Mercian throne after Guthlac's death, but for a while became a refugee in neighbouring East Anglia, which had a definite interest in stirring up the Mercian pot. Aethelbald did eventually leave East Anglia, probably due to heavy Mercian pressure being brought to bear upon the East Angles, themselves in a semi-dependent situation at this time, and there seems no doubt that he sought refuge in the remote recesses of the Fens. This not only provided him with some security, but it also gave him the opportunity for consolation from his probable kinsman, St Guthlac, whom he not only sought out on regular visits to Crowland, but who apparently warmly received the royal refugee and even prophesied that he [Aethelbald] would eventually become King of Mercia.

Harbouring and giving succour to a royal refugee such as Aethelbald must have placed Guthlac in even further danger from King Coelred, particularly if the king's retainers were scouring the Fens on Aethelbald's trail; and in the pursuit of this object unwelcome and unfriendly visits may well have been paid to Crowland, such visits having been the later cause of remembrance as Guthlac's physical assaults by 'demons'. (Even Bettelin's murderous temptation could have links with this possibility!)[31] At some time during his Crowland sojourn, Guthlac was joined by other ascetical strugglers, two of whom are named as 'Cissa' and 'Ecgberht'. A very late chronicler for Crowland, Ingulphus, says that Cissa had sprung from a noble family and had, in former times, been 'of great influence in worldly matters',[32] which tends to suggest that he may have been another 'Mercian royal' linked to Guthlac and perhaps to the fugitive Aethelbald. Of the others we know virtually nothing, though it seems that Ecgberht became Guthlac's closest confidant, and most probably his confessor, and was perhaps the eventual source for much of the information that related to Guthlac's most intense struggles.

Much of the material in the 'Life', as we have said, bears close parallels to similar accounts of earlier saints who were desert-strugglers and probably derives from them rather than from actual events in Guthlac's own life, though it is worth looking at some of them for their own sake. One such story tells of a man visiting Guthlac with a written parchment which was stolen by one of the island's many ravens who flew off with it into the fen. St Guthlac, seeing the man's obvious distress, told him to row after the raven, promising that he would recover his parchment. The man came to an island reed-bed and duly found the parchment hanging upon a reed, whereupon he returned with it to the saint who pronounced it a miracle.[33] Other stories also bear a close resemblance to traditional hagiographical tales, stressing the rapport that Guthlac had with the world of natural creation and telling of how birds, fish and wild animals were all subject to him and of how the saint would share his morsels of food with them. On one occasion, whilst he was talking to one of the monastic brethren, named Wilfryth, two swallows were said to have settled upon Guthlac's shoulders, then upon his breast, his arms and his knees. When Wilfryth questioned this, Guthlac pointed out that the natural creation comes close to those who live their lives according to God's will, and that angels come to those who separate themselves from worldliness.

Probably at Easter, 715, St Guthlac served Mass and preached the gospel for the last time, having already prophesied the date of his death. It seems that he had been ordained as a priest towards the end of his life by Bishop Headda of Mercia, despite the saint's reluctance and need of persuasion. It may well have been this ordination that had saved Guthlac from assassination by King Coenred and his agents; since he had become part of the Church hierarchy, there would be severe penalties for any such murder (though this was not always a guaranteed shield!)[34] and the ordination may well have been a deliberate move on the part of Bishop Headda and the Church to protect Guthlac. It seems that by the time of his last Mass Guthlac was already very ill, and three days later one of the brethren found him leaning in the corner of the monastery chapel against the altar table. Guthlac gave instructions for his sister, Pega, to be fetched at the time of his death, and for her to be asked to prepare his body in a coffin, wrapping him in a shroud.[35] The next day he is said to have stretched out his arms and, lifting them up heavenwards, died.

St Pega, St Bettelin, St Cissa and St Ecgberht

St Bettelin, who was present at Guthlac's death, later said that he saw his master's cell filled with a 'heavenly light' and that he saw a 'fiery tower' stretching upwards to heaven, with the accompaniment of angelic singing and a fragrant aroma which filled the whole island. Bettelin duly went to fetch Pega, having

St Pega (Window at Peakirk Church)

himself been instructed by the saint to reveal only to her his prophetic and visionary powers, and, on hearing the news of her brother's death, she fell to the ground in a deathlike trance. She faithfully carried out Guthlac's instructions and obsequies and then herself took possession of Crowland for a while, living in her brother's former cell (prior to this she had lived as a hermitess at Peakirk, on the edge of the Fens, not too far away).[36] Another late source for Guthlac, Orderic Vitalis, says that Pega endeavoured to practise even greater austerities than those of Guthlac during her time at Crowland, and it seems that the monastery thus became a 'double' one for a while under what was a hereditary abbacy.[37] Guthlac's disciples stayed on there until their own deaths; Cissa and Wilfryth continued to live there until the 730s, into the time when Guthlac's 'Life' was written by Felix, and they no doubt became important sources for much of the more personal and factually correct details that were later recorded by Felix. A year or so after Guthlac's death, St Pega arranged for her brother's relics to be 'translated' to a specially constructed shrine, the tomb having been opened in the presence of priests, monks and other clergy and the body found incorrupt. A blind man was present in the chapel containing the relics and it would seem that this man had accompanied St Pega to Crowland, she having told him that if he came to Guthlac's tomb he would be healed.[38] Pega led the man into the church and permitted him to lie down beside Guthlac's body. She then scraped some salt that had once been blessed by Guthlac, mixed it with water and let droplets fall upon his eyelids.[39] As the first droplet touched him he recovered his sight and then, with hymns, Pega wrapped Guthlac's body in a new shroud, given by the disciple Ecgberht, and put the relics into the new and more prestigious tomb.

After a relatively short stay on Crowland Pega eventually left for ever and for reasons we are not told,[40] and went off on pilgrimage to Rome where she died and was buried,[41] Guthlac's former disciple, Cissa, taking over as Abbot of Crowland. By 716, the former fugitive Aethelbald came to the Mercian throne, as Guthlac had foretold, and, upon hearing of Guthlac's death,[42] hurried to Crowland to visit the saint's tomb, sleeping the nights in the former monastic cell, during which he received a vision of the saint.[43] Aethelbald had earlier vowed that if Guthlac's prophecy regarding his own accession to the throne was fulfilled, he would construct a fitting monastery building upon the site of Guthlac's simple hermitage. He carried out his vow and, with the assistance of an Evesham monk, named Coenwulf,[44] began the task on St Bartholomew's Day, 716. He is said to have also made a grant freeing the monastery and the island from all future services and payments to the Crown, and to have given £300 in silver (a small fortune then!), together with £100 a year for ten years, to assist with the building of the abbey.[45]

So, in place of the primitive huts that had once sufficed for Guthlac and his simple companions, a fine abbey (by the standards of the day) abbey was erected, set upon great oak piles that were driven into the peaty soil, the buildings having probably been constructed out of wood, wattle and reed-thatch, and the church out of imported stone, in much the same way as Ely. The prized possession of the abbey seems to have been St Guthlac's whip, said to have been given to him by St Bartholomew for the purpose of driving away demons, together with the saint's psalter. When the rest of Guthlac's former companions in turn died, they in time came to be revered locally as saints and were buried in tombs encircling that of their former master where they would be venerated and undisturbed until the arrival of pillaging Vikings in 869, over a hundred years later. We hear a little more of St Bettelin after Guthlac's death, but regrettably in what is quite clearly only a fictional and late tale, which claimed him as the patron saint of Stafford which was clearly a confusion with another saint of a similar name![46]

King Aethelbald, like most of his royal ilk, failed to live up to pious expectations and went on to enjoy a notable reputation as a singularly prolific debauchee, possessed of a proclivity for young girls – even nuns were not spared his attentions – together with the rather noticeable tendency of Mercian kings for church and monastery pillage, all of which succeeded in earning him the stern reproval of the great English missionary saint, St Boniface. In 757 he was murdered by a rival claimant, Beornred, his power having been in decline for several years. His supplanter was in turn soon ousted by another contender, Offa (of Welsh dyke-building fame), who went on to reassert waning Mercian control over East Anglia. Interestingly, a daughter of this same King Offa, Aelfthryth (another 'Etheldreda'), later retired to Crowland as a hermitess, though practically nothing is known about her. As we shall see, her retirement and solitude at Crowland were said to be by way of an atonement for the murder of an East Anglian king (a victim of her father); and in time her own relics were enshrined at Crowland where they remained as a claimed source of miracles until the Viking sack of the monastery.[47]

St Ethelbert, King and Martyr

Back in East Anglia proper, King Aelfwald, for whom Felix's account of Guthlac had been written, died in about 749 and the kingdom then either fell apart or possibly was subject to the co-rule of three kings, though how, we are not certain (it is by no means apparent that they ruled concurrently). They seem to have been named Heonn, Beonn and Ethelbert (*Aethelberht*).[48] The latter, St Ethelbert, was still exercising some sort of rule by 794 and had he been a co-ruler, succeeding Aelfwald, would have enjoyed a reign of some forty-five years. All of this is extremely improbable, especially as his 'Life' records that he met his martyrdom after going to Mercia in search of a bride, with the implication that he was quite a young man, probably no more than in his early twenties at the most. The strongest likelihood is that there was a succession of kings after Aelfwald, and that the named Heonn and Beonn were successors and not co-rulers; and there may have been others not recorded or necessarily directly related, reflecting power struggles similar to those that we have seen in neighbouring Mercia, with Ethelbert having been the last in this procession of kings. There is also the likelihood that some of these factional struggles may have been connected with the re-emergence of East

Anglian power and independence, which was probably growing during Aelfwald's time and which had seized its opportunity during the decline of the power of King Aethelbald of Mercia. (It is also likely that East Anglian influence in the Fenland territory was on the reascendant, hinted at by Felix in his dedication of the 'Life' of Guthlac to an East Anglian king.)[49] The murder of King Ethelbert of East Anglia by Offa of Mercia would prove to be a boon for East Anglian anti-Mercian and pro-independence interests and would, as we shall see, be played for all it was worth with, of course, the obliging co-operation of the East Anglian Church in its elevation of the slain king to the status of a martyr.

East Anglia's traditional allies, as we have seen, had been Kent and Northumbria, lined up against, when possible, its traditional enemy Mercia. Whilst Aethelbald of Mercia had been virtual overlord of all southern England until his decline in the 740s, Northumbria had retained its independence, and Kent had managed to reassert and exercise virtual independence between 716 and 725, which may have coincided with similar reassertions in East Anglia. Offa, who was to become the most powerful and feared of the Mercian kings, seems to have exercised little power outside his own territory for the first seven years of his reign, and this may have allowed for a further strengthening of East Anglia's own position until about 764. After that, Offa asserted his power and wider aggrandizement with a vengeance, particularly in Kent – East Anglia's ally.[50] In 792, Offa married one of his daughters to the King of Northumbria, indicating an attempt to exercise some measure of control over that kingdom also. East Anglia, now relatively isolated from its traditional allies, would, it seems, also be brought into the net by a similar device, and we can be certain that Mercian pressure was brought to bear upon its king, Ethelbert.[51] According to his 'Life', he was 'invited' across to Mercia and King Offa's court for the purpose of marrying yet another of Offa's daughters, named Aelfthryth,[52] all of which suggests the extent to which Offa's power and influence over East Anglia had probably been growing from the late 780s onwards.[53]

According to the 'Life of St Ethelbert the Martyr', which needs to be treated very cautiously as it was not written until the late eleventh century (though possibly owing a little to earlier remembered traditions), Ethelbert was a son of a King Aethelraed of East Anglia and was his successor,[54] though unfortunately, there seems to be no historical corroboration for this. Apparently Ethelbert was courteously received by King Offa, but then, within a few days of his arrival at the Mercian court, he was treacherously murdered at Sutton Walls in south Herefordshire for 'reasons of state', which need not surprise us too much! His body was roughly buried on the banks of the River Lugg at Marden and his decapitated head was contemptuously kicked around. Following certain 'visions', his remains were later found and were buried at Hereford, his head, many centuries later, finding a resting place at Westminster Abbey. The Church chroniclers,[55] rather unsurprisingly, attached the blame for Ethelbert's murder to Offa's allegedly conniving wife, Queen Cynethryth, who was said to have warned her husband that the young East Anglian king had been reconnoitring the Mercian kingdom during his journey across it, with a view to eventually invading it[56] (not an impossibility!), though we might well take a somewhat different view of the events. The accusation levelled against Queen Cynethryth should be seen in a more plausible light. Undoubtedly the real culprit was Offa himself who may have decided to take over the East Anglian kingdom in its entirety and thus deliberately lured its king into his own territory. In this he succeeded, for the evidence suggests that there was direct Mercian rule over East Anglia until the 820s, when there would be a brief and rather shadowy reappearance of some native East Anglian rule coinciding with declining Mercian power. Significantly, the brief reappearance of East Anglian independence from the 820s onwards (until its total and permanent eclipse at the hands of the Vikings) undoubtedly went hand in hand with the nurturing of the cult of St Ethelbert the Martyr, particularly in his role as a royal martyr-saint and protector of his people and Church in true Wuffings tradition. The reality of the events was, as usual, embellished by the churchmen with the customary hagiographical devices ('spiritual credentials') suitably supporting the royal interests and propaganda requirements of the Church's patrons and protectors. The cult proved only to be a short-lived one as by the 890s onwards it was virtually superseded by the far more powerful one of King Edmund, East Anglia's far better-known martyr-king. However, as a short-term device the cult was successful and flourished in East Anglia for at least forty years.[57]

The accusation levelled at Queen Cynethryth must, of course, be seen in the context not only of what became a useful East Anglian hagiographical 'propaganda weapon', but as characteristic of the usual ecclesiastical prejudice against women who wielded power.[58] The intense dislike of Offa's queen, as conveyed in the 'Life', probably derived from the East Anglian dynasty's resentment of Mercian power and its queens who were its agents.[59] It would seem also that the Mercians, who retained Ethelbert's relics, were also eager to further the advantages of this new martyr-cult within their own territory, based upon that possession,[60] and would, therefore, hardly have been likely to disparage the memory of one of their greatest and most successful kings – to his wife then the blame! After Offa's death the maligned Cynethryth did in fact go on to become the Abbess of Cookham (she even enjoyed hearty disputes over land with the Archbishop!)[61] and continued to exercise a joint lordship with succeeding Mercian kings over Mercian monasteries, including Crowland; we may be sure that this was the true reason why her daughter, Aelfthryth, was sent there, remorse and atonement apart! Her control over Crowland probably helped retain some Mercian power in the Fenland area and over what Mercia regarded as one of its important royal spiritual institutions.

In East Anglia, we can observe the development of St Ethelbert's veneration and martyr-status from the 830s onwards, with a considerable number of church dedications to him, many of them appearing, significantly, close to probable royal and episcopal seats. All of this tends to confirm that this was indeed a royal cult, developed by the East Anglian kings who were re-emerging

after the virtual eclipse that had come about in Offa's time, and
the clear episcopal support underlines the inescapable fact of the
close interdependence of the kings and the Church. That the
Mercians retained Ethelbert's relics and made good use of them
also indicates the power of such instruments of devotion which,
as we shall see in the case of the later cult of St Edmund, would
eventually be used to the fullest by the Church as well as the
Crown in centuries to come. The possession of relics of such
status, particularly royal ones, was treated like the possession of
prize booty. These relics (genuine or 'discovered'), when within
the control of the royal monasteries, substantially promoted the
prestige of the kings,[62] as in a later age they would serve to enhance
the prestige of the most powerful monasteries that had become
free of royal and secular control following the Monastic Reform
Movement of the tenth century. (Ely Abbey under its later rulers
was to become a prime example of 'relic-hunting', as in the
recorded case of the pillage of St Witburgha's relics from Dereham.) The kings could and did gain increase in their political
influence by associating themselves with monasteries that were
the centre of royal relic-cults, and this was even more the case in
the territories where they were asserting, or reasserting, claims
to rule and where their own traditions were shaky.[63] Mercia's
possession of Ethelbert's relics was an advantageous countermeasure against East Anglian resurgence, and the placing of
Offa's daughter at Crowland was unmistakeably part of that
countermeasure. Her elevation to the status of a saint after her
death and the attribution to her of miracles were also part of a
Mercian, rather than East Anglian, cult and instigated for the
same reasons. As we have seen, these traditions were developing
for some forty years or so both in East Anglia and Mercia but
they were soon to be held in temporary check and to be overtaken
by unforeseen events, the clouds of which were already gathering
on the horizon and which would bring to an end the East Anglian
kingdom together with a shattering of its Church. The Church
would eventually recover from that coming storm, but in a very
changed form. We might well remark that, if East Anglia had

received its 'baptism' in the early seventh century, it was about to undergo a second one in the late ninth century – one of blood and fire!

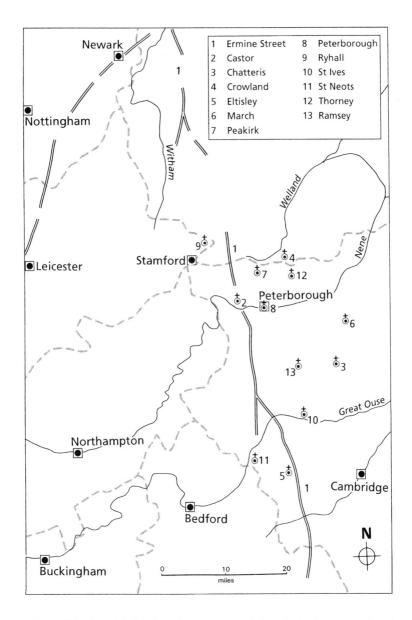

1	Ermine Street	8	Peterborough
2	Castor	9	Ryhall
3	Chatteris	10	St Ives
4	Crowland	11	St Neots
5	Eltisley	12	Thorney
6	March	13	Ramsey
7	Peakirk		

Map 3 *The East Midlands – showing some of the principal sites mentioned in the text*

7

The Storm

The Pagans Return

'*From the wrath of the Northman – Good Lord deliver us!*' So ran a petition in a litany of the early English Church, a reference to the warlike Scandinavian bands of predators who, like the early English themselves three to four hundred years previously, began to attack the coastal and exposed areas of England and Western Europe from the late eighth century onwards.

The first recorded Scandinavian attack upon England was mentioned in the *Anglo-Saxon Chronicle* in the entry for 789, when we are told that three ships of Norwegians landed on the south coast of England, killing the king's reeve who tried to parley with them.[1] Given that Scandinavian ships carried up to about thirty men, this amounted to a war party of some fifty to eighty warriors. Further attacks were recorded for the 790s and the early decades of the ninth century. The earliest attacks seem to have been mainly Norwegian and somewhat sporadic, but by the 850s they had started to increase in frequency and ferocity, this time taking on a Danish preponderance. The references indicate that attacks were concentrated on the eastern coastlines of England, and, though in the earlier stages we have no specific references to attacks on East Anglia as such, they are likely to have occurred. St Felix's episcopal seat of *Dommoc* seems to have rapidly come to an end at about this time and was probably moved to somewhere deeper and safer inland, Hoxne in Suffolk having been a possibility, the transfer having undoubtedly been precipitated by coastal raids and attacks.

It is now generally considered that the Scandinavian armies were relatively small,[2] but highly mobile, and were aided by their use of a superior naval technology. They came primarily as raiders and plunderers, their targets having been wherever there was moveable wealth (coinage, precious objects and manpower – suitable for slaving and ransoming), and thus they noticeably singled out the Church, particularly the monasteries, for attention, given that it had much to offer in this direction, together with the added bonus of undefended vulnerability. The ninth-century Kingdom of East Anglia, exposed as it was on two sides to the sea, was not only amongst the richest kingdoms in England, but its Church was very rich also.[3] There is no particular evidence to suggest that the Vikings had any particular mission in killing priests and monks, or in slaughtering Christians simply because they were Christians, despite the claims of later Church polemicists, nor were they out to destroy churches and monasteries as such: it was simply that the Church had become the repository of vast material wealth over the previous two centuries, and it was for this reason that it bore the heaviest brunt of Viking attention. Apart from anything else, the monasteries were invariably situated in remote locations, often accessible by waterways, all of which amounted to a 'god'-send to these entrepreneurial Norsemen.

It seems that the Scandinavian invaders were mainly young and of aristocratic background and were still pagan. We do not really know what prompted their eruption from Scandinavia, just as we cannot really be certain what had triggered the movement of earlier Germanic peoples, such as the Anglo-Saxons, other than the lure of wealth. Though pagan, the Danes particularly had had some contact with Christianity due to a small-scale Christian influence which had penetrated into southern Denmark as early as the mid-ninth century onwards, arising from contacts with the Western Empire of the Franks. English missionaries had been involved in the Christianizing process that went hand in hand with the empire's domination of the German tribes up to the Danish border and this may well have brought English churchmen into contact with Scandinavians. Such contacts may have served to increase the Scandinavians' awareness of the wealth of the western lands (if they were not already aware of it through trading contacts) and of the concentration of wealth in the Church particularly. This, perhaps, combined with a 'tit-for-tat' attitude towards the missionizing of the Church, may go some way towards explaining the ferocity and targeting of attacks on ecclesiastical centres which would have been particularly apposite had the Church and the missionaries been perceived as 'agents' of the Western imperial interest.

An entry in the early *Anglo-Saxon Chronicle* for 841 refers to 'many' in East Anglia having been slain by the pagan host, but it also goes on to say that the Norsemen were defeated and beaten off.[4] Local traditions in Norfolk (and they are no more than that) speak of an attack near Thetford, and ancient burial mounds at Ringmere are popularly, though probably incorrectly, identified as Scandinavian burial sites following such battles. The lack of surviving records for East Anglia during this period, to a considerable extent itself a consequence of the attacks on the ecclesiastical sites, makes it impossible to assess how heavy these early attacks were, though it is likely that the coastal areas were the most severely affected. There may have been some similarities between these raids and those of the Anglo-Saxon freebooters of the earlier centuries. First came a phase of plundering; then most probably arrangements were made with local kings and chieftains who tried to contain the problem; then would follow the final objective of the wholesale takeover of kingdoms – the Church, due to its overdependence upon the kings, becoming one of the major casualties of the process. However, we should not stretch the parallels too far for there seems to be no evidence for any earlier Scandinavian infiltration into the country comparable to the settlement of Germanic peoples in the late Romano-British period of the fourth and fifth centuries, and the Scandinavian raids may have involved much smaller numbers, the duration of Scandinavian activities having extended over a shorter period of time. Though we know more about Scandinavian paganism than we do of its early English predecessor, it seems that it was not so deeply entrenched, for the conversion to Christianity of the Scandinavian settlers in England was to prove far more rapid and occurred within a much shorter space of time following their settlement than had been the case of the English, three centuries earlier. The Church of the ninth and tenth centuries, though a major casualty of the Viking attacks, demonstrated an ability for rapid recuperation, and thus appears to have been far more powerfully established than had been its Romano-British predecessor of the fifth century.

By the 850s, serious Scandinavian attempts at conquest were taking place, with the Danes wintering and setting up permanent bases and seeking to take over whole kingdoms, eastern England having been a primary target, notably Northumbria and East Anglia. The *Anglo-Saxon Chronicle* records for 865, that 'a great heathen host arrived in England and took winter quarters in East Anglia, where it was provided with horses, a truce having been made with the East Angles'.[5] The *Chronicle* also tells us that in the same year a heathen host wintered in the Isle of Thanet under similar arrangements.[6] Here the Danes were promised tribute, but devastated the area nonetheless, and we may well suppose that a similar scenario was enacted in East Anglia. It has been suggested that this particular incursion was in fact a concentration of war bands from all over Europe under an ambitious leadership, numbering some several thousands of warriors. They certainly had been active in France prior to this descent upon England but with varying degrees of success, having left France for England in 865; and they may have been a part of the 'Great Army' of Bjorn Ironside, the supposed son of Ragnar – often incorrectly identified with Ragnar Lodbroke, the legendary father of St Edmund's slayers.[7] The force that landed in East Anglia was said to have been led by three chieftains, recorded as Halfdan, Ubbi, and Ivarr 'the Boneless',[8] who would go on to carve out an empire stretching from Northumbria to Ireland. It seems that they made the most of exploiting English internal divisions to the full, for both Northumbria and Mercia were factionally divided and, though we know nothing of what was happening in East Anglia, it was almost certainly trying to resist a long legacy of Mercian domination. The extensive coastline of East Anglia and its various water routes rendered it highly accessible to these seafaring raiders, and, as we have noted, the indisputable wealth of the kingdom and its Church was also to be a powerful magnet, not only in terms of tribute-exaction and plunder, but also for potential takeover. The geographical situation of the kingdom also made it a useful territorial base for further attacks into other parts of England.

By the 860s East Anglia seems to have enjoyed some measure of independence, arising from Mercian weakness. The possibility has to be considered that the Scandinavian intruders may have been perceived not only as a threat, but as potentially useful mercenary allies for the purpose of resisting Mercia. This would have been similar to the late Romano-British policy of the fourth and fifth centuries.[9] The Danish host stayed in East Anglia for a year, securing horses and raiding throughout the local countryside, and compelled the local inhabitants and their king, Edmund, to buy peace, and it may well have been during this period that many of the smaller monasteries and *mynsters* were plundered, disappearing from the scene for ever. A fairly large and important monastic site that had existed at Brandon in Suffolk shows evidence of having been possibly abandoned and destroyed due to Scandinavian attack and it could well have been a victim of this phase of Viking activity. It seems that the larger monasteries, notably those of the Fenlands, suffered a little later, and this may have been the time when the episcopal seat was moved inland to Hoxne and close to what may have been a royal inland base. Devastation may have been heavier in Norfolk than Suffolk during this first stage of occupation, though we cannot be sure, and we cannot rule out the possibility that some sort of division of the kingdom occurred, leaving King Edmund as the client-ruler for the parts occupied by the Danish army and with direct control only over part of the southern Suffolk base, the traditional Wuffings area. Direct control over Norfolk and western Suffolk would have been of more use to the Danes as it provided access by land and sea to both Mercia and Northumbria, to which they would now turn their attention for a while, whilst King

Edmund was probably left with little option other than to accept terms and to play for time.

Martyr-Monks

After a year's occupation, the Danish army left East Anglia in order to attack Northumbria where they brutally killed its kings, installing their own English puppet ruler and exacting a heavy tribute. Following a confrontation with Mercia and a buy-off by the Mercians of the Danish host, the latter returned once more to East Anglia in the late autumn of 869. It seems that they returned from their base at Nottingham moving southwards and down across the Fens (the *Anglo-Saxon Chronicle* clearly indicates that they returned to East Anglia by land and not by sea).[10] In their path lay the great Fenland monasteries, and the Anglo-Norman chronicler, Matthew Paris, lists the monasteries that suffered plunder and devastation. He states that they were Crowland, Thorney, Ramsey (he was wrong)[11] and Peterborough. These were obvious and highly accessible targets and the Vikings, returning home to their base in East Anglia, were doubtlessly already possessed of considerable wealth from their exactions in Northumbria and Mercia and definitely not prepared to miss another opportunity of adding to it – we must assume that they were already fully aware of the potential booty that these ecclesiastical centres offered!

Peterborough was probably hit first, and the *Chronicle* entry for 869 tells us that the Danes reached there, burned and beat the monastery down, slew its abbot, Headda, all the monks and all whom they found there, and that 'this place which was once rich, they reduced to nothing'.[12] The total of monks killed was said to have numbered eighty-four, which seems a somewhat large figure, but it probably includes the outer retainers and lay servants of the monastery and the scale of the slaughter may have had something to do with resistance and defence offered by the latter. Moveable treasure was undoubtedly seized, i.e. money, gold, chalices, vestments and so on, though manuscripts and relics would have been of no particular use or interest and were therefore

unceremoniously burned together with the wood and thatch buildings and the bodies of the slain. From Peterborough the host may
have fanned out across the Fens, using punts and boats, and then
struck at Ely, Thorney and Crowland. Ely was burned to the
ground, its gold and silver treasures, vestments and manuscripts
all disappearing, though its sacred relics and tombs survived
(according to later Ely claims). Maybe not all of its monastic
community were killed; some may have fled in advance, and some
are said to have eventually returned to the dereliction that was
once their great monastery. Next came Crowland. The sources
that describe its sack are very late and may not be too reliable.
They say that the monks knew of the impending arrival of the
Danes and planned an evacuation to nearby Thorney, with the
intention of taking there St Guthlac's relics, his psalter and whip
and other sacred items, together with the monastery's jewels and
charters. These they loaded on to a boat, burying their sacred
altar-stone and gold and silver plate in a wall of the cloister.
Unfortunately, the Danes arrived before they could make good
their escape and whilst their abbot, Theodore, was still serving
Mass. The leader of the Scandinavian detachment, named as
'Osketyl', murdered the venerable abbot, hacking him down across
the altar, and the rest of the monastic community were tortured
in order to discover the whereabouts of the monastery's treasure.
None of the monks co-operated and were therefore summarily
killed; the only survivor was a ten-year-old novice, named as
'Turgar'.[13] The raiders then broke open the tombs of St Guthlac
and his former disciples, hoping to find treasure, but, enraged
with disappointment, they heaped the relics and the contents of
the tombs into a pile and then burned them, together with the
bodies of the slain and the church and monastery buildings. The
account does go on to say that the Danes did actually find some
of the monastery treasure (maybe the small boy had told them of
its whereabouts), including St Guthlac's whip and psalter (though
these would have been of no value to them), which they then
succeeded in losing in the River Nene, probably a way of saying
that that which was of no monetary value was dumped![14]

Thorney Abbey suffered much of the same, where three of its hermits, named as Tancred, Torthred and Tova (two brothers and a sister) were said to have been butchered,[15] and similarly St Benet Holme in Norfolk, which was supposed to have been founded in the 820s by a holy man – Suniman – who was martyred along with all his community, one of whom would be remembered as a hermit named Wolfeius. (St Benet Holme could have been destroyed during the earlier Danish incursions into East Anglia, or a little later at the time of the death of King Edmund.) There is a slight problem with the names of the Thorney martyrs as these are also the names given to its founders of nearly a hundred years earlier. The claim is most likely to have been a reference to the destruction of the relics of the three founding hermits of Thorney. In the case of Crowland the actual names of those martyred together with Abbot Theodore are given.[16] They are recorded as; Askega (the prior), Lethwin (the sub-prior), Aelfgete (a deacon), Sabinus (a sub-deacon), Grimkell and Agamund (centenarians!), Hereberht (a chanter), Ecgdred and Ulric (servers) and seventy others.[17] The alleged number of victims is rather similar to that given for those who suffered at Peterborough and must be seen in the same light. Some of the names on the Crowland list are clearly Danish and cannot have been those of the monastic community, which probably adds up to the fact that by the time the abbey was refounded and its chronicle written, most of the names of the slain were no longer known or remembered and token names were provided for them. Having accomplished their bloody purpose, the Danes now moved back into the heartland of East Anglia itself, taking up, it is said, a base at Thetford and ready to inaugurate what would prove to be East Anglia's most enduring and famous tradition.

The Martyr-King

We know nothing of what had transpired in East Anglia under its disadvantaged king, Edmund, during the time of the Danish two- to three-year absence, and it is quite possible that the beleaguered king had been able to effect some recovery and control in his territories, hoping to strengthen his position and also, no doubt, hoping that the Danes would not return – if this was so, then he was to be doomed to disappointment and disaster!

The only historical reference that we have to the events of 869 and St Edmund's death (all else is largely legend) is a brief entry in the early *Anglo-Saxon Chronicle* for that year which records that 'the host went across Mercia into East Anglia and took winter quarters at Thetford; and the same winter St Edmund, the King, fought against them, and the Danes won the victory, and they slew the King and overran the entire Kingdom, and destroyed all the monasteries and churches to which they came'.[18] This does seem to indicate that Edmund, during the Danish absence, had had time to raise an army and that he was not prepared to submit to the Danes, have his kingdom divided, or pay them tribute a second time. (Bishop Asser, the chronicler for King Alfred, who wrote not too long afterwards, categorically stated that the East Angles were not prepared to countenance the presence of the Danes again or to pay tribute a second time.)[19] It may also have been that the Danes were now prepared to do away with him and to replicate what they had accomplished in Northumbria by installing a puppet ruler of their own choice rather than trusting the legitimate king. These same Danes had refused to give battle to English forces previously at Nottingham,[20] and, had Edmund known of this, he may have underestimated the Danish strength and determination and perhaps have anticipated some sort of alliance with, and assistance from, King Alfred and his Kingdom of Wessex. The true fate of Edmund, as we have indicated, is mainly hidden in legend, but hagiographically much would be claimed for him and it is to those sources that we now turn.

Most of the accounts of St Edmund's martyrdom are very late (post-1066) and historically untrustworthy, though there is an earlier record, which may give us a few clues and which was written by St Abbo of Fleury at Ramsey Abbey during the tenth century. Abbo claimed that he had based his version of events

St Edmund (showing Sceptre and Arrow; From the Rood Screen of Barton Turf Church, Norfolk)

upon the testimony of Archbishop St Dunstan of Canterbury, who, as a boy, had heard the account of King Edmund's martyrdom from an old man who had been the king's personal armour-bearer and an eyewitness. Be this as it may, Abbo certainly seems to have embellished the original account by adding material that has been demonstrated to have come from other saints' 'Lives', and St Dunstan himself is also known to have been a notorious 'embellisher' in this respect.[21] We must also bear in mind that though Abbo was closer in time to the actual events than any of the later biographers of Edmund, he did have a definite purpose in setting out his account and his purpose was hagiography and not historical biography. By the time Abbo wrote his account very little was probably remembered about the circumstances surrounding Edmund's martyrdom other than a few surviving oral traditions. Abbo's purpose was to present Edmund as a virtuous king, in the Old Testament ideal, and as a Christian martyr who had suffered for his faith and people. He goes to great lengths to stress the king's supposed virginity and purity and we can discern striking similarities between his 'Life' of Edmund and other martyrologies that were well known at the time, such as that of St Sebastian.[22] Abbo also seems to telescope people, places and events in the style common to hagiographers,[23] and he probably incorporated into his work traditions that circulated at Bury St Edmunds Abbey, which by his time was claiming to have possession of the relics of Edmund. The earliest version of his account can be found in an edited rendition, translated into Early English by Aelfric.[24] The later accounts of St Edmund belong mainly to the eleventh and twelfth centuries and are extremely fanciful and elaborated, though we have to allow for the possibility of their having relied upon surviving local East Anglian traditions in some form or other.

According to Abbo, the Danes, under the leadership of Ivarr, sailed to East Anglia in the winter of 869 and slew many people.[25] They sent a message to Edmund the king ordering him to submit and to pay them homage as an under-king. Edmund was in close consultation with a bishop who advised him to submit to the

Norsemen or to flee. Edmund refused to do either and sent a return message saying that he would only submit if Ivarr became a Christian. The bishop informed Edmund that many of his people had already been slain and that the king had no forces for resistance (the later sources contradict this by saying that Edmund did go out and give battle near the Danish base at Thetford). Abbo then says that Ivarr came and seized Edmund in his 'hall', and the later Norman translation of Abbo's account gives extra information to the effect that Edmund defeated the Danes at Thetford (also claimed by the other late sources) and that there were heavy losses on both sides. The same Norman version of Abbo also goes on to say that Edmund retired to Framlingham and it was there that Ivarr sent his demands, which were that Edmund renounce his religion and kingdom. Yet another late account has it that Edmund was residing at a town called '*Haegilsdun*' and, when Ivarr advanced, Edmund retired to a church on the advice of a bishop (named by late sources as '*Hunberht*').

We cannot set much store upon these accounts, and even Abbo's version needs treating with extreme caution, but it would seem that, if there is anything of a trustworthy nature in the accounts at all, the king had fled southwards following defeat or a stalemate, perhaps in the hope of recovering his situation, with the Danes in hot pursuit. If this had been the case he may have been heading back to his royal base in Suffolk, though circumstances allowed him no time for recuperation. The Danes, if the accounts amount to anything, seized and killed him and the sources say that he was first tortured and then finally beheaded without the option of further negotiation. Edmund (according to Abbo, who tells us that he was tied to a tree and shot through with arrows before the *coup de grâce* was delivered) was claimed to have died heroically and as a Christian, calling upon the name of Christ.

The *Anglo-Saxon Chronicle* makes it quite clear that Edmund was killed in the *aftermath* of battle and the late sources indicate that he was killed by the Danes following a brief interval after warring against them. If this was so, then probably no more than a few days had elapsed after the engagement at Thetford; Abbo states in his account that, by the time Edmund sent his message of defiance to the Danes, their army was already advancing upon him, and that the king was consequently captured in flight.[26] There are references in the text to Edmund, at the time of his martyrdom, having had his ribs laid bare, and to his having had numerous gashes,[27] which, if true, could be an indication that he had already been badly wounded in battle and may in fact have been overtaken and captured in flight. Abbo's graphical description of Edmund as having been tied to a tree and shot with arrows 'until he bristled like a hedgehog',[28] resembles the tradition of the martyrdom of St Sebastian,[29] and could be a hagiographical device of portraying the wounds that the king had previously suffered in the engagement with the Danes. What probably happened was that, when the Danes caught up with him, they were determined to be rid of him and he was beaten and decapitated. The Danes apparently threw the dead king's head away in a nearby thicket (we are not told why) and returned to their ships. The story then goes on to tell how a wolf, 'sent by God', protected the slain king's head until the local inhabitants found it (with some assistance from the head, according to Abbo, as it cried out to the searchers, 'Here, here!') and then took it away to the 'town', hurriedly burying it with the body, where in time a simple wooden chapel was erected over the relics. These events were said to have occurred on 20 November 869.

Further serious questions arise straight away even from Abbo's version of the events. Firstly, was there any battle at all at Thetford? The earliest translated version of Abbo's account (by Aelfric) makes no mention of it, though the earlier *Anglo-Saxon Chronicle* reference does. Either the *Chronicle* assumed this to have been the case or perhaps Abbo was ignorant of it. The alleged battle could be a reference to the earlier events of 865 when there was a stalemate enabling the king to reach some terms with the Danes,[30] and, if this was the case and Abbo's version of events was correct, then Edmund was as much defeated in diplomacy as in war and in no position to bargain. Possibly the Danish return was unexpected and crippled the king's power of resistance – there was no

time to raise an army, exactly as the bishop had warned him.
Abbo, as we have seen, was primarily concerned with portraying
Edmund as a 'Christlike' victim who died nobly when he had no
choice, and as a sacrificial victim whose death was a moral choice
rather than the traditional battle death.[31] As we have already noted,
the parallels with other saints' 'Lives' are unmistakeable. Apart
from the resemblance to the death by arrows of St Sebastian,
there is a similarity between the account of Edmund's head calling
out to his followers and the story of the head of St Dionysius of
Paris (a martyr of the Roman period), which was also supposed
to have spoken after decapitation.[32] The wolf sent by God to guard
the king's head bears some similarity with a tradition in the 'Life
of St Mary of Egypt', where the saint's dead body was said to
have been guarded by a lion.[33] Interestingly, the bodies of both
St Sebastian and St Dionysius were said to have been faithfully
tended by holy women – Abbo says that Edmund's body was
cared for by a holy woman, whom he names as 'Oswin'.[34] As a
professional hagiographer, Abbo would, of course, have been very
familiar with these Church tales and traditions, and we can therefore safely assume that little of what he wrote, as in the case of
the earlier hagiographies upon which he based some of his tale,
bore any accord with the real events. We have already noted that
Abbo would also have been at great pains to establish the king's
personal purity and virginity, as this was a prerequisite for bodily
incorruption after death, and Edmund's alleged remains were to
be claimed as incorrupt for at least the next three hundred years
or so.[35] Finally, to have been slain by pagans was sufficient guaran-
tee in itself for elevation to the status of saint and martyr, and
in this respect, Edmund certainly seems to have met the
requirements.

It is worth examining the time and conditions in which Abbo
actually penned his account of St Edmund's martyrdom and realizing why the king's death was raised from virtual historical obscurity to cult level, not only on an East Anglian scale, but, in time,
on a national and even international one, which would persist until
the sixteenth-century Reformation and beyond. Abbo wrote his

story some hundred and twenty years after the events and at the height of what came to be called the Monastic Reform Movement.[36] Of this, Abbo was himself a part, and his abbey, Ramsey in the Fens, had been founded by one of the leading personalities of the movement, St Oswald. Significantly, St Dunstan, Abbo's source for much of his Edmund material, was another leading and powerful light in the same movement, and the movement had a powerful base in East Anglia, where many of its reformed monasteries were situated. St Dunstan had already been heavily involved in the canonization and royal cult-promotion of St Edward the Martyr which had also, paying scant regard to the real facts, portrayed St Edward as an ideal king and a sacrificial victim.[37] The cult of St Edward was primarily a Wessex-based one and, by the late tenth century, when East Anglia had long been wrested from Danish control and absorbed into the expanding domain of Wessex (which was unifying the whole country), East Anglia's cult of St Edmund proved a boon to the zealous churchmen of the Monastic Reform Movement, the cult transpiring to be a far more powerful one than that of St Edward.[38] The concept of 'ideal kings' (as defined by the tenth-century Church and the reformers) was to be used as a powerful weapon by the Church in dealing with kings and at the same time, by stressing virginity, was a valuable propaganda weapon against the married clergy and what were regarded as 'pseudo-monks'.[39] It gave the reforming churchmen a reason for rejecting the commands of bad kings and it heralded the further increase of the worldly power of the Church, an aspect that would become the most striking feature of the several centuries that lay ahead and which, in effect, gave the later medieval Church much of its shape and form.

Facts and Fictions

We can trace the development of the cult of St Edmund from the very beginning of the tenth century within only a generation of his death. No later than 900, coins were being minted by the Danish ruler of East Anglia, Guthrum (also known as '*Aethel-*

stan'),[40] who had made a treaty with King Alfred the Great, and had accepted baptism.[41] This suggests that the memory and popularity of Edmund and the fallen Wuffings dynasty remained strong in the former kingdom, and that Guthrum had no personal qualms or reservations about encouraging the devotion to a former enemy, no doubt with his own interests in mind as the de facto Christian successor of the slain king. According to a Bury St Edmunds' tradition, the dead king's relics were translated from their humble resting place to *Beodricesworth*, now to be renamed St Edmund's Bury, thirty-three years after his death,[42] which might roughly coincide with the issue by Guthrum of the memorial coinage. The body was claimed to be incorrupt and still fresh, the original wounds having now disappeared, and the neck wound was said to be marked only by what was described as the semblance of a 'silk red thread'. The holy widow, Oswin, continued to pray and fast by St Edmund's relics and would, it seems, annually cut his hair, beard and nails which apparently still continued to grow![43]

There is a lot of evidence to show that Bury St Edmunds was an important royal centre under Danish Guthrum,[44] and he was no doubt keen to establish his own credentials there as the promoter of a cult in which we can rest assured he was suitably encouraged by the local Church which had been savagely mauled by his own kinsmen earlier. By 910, East Anglia had been returned to English control by Alfred the Great's son, King Edward the Elder, and was now within the control of the expanding Kingdom of Wessex. St Edmund's cult proved highly useful to the Wessex kings as a national symbol of resistance to the Danes and a powerful rallying symbol for the kings as well as for the Church. Fresh Danish attacks in the early eleventh century, this time by ostensibly Christian Danes, saw St Edmund's body reputedly moved to the safety of London, and, three years later, back to Bury once more.[45] There it was mocked by the Danish claimant to the English throne, Sweyn Haroldsson (father of King Cnut), who was feasting at Bury on 2 February 1014 and for his irreverence was allegedly punished by the saint through choking to death![46]

The Site of St Edmund's Shrine (Bury St Edmunds)

In King Cnut's time, the great Benedictine Abbey was refounded at Bury to house the saint's relics, and Cnut showed his eagerness to adopt Edmund as a patron, no doubt for the same reasons as Guthrum (they were both usurpers!), and, of course, in order to show himself as an 'ideal' Christian king and a great patron and protector of the Church. A Bishop Theodred[47] had opened St Edmund's tomb earlier in 951, inspected the body, verified its intactness, and washed and reclothed it, replacing it in its coffin which was described as having Danish ring-handles – probably the same coffin provided by Guthrum. Then, in 1032 the coffin was reopened on the occasion of the dedication of Bury's new church, and the body was once more inspected and verified, this time by Archbishop Aethelnoth of Canterbury and in the presence of witnesses. Yet again, in 1050, the coffin was opened,[48] inspection and verification of the body following, and identification corroborated by one of the original 1032 witnesses[49] who was present again, the body this time being described as though 'sleeping' and giving off an odour of sanctity. The burial clothes were pierced with bloodstained arrow holes and the head was solid with the trunk. Two more viewings were still to take place, the next one being carried out by Abbot Baldwin in 1095. Baldwin was anxious to improve the reputation and fortunes of the abbey and distributed some of the relics of St Edmund's clothing far and wide, even visiting Lucca in Italy, where he gave the local church some relics of Edmund, thus establishing the saint's cult there.[50] The final recorded viewing came in 1198 and was carried out by Abbot Samson, though this time the body was not unwrapped but only felt in outline through its clothing;[51] and there it presumably rested undisturbed until the Reformation of the 1530s, though there was a great fire in 1465 which severely damaged the shrine, and which could possibly have actually destroyed its content. Surprisingly, when Henry VIII's Commissioners suppressed the abbey and the shrine they made no mention of any alleged body or relics of St Edmund.[52] In 1634 a search was carried out in the grounds of the derelict abbey, on the presumption that the monks had pre-empted the King's Commissioners and had buried the body there, but nothing was ever found.

From the sixteenth century onwards, the French Abbey of St Sernin, Toulouse, claimed to be in possession of St Edmund's body, by now reduced to bones as we might expect, the story having been put out that, in 1216, the monks of Bury had smuggled the relics out to Louis the Dauphin of France and that the relics had circuitously reached Toulouse by 1450.[53] Needless to say, from the seventeenth century onwards Toulouse Abbey made much of this unlikely tale! In the early part of the twentieth century, these Toulouse 'relics' of St Edmund (minus the skull) were sent to England for installation in the (then) new Roman Catholic cathedral at Northampton, only to be greeted by serious academic objection regarding their authenticity, which threw the Church hierarchy into something of a quandary. The bones were subsequently, and temporarily, interred in the private chapel of the Duke of Norfolk pending further investigation and verification. There they remained until 1994, when a committee was set up under the patronage of the Duke of Norfolk for the purpose of making a thorough scientific examination of them. This was duly undertaken, the bones being sent on to London for further tests and examination. The verdict is still to come.

Was there ever a body of St Edmund at Bury at all? It seems unlikely. There obviously were alleged relics of some description or other kept there until the late Middle Ages, and there they were venerated as such. If we can even assume that Edmund's body was recovered and identified after his death[54] (and this must remain very uncertain), it is likely that it was embalmed, the head having been wired back on to the body,[55] as embalming and preservational skills were not beyond the capacity of the church-men of Edmund's time, particularly as it suited lucrative pur-poses,[56] and the practice was well known and widespread, though with varied results. The purpose was to retain some likeness and form of the body in its living state, the main objective having been to demonstrate the incorruption of the body as a testimony to the saint's purity and virtue, all of which would, of course, be claimed to have been 'miraculous'. It seems that even mummifi-cation sufficed for these dubious purposes,[57] and early accounts of the inspection of Edmund's supposed body do seem to indicate the use of embalming aromatics.[58] The later inspections, which entailed confirming the outline of the body through its wrappings, also suggest some measure of mummified preservation, though the last inspection account of 1198 made no reference to aromatics, which also tends to suggest that what was there by then was no longer preserved.[59] The only final observation that can be made about this strange sequence of events regarding the cult of St Edmund is that, if the alleged relics currently under examin-ation are found to be of the right period and show any consistency with the traditional accounts of the king's martyrdom, then this will go no little way not only to establishing the Toulouse claims, but also to giving some serious credibility to the traditions and accounts (notably Abbo's) surrounding Edmund's martyrdom (it would also require us to reassess the skills of the medieval embal-mers!). Anything less than this will dispel most of the St Edmund cult, as it developed from 900 onwards, and it would have to be seen, along with so many of the royal-saint cults, as having been little more than a pious and politically-motivated myth based upon obscure historical facts.

A Confusion of Places?

Having looked at the controversy regarding Edmund's relics, we are still left with a further one – and one which grinds on till this day – the location for his martyrdom. Traditionally, this has been claimed for Hoxne in Suffolk, and, as such, this pretty and quiet Suffolk village enjoyed a small measure of pilgrimage down to the Reformation. Throughout a considerable part of the Middle Ages, Hoxne possessed two chapels (there was also a third dedicated to 'Our Ladye of Chickering' and not apparently connected to the cult), both said to commemorate the site of Edmund's martyrdom. They were believed to have marked the spot where his head was found and the site of his execution, one of the chapels supposedly indicating the site of the king's capture and the place where his remains first reposed, and the second marking the site of the tree where he was said to have been executed. The first chapel was known as 'Great Chapel', i.e. where Hoxne Priory once stood (now Abbey Farm) – the martyrdom site. The second chapel was known as 'New Work' (its original location is now vague) and is supposed to be where the slain king's head was found.[60] Close to Great Chapel was also an oak tree, the site of which is now marked by a stone memorial cross (the tree fell in 1848),[61] and which was claimed to have been the actual tree to which Edmund was tied at his martyrdom. The tree when it fell was said to have contained an arrowhead which, it was claimed at the time, was Danish, though this was never verified. However, the claim regarding the tradition of 'St Edmund's Oak' was refuted not long after it fell, by a Suffolk resident, who denied on the strength of fifty years' knowledge that there had ever been any oak at Hoxne traditionally connected with any such martyrdom or known by that name! It seems that Great Chapel was the more important of the two and at one time the principal resort of pilgrimage. Hoxne Priory, which contained it, was once the temporary seat of the East Anglian bishops in the post-Danish recovery period and had between six and eight monks who, from the twelfth century onwards, were subject to the Prior of Norwich Cathedral. The rather more elusive second chapel, New Work, seems to have been about a mile away from the Great Chapel[62] and the supposed place of Edmund's capture has been popularly identified since the nineteenth century as Hoxne's Goldbroke Bridge under which the king was said to have been hiding.[63]

That Hoxne has had a long association as the traditional place of Edmund's martyrdom, correctly or spuriously, there is no doubt, and its established tradition can be traced back at least as far as 1200 (i.e. 350 years after the events) – but is there anything really to justify it? Abbo (in the earliest Aelfric translation) made no mention of it and gave no identification of Edmund's place of martyrdom, though in the later Norman translations of Abbo's 'Life' of Edmund, the location was named as '*Haegilsdun*' (and these later translations have quite clearly been 'doctored').[64] Modern scholarship has adequately demonstrated that the name '*Haegilsdun*' cannot be equated with the later name of 'Hoxne',[65] and in fact Archdeacon Hermann of Bury, writing in 1095 of the events surrounding Edmund, states that Edmund was martyred at a place called '*Suthtuna*' (i.e. Sutton). There was, though, a 'Sutton' which was a hamlet within the Hoxne parish which might seem to strengthen the Hoxne tradition,[66] but we must give some regard to Abbo's reference to the Danes' having 'taken to their ships' after killing Edmund, which tends to suggest a sea journey, and (if we assume Abbo was right) can hardly be reconciled with a land pursuit from Thetford to Hoxne! On the assumption that Abbo *was* right, which is difficult, it would seem more likely that the Danes journeyed around the East Anglian coast to strike at the king where we might most reasonably expect him to have been or to have retreated to, i.e. the traditional base of the East Anglian kings at Rendlesham, near Sutton by Woodbridge, which was highly accessible from the sea via the Deben estuary.[67] There is to this day a place near Sutton by Woodbridge, called 'Hacheston', close to what was the Staverton Forest, which by way of confusion could have been the '*Haegilsdun*' of the Norman recensionists of Abbo. There is some evidence that Hacheston was a late Roman site and it was very close to the royal Wuffings seat of Rendlesham. There is also strong evidence that Staverton Forest was an ancient royal hunting park and Abbo's account of Edmund's martyrdom seems to indicate that it occurred in a woodland area. Sutton (i.e. Sutton by Woodbridge) near royal Rendlesham, where we might expect Edmund to have been, has close to it a traditional place of execution (Wilford), which in turn is close to Bromeswell Church, the bearer of an old dedication to St Edmund. Finally, another nearby village, 'Eyke', indicates a settlement, or foundation, of Scandinavian origin and the name means 'oak'. It all looks rather suspiciously as though this was, as we might expect, the area in which Edmund met his fate, and suggests that there were perhaps lingering memories of the tradition in the locality. There may be yet one final clue to the true place of Edmund's demise. Abbo's account of events does say that after the Danes had killed Edmund they departed 'returning to their ships'. Assuming that Abbo was correctly informed, this is hardly suggestive of their having pursued and surprised the king at such inland locations as Hoxne. It tends to suggest that they mounted a surprise attack or foray from the coast, and if Edmund was down at Sutton by Woodbridge, his position was accessible from the sea via the Deben estuary close by. The reference to the bishop having been close at hand could lend strength to this possibility if we accept *Dommoc* as having been at Felixstowe/Walton, as suggested earlier, though we must take account of the possibility of the episcopal seat having been abandoned by this time; but, even so, the bishop may well have sought temporary refuge with the king. Sutton could well be the true location for St Edmund's martyrdom, though, as with the enigma of Edmund's relics, we shall probably never know the full truth and we are simply left with popular and enduring legends, doubtful traditions and arguable possibilities.

The remaining complication is that *Haegilsdun* can in fact be rendered as the modern name of 'Hellesdon' and there have been

two Hellesdons in East Anglia, one in Norfolk (near Norwich),
which is now dismissed as having been unlikely, and another
which recent research has confirmed[68] as having been near Bury
St Edmunds near Bradfield St Clare, and which seems a possibility. The basis of this suggestion is that there was a field named
Hellesdon, which appeared on a map as late as 1840. Two miles
north was a 'Kings Hall', which is suggestive of a former royal
residence, and a mile south there is a 'Sutton Hall'; and records
of Bury St Edmunds Abbey also indicate that this area was once
part of the 'patrimony' of St Edmund.[69] The difficulty remains,
however, that for neither of these two places (nor indeed for Sutton
by Woodbridge) is there any recorded tradition of a veneration of
St Edmund, but there is for Hoxne; so we might well ask ourselves
whether there is more to the Hoxne tradition than meets the eye
– it would seem that there is. The claim of Hoxne for St Edmund
can be linked to the well-recorded rivalry between the bishops of
East Anglia and Bury St Edmunds Abbey. Archdeacon Hermann
of Bury first made a claim for a 'Sutton' as having been the
martyrdom site back in 1095 and we do not know which Sutton
he had in mind, even if he knew where it was. The Anglo-Norman
versions of Abbo's 'Life' of Edmund, which appeared about the
same time, gave *Haegilsdun* as the location. Hoxne was then
claimed for the first time by Herbert de Losinga, Bishop of Norwich, in a charter of 1101 (and in exactly the same year that the
dedication of the church at Hoxne was changed from St Ethelbert
the Martyr to St Edmund the Martyr – clearly more than a
coincidence!). The year 1095 was also the year of the translation
and verification of Edmund's supposed relics at Bury Abbey. Norwich had become the episcopal seat in 1091 (the seat having been
previously transferred from *Elmham* to Thetford) and Bishop de
Losinga had wished to locate his new see at Bury, which was
fiercely resisted by Abbot Baldwin of Bury. Losinga very conveniently came up with the argument that Bury had at one time
been the site of the East Anglian See (which was an outright
falsehood!) and that St Edmund's Shrine had thus once been
attached to the East Anglian See. He further claimed that Edmund

was martyred at Hoxne, which was within the bishop's own episcopal territory (certainly Hoxne had been an episcopal seat, but only temporarily and from no earlier than the mid-tenth century onwards). It would also seem that the bishops had exercised some control over Bury Abbey until the early eleventh century, but by the later part of that century Bury was rigorously claiming and exerting its freedom from episcopal jurisdiction.[70]

The Hoxne claim, probably dating from no earlier than 1101 and from de Losinga, was nothing more than a deceit on the part of the bishops of Norwich. The most that can be said for the Hoxne tradition, in the unlikelihood of there having been even a fragment of truth in it, is the existence of an outside possibility of a lingering martyrdom tradition which the bishops of Norwich used for full propaganda advantage against the powerful abbots of Bury and their treasured relics of the martyr, though it all seems very unlikely. Those who favour Hoxne as the martydom location do so on the basis of its having traditionally been held as such since the twelfth century, and they buttress their position with the apparent fact that there is no such tradition for either Hellesdon or Sutton by Woodbridge (which should not surprise us given the power of the interests that formerly advanced the claim of Hoxne). It can be argued against this that, if the Hoxne claim was, as we have suggested, an invention of the twelfth century onwards, with all the weight and influence of the bishops of Norwich behind it, it was probably based on no known or remembered tradition of a site of martyrdom, and by the time of the twelfth century no one probably knew exactly where Edmund had been killed, save that names like *Haegilsdun* and Sutton may have lingered on in dim recollections and oral traditions with little certainty as to where they had once been. The point is that, from the early tenth century onwards, Bury St Edmunds was the focal point for Edmund's veneration on account of its possession of his alleged relics – by 1100 earlier associations were forgotten. The Church conveniently 'discovered' them! At the end of it all, the most that we can really and sensibly say about St Edmund is that he was, as a Christian king, undoubtedly killed by the Danes defending his kingdom and people, and that in itself gave him a deserved place in history and Christian veneration.

Bishops and 'Relations'

Very late medieval traditions give us the names of others who were supposed to have been associated with St Edmund's martyrdom. One Norman chronicler, Symeon of Durham, actually named the bishop, whom Edmund had consulted, as having been a '*Hunberht*' of *Elmham* and went on to claim that he was martyred on the same day as the unfortunate king.[71] It is impossible to know whether any bishop was killed in East Anglia during the course of the events of 699, though it is not improbable, and, if it did occur, as the Norman chronicler claimed it did, it was very unlikely that the victim was Bishop *Hunberht*; the likelier candidate would have been Bishop Aethelwold of *Dommoc*.[72] Other legends of the time (again, no more than legends) give us accounts of two other saints who were supposed to have been related to Edmund, one of whom was also supposed to have suffered martyrdom at the hands of the relentless Vikings. The first alleged relative of Edmund was St Eadwald, who was said to have been a brother of the king and who was offered the crown after Edmund's martyrdom, but refused it, respectably going off to Cerne in Dorset to become a hermit and said to have been buried there. The second was supposed to have been a nephew, Fremund, Prince of Mercia (historical evidence clearly shows that there was no such person), who reigned for a year and then abdicated, also becoming a 'holy hermit'. According to this fanciful tale, after Edmund's death, Fremund sought to avenge St Edmund by slaughtering as many Danes as possible, but unfortunately for him, the dreadful Ivarr 'the Boneless', Edmund's named slayer, tracked him down first and beheaded him. These tales are, of course, only myths, but they could preserve some memory of the puppet kings who were installed both in Mercia (in 875), and in East Anglia itself between the time of Edmund's death and Guthrum's takeover (two shadowy names of apparent puppet kings do in fact appear for East

Anglia – Oswald and Aethelmund), and it is not impossible that such compliants could have been drawn from surviving Wuffings who had been related to Edmund. It may have been that the Danes soon drove them out or killed them in order to exercise their own direct rule, and, if this was so, then perhaps these legends represent a posthumous attempt, originating in East Anglia, to permit them a share in some of Edmund's sanctity. The same could be said of the supposed 'bishop-martyr', *Hunberht* (a cult that never really got off the ground), though such a cult, if indeed there was any, would have been advanced in the interests of the bishops of Anglia rather than in the interests of the kings, and even the slight references to the same were probably for nothing more than the encouragement of the elevated cult-status of Edmund.

What was left after this devastation? Precious little, it would seem. East Anglia's monasteries, and probably most of her ecclesiastical centres, had been wiped out and along with them much of the religious and cultural heritage that had accumulated over the two previous centuries. The Church organization had all but disappeared along with shrines, relics, and written records, but not the Christian faith nor the recollection of the former kingdom's major saints. It would take about another hundred years for the Church in East Anglia to recover fully from such wreckage and to complete its task of the Christianization of the people at all levels. Renewed impetus would come from outside the region and from within a context of a national ecclesiastical revival, for the old Kingdom of East Anglia was never to be restored. Great abbeys would arise along with powerful Church magnates and a few more saints, though the whole scene would take on a considerably different appearance from that which might be justly described as having once been East Anglia's 'Age of Saints'.

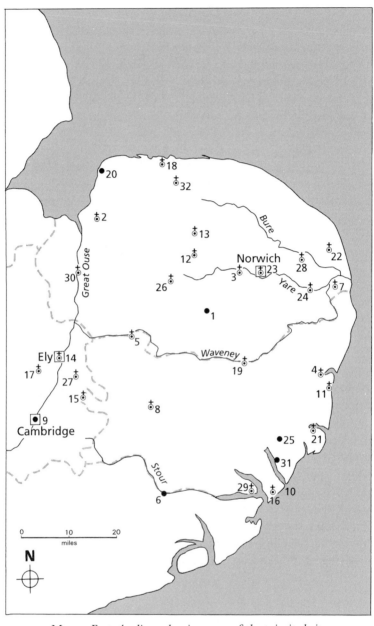

Map 4 *East Anglia – showing some of the principal sites mentioned in the text*

1   Attleborough

2   Babingley

3   Bawburgh

4   Blythborough

5   Brandon

6   Bures

7   Burgh Castle
    (Cnobheresburgh?)

8   Bury St Edmunds
    (Beodricesworth)

9   Cambridge

10 Deben Estuary

11 Dunwich
    (Dommoc?)

12 East Dereham

13 Elmham (North)

14 Ely

15 Exning

16 Felixstowe/Walton
    (Dommoc?)

17 Haddenham

18 Holkham

19 Hoxne

20 Hunstanton

21 Iken
    (Icanhoe?)

22 Martham

23 Norwich

24 Reedham

25 Rendlesham

26 Saham Toney

27 Soham

28 St Benet Holme

29 Shotley
    (Cnobheresburgh?)

30 Stow Bardolph

31 Sutton by Woodbridge

32 Walsingham

8

Changing Times

Before we look at the saints of the period following the upheavals
of the Viking invasions, we would do well to take some stock of
the Church background against which they were set, both before
and after the traumatic, and in some ways mould-shattering, events
of those turbulent times.

The Early Church

What we know of the early Church in East Anglia derives mainly
from evidence preserved outside the region, which indicates that
the East Anglian Church was not in any significant way different
from the Church in the rest of England, and all the evidence
suggests that it was both rich and powerful, as were the kings
who patronized it. Bede refers, in the preface of his *History of the
English Church and People*, to a certain Albinus, the Abbot of the
St Peter and St Paul Monastery at Canterbury, as having been
an information source, and to an account he had received from
an East Anglian abbot, Esi, who apparently provided him with
detail on the early East Anglian Church and the kings.[1] He may
also have obtained some information from Ceolfrith who, as we
have seen, stayed for a while with St Botolph at *Icanhoe*. Apart
from his details on St Felix and St Fursey, Bede was somewhat
sparing with information on East Anglia, but he does mention a
Bishop Bisi who attended the English Church Synod of Hertford
in 672 and who became ill and infirm, which resulted in the
division of the East Anglian See into *Dommoc*(?) and *Elmham*. He
also mentioned a bishop who can now be identified as Cuthwine

of *Dommoc*, who brought from Rome a volume which had many illustrations representing the sufferings of St Paul and which Bede saw.[2] This Cuthwine was a great collector of manuscripts and may have brought several of them back to East Anglia where they would have served as exemplars for the manuscript illuminators in the kingdom's various monasteries. There is also some evidence that several East Anglian manuscripts were sent abroad to assist the English missions on the Continent during the eighth century, where they found a safer home prior to the advent and destruction of the Vikings in the next century; and we may suppose that the East Anglians would not have sent them there if there had been a scarcity at home. Thus was the East Anglian Church clearly rich and powerful and capable of spreading its influence beyond its own territories and even abroad. Felix's 'Life of Guthlac', itself an East Anglian document, indicates not only local access to a wide variety of Church literature but also the presence of many scholars in East Anglia prior to the coming of the Vikings.[3]

As to how many monasteries there were in the kingdom, it is

An Anglo-Saxon Font (All Saints' Church, Warham, Norfolk)

difficult to be certain, though a few clues are given. King Aelfwald, for whom Felix wrote his 'Life of Guthlac', referred in a letter written to the English missionary, St Boniface,[4] to Masses and prayers having been offered for Boniface (indicating a strong East Anglian support for Boniface and his mission to the Germans) in the 'seven monasteries' of the East Anglian Kingdom.[5] We must presume that these consisted of the royal and official monasteries and may have included *Icanhoe*, *Beodricesworth* – a double monastery presided over by the king's sister (which could have been the recently identified high-status monastery discovered at Brandon, Suffolk), the monastery over which Abbot Esi had presided (perhaps King Ana's foundation at Blythburgh), and possibly the episcopal establishments at *Dommoc* and *Elmham*. The identification of these sites with the seven monasteries referred to by King Aelfwald is by no means certain, as there were clearly other high-status houses within the kingdom and the territories in which it had an interest.[6] William of Malmesbury (an Anglo-Norman churchman) made reference to St Felix's relics having been taken to 'Seham', a site also referred to by the *Book of Ely*, which says that it was later destroyed by the Danes. It is generally supposed that 'Seham' was Soham in the Cambridgeshire Fens, though this is by no means certain as it could have been Saham Toney in Norfolk.[7] William also said that St Felix founded a church (monastery?) at Reedham in Norfolk, and other late sources make similar claims for Babingley and Loddon together with Mendham in Suffolk;[8] and Holkham and Dereham, with their St Witburgha associations, could be added to the list of possibilities. Recent research has suggested no fewer than seventeen possible early monastic sites for Norfolk[9] and nine for Suffolk,[10] to which we might add a further nine for the Fenlands where East Anglian influence and interest remained strong. It is virtually impossible to ascertain how far back many of these establishments go in terms of their foundation and how many of them were monasteries in the true sense, thus equating with King Aelfwald's reference. There seems to be a possibility that St Benet Holme, in Norfolk, may have dated back to the late eighth century, and similarly Stow

Bedon, in Norfolk, with its dedication to St Botolph.[11] Monastic *styli* have been found at church sites at Wormegay and Bawsey, both former islands on the edge of the Fens, thus indicating possible monasteries.[12]

It may well have been that some of these putative monasteries were very short-lived and definitely not within King Aelfwald's 'seven', and others may have post-dated his time, surviving only up to the Viking attacks of the ninth century. Some could also have fallen within the category of the 'corrupt foundations' referred to by Bede, where in fact the local landowners styled themselves 'abbots', their families and retainers claiming to be a 'monastery', in order to ensure the permanent alienation of estates which should have rightly returned to the king. Some of the foundations could have represented a genuine stage in monastery-founding by the noble families during the eighth century, following the example of the kings in the previous century (a sort of second wave of conversion). Some of these establishments may also have been what were termed '*mynsters*', having developed from small monasteries that were founded in the seventh and eighth centuries and which had failed to develop as regular monasteries. Such *mynsters* were set up as small teams of priests, sometimes dependent upon a proper monastery, or established upon a noble estate initially to serve the spiritual needs of their founders and retainers rather than for the purpose of proper evangelization, which tended to emanate from the true monasteries; and in the post-Viking period some of these would become the basis for the future parish churches. By the eighth century, the bishop was the apex of Church power and exercised pastoral care over the *mynsters*, the latter carrying out pastoral care within a defined local area whilst the proper monasteries remained more contemplative by nature, once conversion at the top levels of society had been accomplished. In fact, both the *mynsters* and the pseudo-monasteries would be the key to later parish development, but in the case of the latter only after episcopal takeover in the eighth century, which was stiffly resisted and resulted in the compromise of a lay ownership under the bishop's supervision. By the ninth century there is evidence for episcopal control even over the top proprietary churches, i.e. those under royal and noble ownership. The first half of the eighth century saw monasticism at its highest form of development and influence, though even in the properly established houses most monastics did not live by a formal rule, but there seems to have been some sort of communal one.

By the time of the Viking advent the diocesan system was still very unevenly organized and there seems to have been a lot of purely localized provision due to apparent difficulties in finding adequate members of the priesthood, and the dependence of the Church upon the aristocracy; this, as we have seen, resulted in a lot of compromise which must have diminished some of the quality of the spiritual life of the Church. The Vikings were not the only factor to bring about the eventual decline of the Church, and even as early as the eighth century Bede indicated, in respect of the English Church as a whole, a general unease and disquiet, even though we must allow for his having possibly painted a rather too 'rosy' picture of the missionary Church of the seventh century. He says that things were no longer as they used to be and seems to have based his sense of decline and disaster upon the late Romano-British Church polemicist of the sixth century, Gildas,[13] and his account of the decline and plight of the British Church. In his letter to Bishop Ecgberht,[14] Bede criticized the Church for having taken too much advantage of lay concessions (e.g. the secular exemptions of the pseudo-monasteries) and he indicated his concern not only with the implications for secular society, but also with the problem of moral compromise within the Church (it seems that by the mid-eighth century many of the rural clergy were married). By the mid-eighth century, some of the kings took action and some monasteries were closed down, particularly in Wessex and Mercia (we have no surviving information for East Anglia). In Mercia in the 740s King Aethelbald, who had been associated with St Guthlac,[15] was himself accused by a Church synod of 'moral laxity', which included amongst other things the invasion and despoliation of monasteries. We should seriously ask, though, whether some of this accusation was based upon a simple 'clean-up' of a less than satisfactory situation, combined with an overreaction to Church pressures upon the kings (in Northumbria there were attested attempts to deal with specific Church abuses). Disputes between the bishops and the kings became more frequent, some of the tensions no doubt based upon the increasing episcopal jurisdiction over the local *mynsters* (which meant financial advantages for the dioceses), and the bishops came increasingly under fire in this respect. The problem, though, may not have just been due to the moral decline of the Church but as much due to the increasing power of the kings and their authority. Missions to the Continent in the eighth century are clear evidence that the Church had lost none of its fundamental missionary drive, though we might well ask whether or not this led to a deprivation of moral leadership and resources back at home (some resources could have been provided from the suppression of pseudo-monasteries) – the evidence is simply lacking. There is some evidence of there having been a decline in manuscript production at this time which is also matched, as we have noted, by an increase in the number of those appearing in new Continental monasteries; and the diversion may have been significant, given the destruction of the monasteries that would occur at the hands of the Vikings and the likely loss of valuable materials (Peterborough Abbey was said to have possessed a fine library which the Danes destroyed).

The Later Church

Wreckage and desolation are probably the best epithets with which to describe the state of the Church after the Viking storm, particularly in hardest-hit regions such as East Anglia, though historians are under no agreement as to how far this was so. No bishops' names were recorded for the Diocese of *Elmham* between 836 and 934 and the See of *Elmham* was not revived properly until 950,[16] the East Anglian Church – not wiped out – struggling on in an impoverished state. There seems to be some evidence for the co-existence of Danish paganism and Christianity, but there seems to be no indication that there was any need for a general re-

A Late Anglo-Saxon Church (Newton-by-Castle Acre, Norfolk)

evangelization of East Anglia – no new 'apostles' were needed (and indeed, none of any description, nor saints comparable to those of the earlier period, would now re-emerge). King Alfred the Great would complain of the intellectual darkness around him, even though the village priests and some of the local churches and *mynsters* had survived – but then, it was not amongst their number that the learned could be found! Alfred further complained (in a letter to Bishop Wulfsige of Sherborne)[17] of the general ignorance of the English and how few of the clergy could understand the meaning of simple Church services or translate an Epistle into English, all of which tends to suggest that serious decline had been well in place even before the attacks. As far as the ordinary people were concerned, the habits of prolonged warfare and the presence of the Danes probably did lead to a resurgence of paganism, evidenced by the fact that King Alfred instituted severe prohibitions against its practice in his law codes; and the Church would finally deal with the problem of incorporating, or acculturalizing, some of these cults during the course of the next two centuries. The Danes seem to have been fairly ambivalent about religion. The eventually acknowledged Danish King of East Anglia, Guthrum (Aethelstan),[18] who succeeded the martyred King Edmund and had accepted baptism himself, guaranteed the rights – religious and civil – of East Anglia's people, guarding them with penal sanctions and fines. He went on to actively encourage the propagation of the cult of the martyred Edmund, indicating that Christianity, even in areas under Danish control, was still regarded as the state, and required, religion.

We have already noted how monasticism was in a state of decline before its virtual extinction at the hands of the Vikings and the dispersal of the surviving monks had probably resulted in some of them having taken up the married state and owning property, which was probably little more than the exacerbation of a situation in place prior to the coming of the Danes in the ninth century (mainly in the pseudo-monasteries). During the period of the recovery of the Church from the (late) tenth century onwards, which found its apogee in the Monastic Reform Movement, many of these monastics were unwilling to submit to the restraints of traditional disciplines and divided the revenues of the surviving churches between them, living as separate families in former monastic enclosures and content simply to assist in the daily services, or deputing other priests to perform them whilst they retired to holdings attached to their prebends. Much of the shattered remnants of monastery property that had escaped Danish plundering had been seized by the kings in order to defray the costs of war. By the time of the accession of King Edgar of Wessex (959),[19] who exercised a rule over the whole of England, monasticism was on the move again. Throughout England as a whole, up to forty monasteries are said to have been founded by him, including several of the older foundations that had either been destroyed, abandoned or secularized. St Aethelwold of Winchester, a great monastic reformer, who was to exercise a considerable degree of interest and involvement in East Anglia, obtained from Edgar the sites of Ely, Thorney and Peterborough Abbeys, whilst St Oswald of York, another notable reformer, instituted the new Abbey of Ramsey in the Fenlands, all of these being built in comparative grandeur. One problem that the refounders and reformers encountered was that of the 'secular canons', as they were called, the pseudo-monks referred to above, and the attempt to bring them under some sort of control and monastic discipline. Their simple answer was that of expulsion and the enforcement of celibacy and the imposition of the Benedictine rule. A further attempt was made to reconsolidate monastic power in the Church by giving the monks the power to elect bishops. One other problem for the reformers was the need to cope with the problem of the integration into the monastic life of the secular world of kindred and tribal groups, particularly as in the past the family of an abbot or abbess expected to nominate their successors, and in some cases the abbatial office had even been sold for a handsome price. Prior to the tenth-century reform the monks had not been subject to any real form of authority though the abbot or abbess was expected to (and invariably did) exercise authoritarian rule.

Only fifty years before 1066 England had again been conquered by Scandinavians, though this time they were ostensibly (though arguably!) Christian. East Anglia once again received more than its welcome share of their attentions, though the Church was not adversely affected in terms of its structures, nor were the ideals of the Monastic Reform Movement. During the course of the eleventh century, there would be English missionaries abroad again, this time in Scandinavia itself, and a large number of English Church manuscripts were transported there. The Monastic Reform Movement and the revival of the Church in the tenth century had clearly put down deep roots and by the eleventh century we see evidence of vernacular religious literature appearing and a fresh burst of writing about the saints. Monasticism was again securely established, though in fewer places, and it was growing, with much attention being given to the laypeople. This period also saw the growth and development of the parish church system and by 1086 no fewer than 604 East Anglian churches were mentioned as having existed – and there may have been more – 243 in Norfolk and 361 in Suffolk, though only 4 in the Fenlands. This phase of final expansion of the Church saw the ultimate Christianization of all levels of society and the integration and acculturalization in the remotest rural areas of the most persistent of the lay and semi-pagan cults which, as we shall see, were represented notably in East Anglia by the cults of St Walstan of Taverham and the Virgin Mary at Walsingham.

By the eleventh century there was also much corruption and scandal in the Church, chiefly associated with the accumulation and fabrication of relics, and Ely Abbey would show itself to be in the forefront of such matters. There also appears to have been evidence of scandal at episcopal level, which would continue into the Norman period with the relentless growth in the power of the Church. Stigand, Archbishop of Canterbury (deposed by the Normans in 1070) and previously Bishop of Winchester and of *Elmham* (from which see he was briefly deposed), may have been of Danish East Anglian origin and, it seems, had uncanonically superseded the previous Archbishop of Canterbury (a Norman – Robert of Jumièges).[20] He had also amassed ecclesiastical offices and was even reputed to have bought them! Even by the standards of the time, it is clear that there was something wrong with him.

By the eleventh century, too, laxity and decadence were again pervading the Church at all levels and were starting to accelerate, setting the stage for the Norman and later medieval Church. The monasteries were often treated as 'finishing schools' for the aristocracy, particularly the nunneries, and the hermits, who had been a characteristic of the monastic life of the earlier centuries, seem to have disappeared from the tenth century onwards. Despite the efforts of King Alfred the Great and the monastic reformers not many of the ordinary clergy seem to have been very Latinate, which was probably the reason why Church literature and the 'Lives of the Saints' started to appear in English during this time: it was probably for the local clergy and the edification of the laity that they were written. To what extent genuine piety was affected by the 'comfortableness' of the clergy (particularly the senior clergy) is difficult to assess, and the Norman churchmen of the eleventh century were clearly not impressed by what they found – though allowance must be made for Norman propaganda. The Normans certainly indicated that they were appalled by English intellectual standards (little was said of spiritual ones) and they showed a patronizing and contemptuous attitude towards the native Church, clearing out the English at episcopal and abbatial level within one generation, and remoulding the English Church on Continental lines. They also marginalized, or even suppressed, the strong attachment and devotion to the local native saints, many of whom were relegated to a lower status, some disappearing from the calendars altogether (in this respect, East Anglia fared a little better than Cornwall), though a few were retained who had national significance. Throughout the Middle Ages, St Edmund, St Felix, St Etheldreda, and even St Walstan, would continue to be portrayed on the rood screens of churches in East Anglia and beyond.

Of the great abbeys of East Anglia, the most important were Bury St Edmunds and Ely, whose primary cults (of St Edmund and St Etheldreda) were national and enduring and also assisted in the growth of their associated towns. We have already noted the importance and power of Bury, refounded by St Aethelwold in the tenth century and restaffed in the early eleventh century by monks of St Benet Holme, in order to accommodate the increasing importance of the St Edmund cult. Ely had been refounded by St Aethelwold in 970 along the principles of the Monastic Reform Movement, but this time only for men. Aethelwold went on to restore Thorney and Peterborough, and it seems that his policy was to provide, in areas of former Danish occupation, a centre of loyalty to the Wessex kings who now ruled over the whole of England. Thorney was smaller than Ely and Crowland (which were also restored) and was noted for its natural beauty with its orchards and vineyards. Aethelwold, in 972, endowed Thorney for a year and enriched it with many relics, notably those of St Benedict Biscop, Sts Botolph and Adolph, St Herefrith (a little-known East Anglian bishop – perhaps at Louth), St Cissa (one of St Guthlac's hermits) and the early founders of Thorney – Sts Torthred, Tancred and Tova – and the abbey became notable as a centre of learning and for its discouragement of female visitors! Peterborough, which was also restored by Aethelwold, claimed to have had St Wilfred of York as one of its original seventh-century founders and was regarded as an abbey of importance. For the purpose of enhancing its prestige (there was much rivalry and competition amongst neighbouring major monastic institutions) it added to the relics that it still claimed to have of its original founders and patronesses, Sts Cyneburgha, Cyneswitha and Tibba. Aethelwold apparently 'knew where to look' for the bodies of Sts Cyneburgha, Cyneswitha and Tibba and promptly exhumed them, offering them to St Peter (via the restored abbey) on the same day.[21] The Abbey paid £500 (the equivalent today of half a million!) for the body (minus the head) of an obscure French saint, Florentius of Bonneval, and took advantage of the monks of Bonneval, the guardians of the relic, by offering a lower than market-value price, which they were forced to accept as they needed the money to survive and to give relief to the local population who were stricken by famine.[22] Peterborough also claimed to have an arm of the seventh-century martyr-king of Northumbria, St Oswald, together with some of his ribs and the soil upon which he fell, though its most prized relics were the 'actual manger of Christ and His swaddling clothes'; parts of the 'original five loaves and two fishes for the feeding of the 5000'; 'some of the original clothing of the Virgin Mary'; part of the 'rod of the Holy Patriarch Aaron' [Moses' brother]; and the 'bones of St Simeon the Elder' (who greeted the infant Christ in the temple)![23] When refounding Peterborough, Aethelwold is supposed to have claimed to have found hidden in the ruined walls of the former monastery documents of the slain Abbot Headda, telling of how the monastery was originally founded in the seventh century and how it had been free for evermore of king, bishop and all secular obligations, all of which had been confirmed by Pope St Agatho at that time.[24] Regrettably these foundation accounts derived from a later forged charter and the reference to Pope Agatho has been found to have been spurious (clearly either St Aethelwold or the charter forgers had a somewhat over-exercised imagination!). As we have noted, Ramsey Abbey had not existed in the pre-Viking period but was endowed by St Oswald of York; and it went on to become even wealthier than its restored neighbour, Peterborough (formerly *Medeshamstede*), and acquired extra fame due to its association with St Abbo of Fleury, another leading figure in the Monastic Reform Movement. Its most important relic was claimed to be that of St Felix, allegedly translated to Ramsey from its former resting place at Soham(?), to which were added those of the legendary Kentish martyr-princes, Sts Aethelraed and Albricht, and a rather obscure (and very dubious!) Persian hermit, St Ives.

It is against this somewhat depressing background that we must now turn to examine the few known (and somewhat uninspiring) saints of the later period, reflecting, as they do, the trends and Church conditions that we have noted above.

The Later Saints

St Aethelwold

Though Aethelwold really belongs amongst the saints of Wessex, his heavy involvement in East Anglia, which we have outlined, entitles him to some mention as a type of 'honorary' East Anglian saint. He was in fact a native of Winchester and was priested about the same time as St Dunstan and became a Benedictine monk at Glastonbury Abbey under the latter. He became the Abbot of Abingdon in Berkshire and with the help of Glastonbury monks reformed it according to strict Benedictine principles, and then went on to resurrect many of the former monasteries that had been destroyed by the Danes. He instituted the Winchester school of illumination which flourished in his monasteries and inspired metalwork, music and painting. He was an assiduous relic collector and enthusiastically promoted the cult of St Etheldreda at Ely, together with those of her sisters and nieces – St Wendreda's relics eventually went to Dorchester. He inspired King

Edgar to expel the secular canons from their tenures in East Anglia; he purchased the ruins of Thorney and restored it in 972, and similarly the land and ruins of Ely, establishing them as Benedictine abbeys. He directed and assisted Ealdwulf, King Edgar's chancellor, to buy the ruins of Peterborough Abbey for the purpose of rebuilding and repopulating it. Ealdwulf gave his whole estate to the abbey, becoming a monk in it, and was chosen as its first abbot. Aethelwold's reforming proclivities and activities aroused much bitter opposition and he earned the epithets 'terrible as a lion' from his opponents, and 'more gentle than a dove' from his supporters, together with 'father of the monks' from posterity. When he died he was buried before the high altar at Winchester and claims of miracles through his intercessions were subsequently made.[25]

St Abbo of Ramsey

St Abbo (usually referred to as Abbo of Fleury) was one of the most learned monks of his age. A delegation from Ramsey Abbey, founded by St Oswald in 971, arrived at Fleury-sur-Loire to ask for a renowned teacher as part of the Monastic Reform Movement. Fleury had been linked to England for a while and St Oswald, the nominal Abbot of Ramsey, had been educated there; and, as it seems that Abbo had previously been passed over for the abbacy of Fleury, he may have been eager to realize his ambitions elsewhere. He became, during his time in England, a close friend of St Dunstan to whom he dedicated his 'Life of St Edmund', for which he is chiefly remembered during his two-year sojourn here, and from whom he apparently gleaned information regarding the king-martyr (as we have seen, Dunstan claimed to have heard the account of Edmund's martyrdom from the latter's sword-bearer). He probably first heard the oral traditions already circulating about King Edmund at Ramsey and he seems to have written the work in about 987 or 988. Though the historical St Edmund was barely distinguishable within Abbo's hagiography (doubtless the result of St Dunstan's influence and contribution) or within local folklore (much probably emanating from Bury St Edmunds Abbey), there still seems to remain, on the whole, what appears to be a very small sediment of fact in the account.[26] Having held the abbacy of Ramsey for two years, Abbo returned to Fleury to resume his studies which were notably in philosophy, mathematics and astronomy. He struggled to keep the monasteries free from episcopal control and played a role in bringing mediation and peace to disturbed monastic communities. In 1004, he tried to bring order to bear upon a monastery at La Réole in Gascony, intervening between brawling monks and their servants, one of whom stabbed him to death, and he subsequently came to be venerated in France as a martyr.

St Herefrith of Thorney and Louth

Herefrith, one of the most obscure – though probably historical – saints of this late period, was commemorated in the Thorney calendar as a bishop and also as such in the Bury St Edmunds and Deeping calendars, which indicates a strong East Anglian interest, perhaps reflecting his origins.[27] He may have been the Bishop of Lindsey (in south-east Lincolnshire) when it was a diocese in its own right and under the administration of the Archdiocese of York. No trace of his name appears on the surviving episcopal lists, but this could have been in the twilight years of the diocese which disappeared under the ravages of the Danes (and possibly the records with it). He could have been the last Bishop of Lindsey and possibly a victim of the Danes when they wintered at Torksey, in that area, in 873, though he is not categorized on the Church calendars as a martyr (some sources refer to him as an 'East Anglian hermit'). He was commemorated at Louth on the same day that Thorney kept his feast (27 February) and there is some evidence for a former shrine to him, which originally housed his relics, at Louth.[28] It is said that St Aethelwold, when re-founding Thorney, heard of the 'merits' of St Herefrith whose relics rested at Louth, and that, when all who guarded the church and shrine there had been put to sleep 'by a cunning ruse' (alcohol?), a trusty servant of Aethelwold's took the relics of the saint out of the ground, 'wrapped them in fine linen cloth, and with all his fellows rejoicing, brought them to the monastery of Thorney to be re-interred'.[29] All this is suggestive of a shrine with custodians and a similar scenario to the despoliation of St Witburgha's former shrine at Dereham, when Abbot Byrhtnoth of Ely came there with his monks, plying the townspeople with food and 'drink', and making off with the relics back to Ely.[30] Significantly, the Dereham/St Witburgha plunder occurred at almost the same time as Aethelwold pillaged Louth's sacred relics (which should not unduly surprise us, as the two, Aethelwold and Byrhtnoth, were notorious collaborators – one is almost tempted to say 'partners-in-crime'!).

St Eadnoth

Eadnoth was not only a monk of Winchester but also Abbot of Ramsey and Bishop of Dorchester (1012), and another zealous church builder and endower of monasteries; his sister, Aelfwin, was the Abbess of Chatteris. He was killed whilst serving Mass at Assendun and his body was brought to Ely en route for Ramsey. Aelfgar, the retired Bishop of *Elmham*,[31] was staying at Ely and arranged for the body to be secretly buried whilst its guards were drunk. This was done and the body remained at Ely where it came to be greatly honoured.[32]

St Ives

Ives was claimed to have been a hermit and supposedly a Persian bishop, though there is some justifiable doubt even as to his existence. There is some reason to think that the name may derive from the Old English '*ifig*', meaning 'ivy' (indicative of the Christianization of an existing pagan cult). Apparently four bodies were 'discovered' in 1001 at the monastery of Slepe (later renamed 'St Ives' and now in Cambridgeshire), which was a small dependency of Ramsey Abbey. The 'Life' of St Ives was written by the

Anglo-Norman writer, Goscelin de Brakelond, who in turn notably embellished an earlier account by Withman, Abbot of Ramsey, who had visited the Holy Land in the 1020s and had heard much of the fame of St Ivo, a Persian bishop venerated in the Christian East since the sixth century. The story goes that a farm labourer was ploughing in a field near Slepe, and in the course of his work his ploughshare struck against something solid. He went to see what was the matter, and to his astonishment found that the obstruction was caused by a large and handsome stone coffin lying below the surface of the ground. The ploughman immediately reported his discovery to the Abbot of Ramsey (presumably St Eadnoth), who came without delay and caused the coffin to be opened, and inside was found an 'incorrupt' body dressed as a bishop, with a golden chalice by its side. There was an inscription on the coffin, and the Abbot gathered from this that the body was that of the Persian bishop, Ivo, and that it had thus lain there for five hundred years! Further searching revealed two more coffins and 'a nobleman's monument', all containing bodies which, it was decided, belonged to St Ivo's companions. Later, in a 'dream' St Ivo appeared to the peasant, confirming his identity and those of his companions. He apparently told the peasant that he had been a Persian and a bishop who, with his three companions, had run away from the honour and comfort that he had once enjoyed in his own country and had found his way to England. There he had settled in the wild fen country and, after being mocked at first for his 'barbarous speech', he had been left alone to live and die unnoticed. The bodies were duly buried at Ramsey Abbey, a chapel being erected over the site of the discovery of the relics, and a 'miraculous spring of water' obligingly appeared at which many miracles were reported. The Anglo-Norman writer, William of Malmesbury, even claimed to have been an eyewitness to the remarkable cure of a man suffering from dropsy. The relics remained at Ramsey for a century until a 'miraculous light' was seen stretching from Ramsey to its dependency at Slepe, indicating that St Ivo's companions, at least, wished to return there. This was accordingly arranged and a subsidiary shrine and dependent priory were established at Slepe, whilst St Ivo remained at Ramsey, thus providing a useful source of revenue for both monastic houses, as pilgrims resorted thereto from all over the country for many centuries. The whole cult of St Ives, needless to say, bears all the hallmarks of the propagation of the prestige of Ramsey and its dependencies through the acclamation of relics, probably integrating a surviving pre-Christian cult in the locality.[33]

St Thurketyl

Thurketyl was the monk who refounded Crowland Abbey in about 971 after its destruction by the Danes. It appears that previously he had been the Abbot of Bedford, though he was at one stage expelled from there and according to the Anglo-Norman chronicler, Orderic Vitalis, was a friend of the monastic reformers, Sts Aethelwold, Oswald and Dunstan (he may have been related to St Oswald). He apparently asked the then Bishop of London to admit him to his confraternity at St Paul's, a request which was initially refused but then granted when he gave them an estate of land at Milton (near Cambridge), which they in turn exchanged for a similar holding of Ely. He also bought and sold several estates to St Aethelwold and bought from him several in the East Midlands (from where he may have originated – his name seems to be Danish) and used them to endow Crowland. He was said to have been noted for his chastity, somewhat obligatory for a monk, and according to the chronicler of Crowland (pseudo-Ingulphus) refused to become Bishop of Winchester or Dorchester, both of which sees were offered to him. He was supposed to have gone on a mission to Cologne and to have restored many monasteries and churches, and even to have gone so far as to present St Dunstan with a golden chalice. During his tenure as a monk and Abbot of Crowland, he compelled some recluses who had established themselves at St Pega's former cell at Peakirk to become regular monks at Crowland, subsequently reforming Peakirk itself as a dependency, a certain priest-monk, Reinfred, becoming its first abbot. He obtained a foundation charter from King Edgar, for Crowland, and restored to it much treasure and many relics.[34]

St Neot

In the tenth century some monks settled at the town which bears Neot's name, and established a small monastic cell which was a dependency of Ely Abbey. An Earl Leofric, who seems to have lived at Eynesbury, is named as the actual founder of the monastery, having granted the land in around 974.[35] For due sanctity relics were required and, thanks to the connivance of Byrhtnoth, Abbot of Ely, and with the help of St Aethelwold, the bones of St Neot, an obscure Cornish hermit of the ninth century, were stolen from Neotstoke in Cornwall, much to the rage of the Cornish, who were thwarted by the joint endeavours of King Edgar and Bishop Aethelwold. There has been a suggestion, though, that this St Neot was an English saint of the same name as the Cornish one and was a monk at Glastonbury in the ninth century. If that is the case, it was claimed that he had enjoyed royal connections with both the East Anglian and Wessex dynasties, and whilst he was at Glastonbury, his counsel was sought out by King Alfred the Great, and he was supposed to have appeared to the king on the eve of the Battle of Eathundun against the Danes.[36] It was probably Neot's supposed royal connections with King Alfred the Great that encouraged the activities of Byrhtnoth and Aethelwold in purloining his relics.

St Arnulf of Eynesbury

This obscure saint was said to have been greatly venerated and his tomb to have been the location of many miracles before the Danish invasions. There is no surviving information on him other than that he was supposed to have been of Romano-British origin and a hermit on the Fenland border area. He may have been the same as a French St Arnulph whose relics were translated to

England (and who was commemorated on the same day) and which thus eventually found their way to St Neots. He gave his name to the town, but seems to have been forgotten by 1000. The French Arnulph was in fact a seventh-century bishop who became a hermit.[37]

St Pandwyna (Pandiona) of Eltisley

St Pandwyna was supposed to have been the daughter of an Irish chieftain or from north Britain (the name appears to be British rather than Irish and is certainly not English), who fled to England to escape her father's tyranny and the pursuit of those who wished to dissuade her from the monastic life and her desire for permanent virginity.[38] She took refuge with a relative who was the abbess of a small nunnery at Eltisley where she settled down as a hermit, becoming noted for spiritual perfection and a life of great sanctity. When she died, she was buried close by a well, which took its name from her and which was reputed to have been a source of healing and miracles. She is supposed to have died at the beginning of the tenth century and was listed by one source as a martyr, which seems extremely unlikely (and was probably an error). Her relics were translated into Eltisley Church in the fourteenth century, and there appears to have been a local 'Life' written for her at about the same time but this no longer survives.[39] Eltisley is only four miles from St Neots and the cult may have something to do with status relic acquisition and the late Christianization of a pagan water-cult associated with the 'holy' well.

St Walstan of Taverham

The two, and only, surviving sources for St Walstan date back to the fifteenth and sixteenth centuries ascribing a date of death for him as 1019. The sixteenth-century source is a Latin 'Life', probably deriving from an earlier fourteenth-century compilation of saints' lives and traditions by the chronicler John of Tynemouth, and based upon earlier local church calendars, menologies and

St Walstan (A Contemporary Church Icon)

breviaries, and further recensed by an early sixteenth-century friar, John Capgrave. The second source is a poem of the fifteenth century, written in Middle English, and originally attached to a triptych that once graced St Walstan's shrine at Bawburgh; this is now kept in Lambeth Palace Library. This poem was probably a compilation of local church legends and traditions surrounding the saint, and was no doubt written for the edification of the numerous pilgrims who once thronged to the shrine.[40]

According to the sources, St Walstan was born in the time of King Aethelraed 'Unraed' (Ethelred the 'Unready') and was of royal stock, his mother having been a 'princess' named Blide and his father a nobleman, Benedict. At the age of twelve, he renounced his inheritance and left home to seek work as a common labourer, arriving for this purpose at a farm in Taverham (near Norwich). The farm is supposed to have been close to the present church, and his true identity (as a nobleman) to have been kept secret until his death. Whilst not a monk, he lived like one, spending most of his time in fasting, prayer and penance, and in time he became noted for his humility and generosity, often giving away his daily food and worldly possessions to those in need.[41] So he lived until the approach of his death, which was announced to him by the visit of an angel, a vision apparently also witnessed by a fellow-labourer. Accordingly, he sent for a priest to administer the final sacrament but the priest had unfortunately omitted to bring with him any water to mix with the communion wine. St Walstan offered prayers and a holy spring of water gushed forth close by the church. Just before his death, St Walstan's master had indicated his wish to name him as his heir and legatee but the saint had refused this offer and made a simple request, which was that at his death he be granted two white bull-calves to carry his body wherever they might wish to go. This was duly granted and Walstan, three days later, at noon, died in the meadow where he was working. Accordingly, his body was placed upon a cart drawn by two white oxen who wended their way through nearby Costessey Woods. They crossed over the River Wensum, miraculously leaving the marks of their hoof-prints upon the waters (which were still to be seen until the time of the Reformation, it was said!), pressing onwards until they reached another resting place (identified as having been where Costessey Park is now situated) where another sacred spring of water sprang up. Finally, reaching the foot of the hillock upon which Bawburgh Church stands, the oxen paused and urinated, another sacred well springing up at the spot. Sufficiently refreshed, the white oxen passed 'miraculously' through the north wall of the church, which opened up for them, to where Bishop Aelmar (whom one of the sources erroneously describes as having been the Bishop of Norwich) and forty monks were waiting to perform the burial rites of the saint, whose true noble identity had by now been revealed. Thus was Walstan duly and reverently buried.[42]

In due course a splendid shrine was erected over the site of St Walstan's burial place which, by all accounts, was visited by numerous pilgrims down through the centuries. The reports of the miracles increased, many of which are preserved in the poem, two notable ones having been the resuscitation of a man who had lain drowned in a pond for two days (!), and a woman who had been shot through with arrows. It came to be said that the deaf and dumb were restored to fullness and that many were freed from insanity and 'demonic possession' by Walstan's intercessions; even farm animals were taken to the shrine on a regular basis for the healing of their various maladies. Such was the munificence of the pilgrims, no doubt enthusiastically encouraged by the local clergy, that by the thirteenth century the present church at Bawburgh could be built, supporting six chantry priests and a vicar. At the Reformation the shrine was demolished and the reputed bones of the saint burned, though traces of the shrine can still be seen by the north wall of the present church, together with the interior chancel arch that once formed the entrance. Near Bawburgh Bridge in the centre of the village, stand some flint cottages said to have been built from the rubble of a hermit's cell and chapel that once stood close by. There pilgrims, having been sprinkled by the hermit with holy water, requested his prayers for their needs, and would leave their footwear and journey up the hill to the shrine. Even after the demolition of the shrine in the sixteenth century, the tradition of Walstan persisted in the locality into our own times. Mowers and husbandmen continued to use the three 'holy wells' for the gathering of mosses and waters until as late as the nineteenth century, believing in their curative powers. The twentieth century has seen a revival of interest in and devotion to St Walstan and annual pilgrimages take place once again to Bawburgh, St Walstan having even been proclaimed as the 'Patron Saint of British Food and Farming' in 1989.[43] Such seems to be the abiding attachment to him that we might well explore the reasons for this.

Firstly, was St Walstan even an historically verifiable saint? It is very difficult to be certain and the balance of probability, as in the cases of St Pandwyna and St Ives, would seem to be against this. His name, sometimes rendered as 'Walston' or 'Walstane', can mean in Old English 'well stone' or 'sacrificial stone' and, given his associations with cattle, agriculture and water wells, is immediately suggestive of a barely Christianized fertility cult. St Blide, or Blythe, his reputed mother, of whom there are virtually no other traces or information, may have been mythical (there is no evidence for there having been an official feast day for her, which heightens suspicion); and it has been suggested that she was mistakenly identified with St Bride (Bridget)[44] who was herself clearly a substitute for a pagan Irish goddess of the same name, and formerly known in Romano-Celtic Britain as '*Brigantia*', one of the great mother-goddess figures of the old Celtic pantheon. The Irish Bride had agricultural associations, including those connected with cows, and was also a protectress of fire and hearth, and seems to have had a status as a patroness of motherhood.[45] Even if the identification of Blide with Bride is wrong, she seems to represent a similar female fertility deity. The traditions surrounding her, and they are precious few, refer to her as having been a 'princess', which is an impossibility.[46] (Former Celtic and early English gods and goddesses who were incorporated into later popular Christian mythology were often accorded a new and more respectable status of 'kings' and 'princesses', as we see clearly in Welsh mythology.) The Celtic female deity *Boann* had cow associations and was supposed to have been married to a deity who was a well-guardian, whose well she was forbidden to visit. When she broke the taboo she was engulfed by the well-water which formed a river, the River Boyne. She was associated with laughter and merriment as well as with fertility and sovereignty. Blide's name is also the name of a river – Blythe![47] – and her name means 'the friendly one'. John Bale, the Tudor writer and bitter attacker of what he regarded as superstition attached to the cults of the saints, wrote:

> If you cannot sleep or slumber
> Give oats to St Uncumber,
> And beans in a certain number
> To St Blaise and *St Blythe*.[48]

This, then, is a clear reference to an old ritual involving the offering of beans to St Blythe as an antidote for insomnia (St Blaise was traditionally regarded as the patron saint of wool-combers and animals, and had a strong devotion in nearby Norwich).[49] Walstan's father's name is given as 'Benedict', and he is referred to as a 'king' in the poem (the Latin 'Life' only says Walstan was of 'noble parentage').[50] Benedict of course means 'blessed', but in this case could represent a Christianized form of two Old English words, '*bean-dic*', meaning 'bean-ditch', and we have noted the association of beans with St Blythe. Walstan's feast day was on 30 May, and the month of May, according to Bede,[51] was known in pagan English times as '*Thrimilci*' (i.e. thrice-milking) and strongly associated with cows. One recent writer on the subject of St Walstan[52] (who favours his historical existence) says Blide may have been a member of King Aethelraed Unraed's household and this supposition is based upon the fact that the king had two wives and probably a large number of in-laws and may have represented East Anglian aristocracy displaced by the Danes; thus Walstan was said to claim kinship with Edmund 'Ironside', the son of King Aethelraed.[53]

King Cnut (between 1020 and 1023) forbade allegiance to pagan gods – 'It is heathen practice if one worships wells or stones or any kind of forest trees, or takes part in such delusions'[54] – which indicates that the problem was widespread and that there may have been a revival of it during the earlier Danish incursions, particularly where Danish occupation had been significant,[55] as it had been in East Anglia (on two occasions). Thus the cult of St Walstan and its links with St Blide may have been used to overlay a strong pre-Christian cult observed in May. Significantly, there seems to have been another date for St Walstan – 28 December – which coincides with the pagan midwinter festival of *Giuli* (Yuletide) and *Modra Nect* (Mothers' Night) – both fertility festivals having been mentioned by Bede,[56] when cattle may have been slaughtered in honour of the old gods and for winter sustenance (though Bede says this took place in *Bloodmonath*, i.e. Hallowe'en). Bulls are associated with ancient Celtic religion, and cult-wagons associated with bulls are found in Germanic religion where they were pulled around the countryside for the preservation of fields and crops. The bull-cult's main centre seems to have been amongst the Danes.[57] The legends of white calves and holy wells are very similar to those that abounded in Wales and Ireland and may be indicative of surviving paganism going back even as far as Romano-British and early Anglo-Saxon times. The fact that the saint was invoked for blessings upon the neighbouring crops and fields is also highly significant, as is the tradition that he was regarded as efficacious for the restoration of men and male animals deprived of their genitalia or potency. Bale, writing not too long after the sixteenth-century suppression of the cult, likened Walstan to the old classical god, Priapus, a god of fertility,[58] who was always depicted as having enormous genitals; and in fact a pilgrim offering-box, still to be seen in the ancient church and dating from the twelfth century, is unmistakeably phallic-shaped and points to this curious mix of semi-Christian and late-surviving pagan fertility cult.[59]

To return to the original question – was there ever a real St Walstan? The only reasonable answer must be that, if there was, then nothing certain is known about him – even the name

The Bawburgh Pilgrim-Box

and date of death may not have been his – other than the possibility of his having been a genuinely common peasant labourer known for his Christian piety and generosity in his locality, and fondly remembered by those who knew him. If this had been the case, then all recollection of the circumstances and details of his life had probably disappeared within a generation of his death and they became absorbed in, and buried under, a popular and pre-existent fertility cult extant in the neighbourhood (there seems to have been a marked devotion to St Walstan within a thirty-mile radius around Taverham/Bawburgh). Such a cult would have been one of those that the Normans were eager to suppress, or that the Church sought to acculturalize, during the mid-eleventh to mid-twelfth-century period; the accommodation of the Church probably arose from the strong attachment of the local laity to the cult and the potential for the Church in terms of pilgrimages and shrine-offerings. Walstan, real or mythological, was clearly a 'people's saint', as opposed to a king or a Church prelate, and as such had to be accorded posthumous respectability by claiming that he was of noble or royal birth and had lived ascetically and celibately, even though he was not a monk. The mistaken reference to the bishop who conducted his funeral as the Bishop of Norwich (the Norwich See did not yet exist at the time of the alleged date for Walstan's death)[60] might be a clue to the fact that the cult of St Walstan may have been given some official local Church recognition from the early twelfth century onwards, when the first hagiographical accounts were written for the benefit of pilgrims, the surviving sources probably having been later recensions of these. Despite this, a people's saint Walstan remained and the persistence of his devotion even into our own times, regardless of its very localized nature, is surely evidence of a 'popular' form of Christianity, deeply syncretist, sometimes submerged, sometimes in partnership with the official forms, and even going on to gain respectability with a strength that would survive the Reformation and the 'Age of Reason'. Before we leave such possibilities it might be worth considering a final example of something similar.

Walsingham and the Virgin Mary

The Shrine of our Lady of Walsingham is supposed to have originated in this very late period, i.e. 1061, though the only surviving evidence for the origins of the devotion is to be found in a fifteenth-century book, which ascribes the date of the foundation of the shrine to 1061, and in a poem of about 1496.[61] The poem records how the Virgin Mary appeared in a dream to a local widow, Rychold, showing her the Holy House of Nazareth and instructing her that a replica be built at Walsingham. The designated place was apparently revealed by the failure of dew to cover two spots in a meadow, and when the carpenters attempted to erect the chapel on the first spot, close by twin wells, they were unable to do so. The next night Mary herself moved the edifice to the second site.[62] The only other pieces of early evidence for the Walsingham Shrine are a twelfth-century pipe roll, and an undated foundation charter for the Augustinian priory which exercised the custodianship of the shrine-chapel. The priory appears to have been established by a Norman, Geoffrey de Faverches, to care for a chapel built by his mother (not named), and does seem to have been established by the mid-twelfth century. The pipe roll, dated about 1130, which refers to the same Geoffrey, would seem to place the foundress of this chapel in about the late eleventh century at the earliest, assuming that this is the same chapel and the legendary Rychold. There is no evidence of anyone so named in *Domesday*, or of any monastic foundation at Walsingham prior to the Augustinian priory.[63] A recent writer on the subject of Walsingham has suggested on the basis of the above evidence that what we are looking at in terms of the origins of the Walsingham Shrine is in fact a foundation of the early to mid-twelfth century rather than the date traditionally claimed,[64] which is probably part of the truth.

We could in fact be looking at a late development and a fusion of several influences and another example of their integration into Christianity by the Church in the twelfth century. Given the lack of evidence one way or the other for Walsingham (unless we are to take the legend contained within the *Pynson Ballad* literally) the twelfth-century possibility of the foundation of a chapel of the Virgin Mary seems likely. It is also a possibility that such a chapel was established to house a devotion to the Virgin, associated with the two wells,[65] which pre-dated this period, the name of the legendary foundress, Rychold, having accompanied such a devotion, which itself could go back as far as the early to mid-eleventh century. The widespread and popular devotion to the Virgin Mary in Anglo-Saxon England seems to have become notable from the time of the Monastic Reform Movement of the late tenth century onwards[66] and many such devotions simply supplanted, or were overlaid upon, existing pagan cults associated, as we have seen, with water wells and female deities, and it is probably in these areas that we should look for the origins of Walsingham. The claims regarding the 'Holy House' of Walsingham and its apparent ability to travel through the air seem to owe more to late medieval traditions relating to similar replicas of the original house at Nazareth.[67] What we are considering at Walsingham is yet another lately Christianized cult which was formally recognized and highly successful at the popular level, surviving, like the St Walstan devotion, into our own times.

Beyond 1066

From the mid-eleventh century onwards, and for the rest of the duration of the Middle Ages, there is very little to note in the way of purely local saints, which need not surprise us as we have reached the time of the centralized medieval Church and the centralized kingdom of which it was a partner. One or two purely localized devotions did appear in East Anglia but none of them were very notable or successful. Of some interest is an apparently East Anglian attempt to have Earl Waltheof, an English noble who was a victim of the Normans and buried at Crowland, recognized as a saint. Waltheof had been an English rebel against William the Conqueror and for this was executed in 1076. From the 1090s onwards there were claims of miracles associated with his relics, with obvious political undertones, but the cult was discouraged by the Normans and never gained more than a local and temporary popularity. A little more successful was the cult of a twelfth-century saint, Margaret of Hoveton, who lived in the Norfolk area of that name and who after her death attracted a purely local devotion though virtually nothing is known about her. We are left to suspect that the reason her veneration came to little on a wider scale was that she was an ordinary layperson, probably married at one time, and possessed of a simple Christian piety which would not have augured well for official canonization (in its now more formalized process) and given the interests that lay behind it. We also have the example of St Godric of Walpole in the Norfolk Fenland area, in the late eleventh century, who distinguished himself by going on pilgrimage by foot to the Holy Land and from thence returning to become a hermit in the north of England, and who seems to have been a man of the ordinary people.

Two further examples can be noted in the cases of St William of Norwich (for whom a 'Life' was written)[68] and St Robert of Bury (for whom there was a 'Life' which has now disappeared), who belonged to the twelfth century.[69] They were children and both were mysteriously murdered (probably in circumstances familiar in our own times) and it was claimed that they had been the victims of ritual murder by the Jews. These cults must be seen as a particularly odious form of anti-Semitism which seems to have represented an attempt at resistance to Jewish moneylenders, who enjoyed the protection of the Crown, by churchmen who resented the exorbitant interest rates levied on some of the monasteries in respect of necessary and heavy financial loans. Apart from inflaming anti-Semitic feeling, these cults in themselves never really got off the ground and it does seem that the Church on a wider level (to its credit) found them to be an embarrassment and distanced itself from them. From their time onwards, nobody of note appears in East Anglia save Dame Julian of Norwich, a much acclaimed mystic of the fourteenth century who has received a considerable renewal of interest in the late twentieth century, though she was never formally canonized and thus falls outside the remit of this book, bringing us to the end of our journey.

Our search for the East Anglian saints began on the Suffolk shores and finished, to all intents and purposes, at Walsingham in the north of Norfolk, having also taken us from the seventh century to the eleventh where we must end it. We cannot fail to have noticed the contrast between the apparent missionary and apostolic zeal of the saints and the Church of the earlier time (whilst not over-romanticizing that age or its Church) and the rather dismal picture that appears from the tenth century onwards, which reflects the changing nature and conditions of the intervening ages and of the Church which found itself enmeshed within them. It might be fair to say that perhaps the Church never entirely lost its evangelical zeal and purpose (though retrospectively this is difficult to discern in some of those centuries through which we have travelled): throughout history the Church has always demonstrated a remarkable capacity for recovery and renewal (particularly in times of adversity and persecution) and this is always a basis for confidence.

What of the saints? It has to be said that, in many of the cases we have looked at, they represent concepts of sanctity held by the age and Church of which they were a part and we must allow for the fact that those concepts were often somewhat different from our own. In truth, it might be said that the saints are with us in every age and that the majority of them appear to go unrecognized, not being found amongst rulers and Church prelates or even amongst the clergy and the monks. Rather are they amongst the ordinary people who live, work, bear children, and struggle amid the precarious circumstances of everyday life, and we will not find their names recorded in service books or hagiographies, but instead (from a perception of faith) in the 'Book of Life',[70] the Church collectively commemorating them on the Feast of All Saints.[71] Recent years have witnessed a revival of interest in those who were acknowledged as saints by the Church, for a variety of reasons. For the period of history that we have been examining such acknowledgement usually began at a local level and it seems not a bad idea that this is where we should start, if we are to know at least who they were – which was why this book was written.

Travelogue

Places traditionally associated with the saints

Norfolk

Attleborough:
A late and unreliable claim says that St Edmund lived here for one year, learning the psalter by heart.

Babingley:
St Felix is claimed to have landed here and to have evangelized the surrounding area.

Bawburgh:
Claimed to have been the burial place of St Walstan. There was a shrine here until the sixteenth century; also a 'holy' well close by.

Burgh Castle:
Claimed, since the sixteenth century, to have been the site of St Fursey's monastery of *Cnobheresburgh* – and a possibility (amongst others).

Costessey:
Where St Walstan was supposed to have toiled as a labourer. One of his 'holy' wells (now dried up) is in Costessey Park.

East Dereham:
A possible site for St Witburgha's monastery. A holy well associated with her is in the churchyard of St Nicholas' Church (formerly there were two wells).

Holkham:
Where St Witburgha was said to have been born and educated, and where she had a hermitage until her move to Dereham. The parish church is dedicated to her.

Hunstanton:
A headland with the ruins of a chapel dedicated to St Edmund is said to denote where he landed to take up his kingdom. Nearby, there were some holy springs of water said to have been instigated by the saint.

Loddon:
The church here was supposed to have been founded by St Felix.

Martham:
The alleged burial place of St Blythe (or Blide), supposed mother of St Walstan.

Reedham:
Another church said to have been founded by St Felix.

Saham Toney:
A possible site for one of St Felix's schools and where his relics may have reposed for a while.

St Benet Holme:
The site of a Benedictine monastery whose monks restaffed Bury St Edmunds' Abbey after its eleventh-century refoundation. It is said to be on the site of an earlier ninth-century foundation of St Suniman, the scene of the martyrdom of St Wolfeius the Hermit and his companion monks.

Shernborne:
Yet another church said to have been founded by St Felix.

Taverham:
Where St Walstan was said to have lived, another 'holy' well of his association having been near the church.

Suffolk

Blythburgh:
King Ana and his son (?), St Jurmin, were traditionally, and possibly, buried here – St Walstan (according to one source) was born nearby.

Bures St Mary:
Church of St Stephen, where St Edmund (according to late, and very dubious, sources) was crowned on Christmas Day, 855 (nearby is 'St Edmund's Hill').

Bury St Edmunds:
Formerly *Beodricesworth* and a possible site of King Sigbert's monastery. Better known as the resting place for St Edmund's alleged relics within his shrine. A venue of national veneration until the sixteenth century. It also claimed to have possessed the relics of King Ana, St Jurmin, St Botolph and St Adolph and these were venerated here during the later Middle Ages.

Dunwich:
The 'sunken city' (most of it now gone) claimed since the late Middle Ages to have been the *Dommoc* of St Felix and his episcopal seat, which remains one possibility.

Exning:
Said, by a late source, to have been the birthplace of St Etheldreda, who was supposed to have been baptized in a spring here by St Felix; also said to be the holy well of the unknown St Mindred (*Minthryth*).

Felixstowe/Walton:
Named after St Felix and a possible location for *Dommoc*.

Grundisburgh:
A claimed, and most unlikely, location for St Botolph's *Icanhoe* and his burial place.

Hoxne:
Claimed since the later Middle Ages as the site of the martyrdom of St Edmund, where two chapels stood denoting the actual site of martyrdom and where his head was said to have been found. It also has a

bridge under which he was supposed to have hidden and been captured – all of which are late and extremely unlikely claims.

Iken:
The most likely, and by far the strongest, candidate for the location of St Botolph's monastery of *Icanhoe*. The site, marked by the present church, contains the shaft of what may have been a memorial cross to the saint.

Polstead:
In the village is a dead oak, known as the 'Gospel Oak', beneath which St Cedd, the 'Apostle to Essex', is supposed to have once preached (pure folklore, needless to say!).

Rendlesham:
Once a royal settlement (or *'tun'*) of King Ana and the early Wuffings kings near where there was a church in which St Cedd baptized Swithelm, King of Essex. The present church of St Gregory may stand on the site of a pagan temple, converted to Christian use by the early Wuffings, whilst the royal hall may have stood further to the north (near present Naunton Hall).

Sutton by Woodbridge:
One of the likelier locations for the martyrdom of St Edmund.

Northamptonshire

Castor:
Site of the monastery founded by St Cyneburgha, who was succeeded as abbess there by St Cyneswitha, and associated with St Tibba. A local path still remains known as 'Lady Cunnybarrow's Way'.

Peakirk:
The church is said to be on the site of the hermitage of St Pega (sister of St Guthlac) and contains a medieval stone reliquary once said to have contained her heart.

Ryhall (Rutlandshire):
The site of the hermitage of St Tibba who was supposed to have been buried here prior to her relics being moved to Peterborough. There is a 'holy' well associated with her.

Weedon:
St Wereburgha is alleged to have founded a monastery here.

Cambridgeshire

Chatteris:
Said to have been where St Etheldreda's former chaplain, Huna, had his hermitage at a spot traditionally identified as 'Honey Farm' (Huna's Farm?).

Eltisley:
One of the claimed burial places for St Wendreda (spurious) and also the site of a hermitage of an unknown tenth-century female saint, St Pandwyna (*Pandiona*), said to have been an Irish or British refugee, and for whom there is still a 'holy' well.

Ely:
The cathedral contains the site of the former shrines and relics of St Etheldreda (foundress), St Sexburgha (sister) and St Witburgha (supposed sister) and the former burial place of St Ermenhilda (niece), all of whom were abbesses. It has associations with St Owen, to whom there is a memorial cross, St Huna and St Wereburgha (said to have been an abbess). The relic of the 'head of St Botolph' was also kept here until the sixteenth century, and the relics of St Wendreda were also said to have been kept here.

March:
St Wendreda is said to have founded her monastery and been buried here.

Peterborough:
Formerly *Medeshampstede*. It once contained the relics of Sts Cyneburgha, Cyneswitha and Tibba. Also the site of the martyrdom of Abbot Headda and his '84' fellow-monks by the Danes in the ninth century.

The abbey (now the cathedral) was restored by St Aethelwold, 'Father of Monks', in the late tenth century during the monastic reform period.

Ramsey:
The former abbey (now ruined) was founded during the monastic reform period by St Oswald, Bishop of Worcester. Abbo of Fleury, hagiographer of St Edmund, was once its abbot, and probably wrote the 'Life' here. It once housed the alleged relics of St Aethelberht and St Aethelraed (seventh-century Kentish martyrs), and also those of St Felix, St Ives and St Eadnoth.

St Ives:
Supposed to have been near the hermitage place of St Ives (St Ivo), a 'Persian bishop' whose relics, and those of three companions, were 'revealed' in the early eleventh century. A 'holy' spring was supposed to have marked the site of the relics, where 'miracles' occurred, and a chapel and Benedictine priory were erected by the spot.

St Neots:
The place takes its name from a saint said to have appeared in a dream to King Alfred the Great on the eve of the Battle of Eathundun (Ashdown) against the Danes. A Cornish saint, his relics were translated here in the late tenth century.

Soham:
The church stands on the site of a monastery said to have been founded by St Felix; it may have been home to his relics and the location of his school.

Thorney:
The site of a monastery founded by monks from *Beodricesworth*; also the site of ninth-century hermit-martyrs (under the Danes) – Sts Tancred, Torthred and Tova. It also boasted the relics of Sts Cyneburgha, Cyneswitha and Tibba, St Huna of Ely, St Benedict Biscop (Abbot of Monkwearmouth/Jarrow), and an unknown monk-saint, Herefrith. The monastery was refounded in the tenth century by St Aethelwold.

Lincolnshire

Crowland:

Crowland Abbey (now mostly ruined) is on the site where St Guthlac and his fellow-hermits lived. Also the site of the martyrdom of the Crowland monks who were killed by the Danes in the ninth century, and of the hermitages of St Aelfthryth, daughter of King Offa, and St Thurketyl, a late ninth-century Christian Dane who became Abbot there.

Louth:

The former resting place of the relics of St Herefrith, possibly a Bishop of Lindsey, and maybe of East Anglian origin, whose relics were removed to Thorney.

Appendix 1

The Saints

The East Anglian Saints and their Places of Association

[Italics indicate no known established cult as a saint – places indicated are those that were believed to have housed their relics]

Abbo of Fleury (1004) Ramsey & Fleury
Adolph (680) *Icanhoe* & Bury St Edmunds
Aethelflaeda (835) Crowland
Aethelwold (984) Winchester
Algise (7th c.) Burgh? & Laon
Ana (654) Blythburgh
Arnulf (640) St Neots
Bettelin (8th c.) Crowland
Blythe (11th c.) Martham?
Botolph (680) *Icanhoe*, Thorney, Bury St Edmunds, Peterborough
Cissa (8th c.) Crowland
Corbican (7th c.) Burgh? & Laon
The Crowland Martyrs (869) Crowland
Cyneburgha, Cyneswitha and Tibba (7th c.) Peterborough
Dicuil (7th c.) Burgh? & Bosham?

Eadnoth (10th c.) Ely
Eadwold (9th c.) Cerne
Ecgberht (8th c.) Crowland
Edmund (869) Bury St Edmunds
Ercongota (660) Faremoutier
Ermenhilda (700) Ely
Erpwald (628) ?
Ethelbert (794) Hereford
Ethelburgha (664) Faremoutier
Etheldreda (679) Ely
Etto (7th c.) Burgh? & Liège
Felix (647) Dunwich? & Soham?
Foillan (655) Burgh? & Fosses
Fremund (866) Dunstable?
Fursey (647/50) Burgh? & Péronne?
Gobhan (7th c.) Burgh?
Guthlac (714) Crowland
Haedda and the Peterborough Martyrs (869) Peterborough
Herefrith (873) Louth & Thorney
Hereswitha (7th c.) Chelles

Huna (7th c.) Thorney
Hunbert (869) *Dommoc/Elmham?*
Ives (?) Ramsey
Jurmin (654) Blythburgh
Lactan (7th c.) Burgh?
Mauguille (7th c.) Burgh? & S.
  Riquier
Mindred (7th c.) Exning
Neot (877) St Neots
Owen (670) Ely & Haddenham
Pandwyna (904) Eltisley
Pega (719) Peakirk & Rome
Radolgus (7th c.) Burgh? & Laon
Reginhere (870) Northants?
Saethryth (7th c.) Faremoutier
Sexburgha (700) Ely
Sigbert (637) Bury St Edmunds?
Suniman (869) St Benet Holme?
Tancred, Torthred and Tova
  (7th c.) Thorney

Tatwine (8th c.) Crowland
The Thorney Martyrs (869)
  Thorney
Ultan (7th c.) Burgh? & Fosses
Walstan (1016) Bawburgh
Wendreda (700) March &
  Chester
Wereburgha (700) Hanbury and
  Ely
Witburgha (743?) East Dereham
  and Ely
Wolfeius (869) St Benet Holme?

Post-1066

Godric of Walpole (1170)
Margaret of Hoveton (1170)
Robert of Bury (12th c.)
Waltheof (1076) Crowland
William of Norwich (1144)

Major Pilgrimage and Relic Centres in East Anglia by 1066

Blythburgh (King Ana and
  St Jurmin)
Bury St Edmunds (St Edmund
  and St Botolph)
Crowland (St Guthlac)
Ely (Sts Etheldreda, Sexburgha,
  Witburgha and Ermenhilda)
Peterborough (St Botolph)
Ramsey (Sts Ives, Ethelbert and
  Ethelred)
St Ives ('Companions' of St Ives)

St Neots (St Neot and
  St Arnulf)
Thorney (Sts Botolph, Adolph,
  Huna, Herefrith, Tancred,
  Torthred and Tova)

Post-1066

Bawburgh (St Walstan)
Walsingham (The Virgin Mary)

Note: *Based on primary sources and local traditions.*

Traditional Iconographic Symbols of the East Anglian Saints

St Blythe   Crowned and holding a book and palm branch.

St Botolph   As an abbot, seated and holding a church or book in one hand and the other raised, with a bishop on each side – above the church are depicted a star and crescent.

St Edmund   Crowned as a king and pierced with arrows or holding an arrow in his hand.

St Ethelburgha   Holding the instruments of Christ's passion.

St Etheldreda   As an abbess, crowned, carrying a crozier and book.

St Felix   Fastened to a bed of seashells, with an angel bringing him a crown.

St Fursey   Shown with an angel defending him from the Devil.

St Guthlac   Putting devils to flight, or devils molesting him and angels consoling him. A whip in his hand, his abbey at his feet and St Bartholomew appearing to him.

St Sexburgha   As an abbess, and bearing a palm branch.

St Walstan   In princely robes and crowned, bearing a scythe (sometimes with two white oxen at his feet).

St Witburgha   Holding a church in her hand.

Appendix 2

The Kings and their Saintly Relations

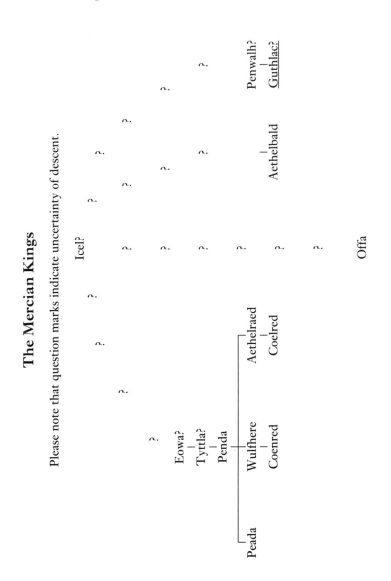

The Mercian Kings

Please note that question marks indicate uncertainty of descent.

The Royal and Saintly Tribe of East Anglia

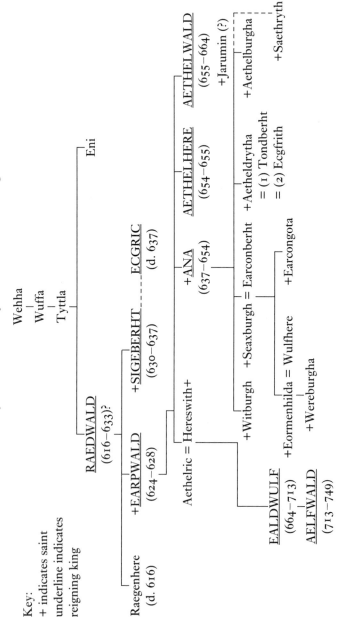

Key:
+ indicates saint
underline indicates
reigning king

Appendix 3

The Chronology of the Kings

The Kings of East Anglia

Pagan

Wehha (?)
Wuffa (?)
Tyttla (?)

Religion Uncertain

Raedwald (?–616?)

Christian

Earpwald (616?–628)
Unknown (628–630)
Sigbert (and Ecgric–Kingdom
  divided) (630–637?)

Ana (637?–654)
Aethelhere (654–655)
Aethelwald (655–664)
Aldwulf (664–713)
Aelfwald (713–749)
Heonn and Beonn (Kingdom
  divided?) (?–?)
Ethelbert (?–794?)
Eadwald (c.797)
Aethelstan (c.825)
Aethelweard (c.850)
Edmund (?–869)

[Probable end of native East Anglian Wuffings dynasty]

Oswald and Aethelraed? (puppet
  kings?) (?–?)
Guthrum/'Athelstan' (Danish
  king) (879–890)

Eohric? (Danish king) (?–904)

*Thereafter, the East Anglian Kingdom and its line of kings came to
an end*

The Kings of England from the Tenth Century until 1066

East Anglia under the supremacy of the House of Wessex

Edward the Elder (son of Alfred the Great) (899–924)
Aethelstan (924–939)
Eadmund (939–946)
Eadred (946–955)
Eadwy (955-959)
St Edgar ('the Peaceable') (959–975)
St Edward the Younger ('the Martyr') (975–978)
Aethelraed ('Ethelred the Unready') (979–1016)

[Edmund 'Ironside'] (Danish) (1016)
Cnut (Danish) (1016–1035)
Harold 'Harefoot' (Danish) (1035–1040)
Harthacnut (Danish) (1040–1042)
St Edward ('the Confessor') (1042–1066)
Harold (Godwinson) (1066)

End of the native English dynasty

Note: Square brackets round a king's name indicate that he never reigned but was legitimate.

Appendix 4

The Bishops and Archbishops

The Bishops

Dommoc
**(Dunwich/Felixstowe/
Walton?)**
St Felix of Burgundy – 'Apostle
   to East Anglia' (631–648)

Thomas (648–653)
Berhtgils (Boniface) (653–667)
Bisi (669–672)

Division of See into Dommoc *and* Elmham

Aecce (672–?)
Aescwulf (?–?)
Eardred (716–?)
Cuthwine (?–?)
Aldberht (731–?)
Ecglaf (?–?)
Heardwulf (747–?)

Heardred (781–793)
Aelfhun (793–798)
Tidferth (798–824)
Waermund (824–825)
Wilraed (825–845)
Aethelwold (845–?)

Interruption due to Danish attacks

Elmham
Beaduwine (672–693)
Nothberht (?–716)
Heathulac (?–731)
Aethelfrith (?–736)
Eanfrith (?–758)

Aethelwulf (?–781)
Alheard (785–805)
Sibba (?–816)
Hunferth (816–824)
Hunberht (?) (824–?)

Interruption due to Danish attacks

Thereafter, a possible temporary administration by Bishops of London until the mid-tenth century.

Restored See of East Anglia | Aelfwine (?–1023)
(Elmham only) | Aelfric II (1023–1038)
Eadwulf (?–966?) | Aelfric III (1039–1043)
Aelfric I (?–970) | Stigand (deposed) (1043)
Theodred I (974–?) | Grimketel (also Bishop of Selsey)
Theodred II (?–995?) | (1043)
Aethelstan (995–1001) | Stigand (again) (1044–1047)
Aelfgar (1001–?) | Aethelmar (1047–1070)

Thereafter the See was transferred to Thetford and thence to Norwich

The Archbishops of Canterbury
from 597 to 1070

St Augustine (597–605)
St Laurentius (605–619)
St Mellitus (619–624)
St Justus (624–627)
St Honorius (627–653)
St Deusdedit (655–664)
St Theodore of Tarsus (668–690)
Beorhtwald (693–731)
St Tatwine (731–734)
St Nothelm (734–740)
Cuthbeorht (740–758)
St Brecguwine (759–762)
Jaenbeorht (763–790)
St Aethelheard (790–803)
Wulfred (803–829)
Fleogild (829–830)
Ceolnoth (830–870)
Aethelraed (870–889)
St Plegmund (891–923)
Aethelm (923–925)

Wulfhelm (928–941)
St Oda (941–958)
Aelfsicge (958–959)
Beorhthelm (959)
St Dunstan (959–988)
Aethelgar (988–989)
Sigeric (990–994)
Aelfric (995–1005)
St Aelfheah (Alphège the Martyr) (1006–1012)
Lyfing (1013–1020)
St Aetholnoth (1020–1038)
Eadsige (1038–1050)
Robert of Jumièges (Norman) (1051–1052)
Stigand (deposed) (1052–1070)

Appendix 5

The Abbots

(Post-Danish Period to 1066)

Bury St Edmunds (formerly Beodricesworth)

Ufi (1020–1044)
Leofstan (1044–1065)
Baldwin (1065–1080)

Crowland

St Thurketyl (971)
Aegelric I (?)
Aegelric II (?)
Oskytel (1012)
Godric (?)
Brihtmaer (1018)
Wulfgeat (also Abbot of Peterborough) (?)
Leofric (?)
Wulfketel (1061–85)

Ely

Byrhtnoth (970–99)
Aelfsige (999–1016)
Leofwine (1019–22)
Leofric (1022–29)
Leofsige (1029–44)
Wulfric (1044–66)

Thurstan (1066–73)

Peakirk

Reinfred (971?)

Peterborough (formerly Medeshamstede)

Ealdwulf (966–92)
Coenwulf (992–1006)
Aelfsige (1006–42)
Earnwig (1041–52)
Leofric (1052–66)

Ramsey

[St Oswald of Abingdon] (969–86 and 988–93]
St Abbo of Fleury (986–88)
Eadnoth (993–1006)
Wulfsige (1006–16)
Wythman (1016–20)
Aethelstan (1020–43)
Aelfwine (1043–80)

Romburgh

Blakere (1047–64)

St Benet Holme

Aelfsige (1019–46)
Thurstan (1046–64)
Aelfwold (1064–89)

Thorney

St Aethelwold (of Winchester)
 (973–84)

Godeman (990)
Leofsige (1016)
Leofsine (1016–23)
Oswig (1049)
Leofwine (1051)
Leofric (also Abbot of
 Peterborough) (1066)

Note: Square brackets round the name of an abbot indicate that he was the founder but was non-resident.

Appendix 6

The Church in East Anglia

Monastic and Major Ecclesiastical Sites in East Anglia (Pre-Danish Invasion Period)

Norfolk

Babingley
Bawsey (?)
Benet Holme (?)
Caister
Cnobheresburgh (Burgh Castle/
    Shottisham?)
Dereham
Dickleburgh (?)
Holkham
Holme (?)
Loddon
North Elmham
Reedham
Saham Toney (?)
Shernborne
Soham (?)
Stow Bardolph
Wormegay (?)

Suffolk

Beodricesworth (Bury
    St Edmunds)
Blythburgh
Brandon
Chadacre (?)
Chedburgh (?)
Chediston (?)
Dommoc (Dunwich/Felixstowe/
    Walton?)
Exning
Eye
Horningsea
Hoxne
Icanhoe (Iken?)
Mendham
South Elmham
Stoke Nayland

The Fens

Chatteris
Crowland
Ely
March
Medeshamstede (Peterborough)
Peakirk
Soham (?)
Thorney

Post-Viking Monasteries (by 1066)

Monasteries

St Benet Holme
Blythborough
Thetford
Rumburgh
Bury St Edmunds
Ely
Ramsey
St Ives
St Neots
Peterborough
Thorney
Crowland

Peakirk
Spalding
Mendham
Stoke by Nayland
Horningsea

Nunneries

Chatteris

**Secular Canons
(Non-reformed)**

North Elmham

The Monastic Reform Movement and its Foundations

**Deriving from Abingdon
(St Aethelwold)**

St Benet Holme
Thorney
Crowland
Peakirk
Peterborough
Ely
Bury St Edmunds
St Neots

**Deriving from Westbury
(St Oswald)**

Ramsey

Appendix 7

Treasures of East Anglia

Treasures of the East Anglian Church

The Benedictional of St Aethelwold (British Library)

Written at the command of St Aethelwold and probably by Godeman, Abbot of Thorney, in 972. It contains texts for use by a bishop at Mass and has twenty-eight miniatures, including one of St Etheldreda, and is beautifully decorated with many colours, including gold leaf.

The Brandon Plaque (Early ninth century – British Museum)

A gold plaque, showing affinities to the *Book of Kells* and found at the high-status monastic site at Brandon, Suffolk. It bears a symbol of St John (showing the eagle head and holding a pen) and may have been one of a set of four Gospel book covers.

Censer (Ninth century – British Museum)

Found at North Elmham and may have been discarded due to Danish attacks. It has similarities with the Seal of Bishop Aethelwold and bears animal heads.

The Crowland Psalter (Mid-eleventh century – The Bodleian Library, Oxford)

Contains a miniature showing Christ trampling upon a lion and dragon (the earliest known example of such) and in its Calendar it refers to Sts Felix, Guthlac and Pega. It was probably produced at Crowland.

Decorations (Eighth century – British Museum)

Bone and copper alloy leaf from a writing tablet found at Blythborough (on the monastery site) with incised runic lettering, suggesting that the writer was attempting Latin verbal forms. It may have been part of a diptych (commemoration list) used at Mass.

The Ely Gospels (1020 – Pembroke College, Cambridge)

Written by a scribe who also wrote a version of Bede's *History of the English Church and People*, it was previously at Peterborough. It contains striking miniatures of the Four Evangelists.

Panel Fragment (Eighth century – Castle Museum, Norwich)

Found at Harling, Norfolk, near a church dedicated to St Ethelbert the Martyr, and may have been part of a book cover or diptych. It seems to show wolf-like beasts and Romulus and Remus (also found on the coins of King St Ethelbert).

The Ramsey Psalter (Tenth century – British Library)

Probably designed for use at Ramsey Abbey, this contains a litany, gold-written, with a triple invocation to St Benedict (to whom Ramsey was dedicated). It is written in fine bold script with magnificent initials and is decorated with acanthus, executed in gold and many colours. It is considered to be amongst the masterpieces of early English Church art.

The Seal of Bishop Aethelwold (Ninth century – British Museum)

A seal die of one of the last bishops of *Dommoc*. It is bronze and engraved with an inscription which translates: '*The seal of Bishop Athilwold of Dommoc*'.

The Wilton Cross (Eighth century – British Museum)

A garnet inlaid cross set in a filigree collar, belonging to an exceptional group of jewellery from East Anglia, including the Ixworth Cross (Ashmolean Museum, Oxford). It may date from the time when Christianity was making a significant impact upon the East Anglian nobility.

This list is not exclusive and only refers to some examples that can be seen in this country. Of particular interest is 'The Red Book of Eye', now no longer extant, and said to have been the original Gospel Book of St Felix containing annotations regarding the early East Anglian kings and their details – it was last seen in the sixteenth century.

Treasure of the East Anglian Kings

The Sutton Hoo Collection
(Early seventh century? – British Museum)
From a royal East Anglian ship burial – Sutton by Woodbridge

Bowls and spears

Bronze cauldrons, wooden bucket and iron chainwork

Bronze stag (mounted on wire ring and bronze pedestal)

Burr-wood cups

Coptic bowl

Drinking horns

Fluted silver bowl

Gilt-bronze bird

Gilt-bronze ring (sword-ring)

Gold shoulder-clasps

Iron axe-hammer

Iron stand

Iron tripod lamp

Large hanging-bowl (Celtic?)

Lyre

Maplewood bottles

Pottery bottle

Purse lid, gold buckle and subsidiary buckles and mounts

Sceptre

Shield

Shield-boss with mounts and fittings

Silver Byzantine dish

Silver cup and ladle

Stone sceptre

Sword pommel and fittings

Ten silver bowls

Two silver (baptismal?) spoons

Thirty-seven Frankish gold coins (tremisses)

War helmet

Appendix 8

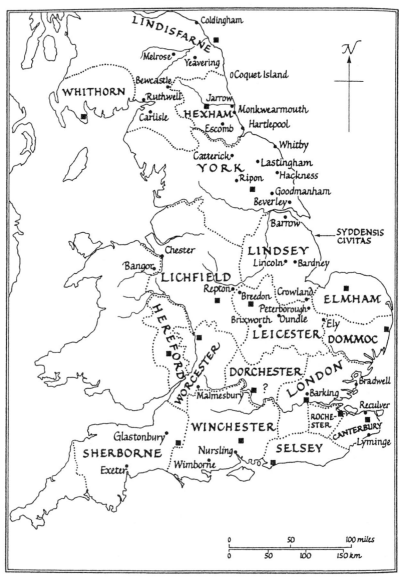

Map 5 *English Dioceses* c *750*

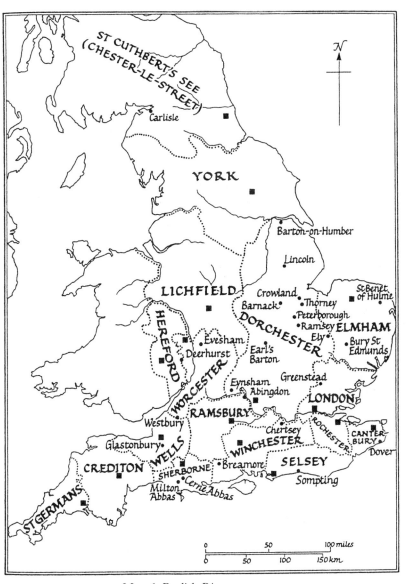

Map 6 *English Dioceses* c *1000*

Glossary

Secular and Political Terms

Anglo-Saxons

A fairly wide and generic term used to describe the various Germanic peoples who colonized a large part of Britain during the fifth and sixth centuries (i.e. the early English).

Annals

Chronicles and records of the kingdoms usually compiled by the monks.

Beserk

A Viking warrior believed to have been possessed by the spirit of the god Odin. In battle he was notable for the ferocity of his fighting, thus inspiring others to determined fighting.

Bretwealda

A king who was claimed to have exercised some form of overlordship over neighbouring kings and their territories.

Burgundy

A Germanic kingdom situated in eastern Gaul and under Frankish control.

Celts

The linguistic/cultural descendants of the peoples and tribes of Ireland, former Roman Britain, and the French province of Brittany (related to similar groups who once dominated a large tract of Western Europe, e.g. the Gauls of France).

Civitas
A former Roman military or civil base.

Connachta
An ancient Irish kingdom roughly corresponding with the western Irish province of Connaught.

East Anglia
An Anglo-Saxon kingdom comprising Norfolk, Suffolk, possibly a strip of northern Essex, and, for a short period, the eastern Fenlands.

Frankia
The kingdom of the Germanic Franks, roughly corresponding to France.

Gaul
A former Roman province comprising present-day France, the Netherlands, and parts of Western Germany.

Gyrwe
A tribe who inhabited the northern Fenlands.

Imperium
The exercise of the rule of a king.

Menology
A summarized collection of 'lives' of the saints read daily in churches [usually at the evening vigil service]. Alternatively known as Martyrology in the Latin Church of the West, or as a Prologue or Synaxarion in the Eastern Orthodox Church.

Mercia
An Anglo-Saxon kingdom comprising much of the Midlands of England.

Munster
An early Irish kingdom in the south-west of Ireland.

Northumbria
A vast Anglo-Saxon kingdom that stretched from the Humber to Scotland (and which included the south-eastern Scottish lowlands).

Romanitas
The concept of Roman rule and civilization.

Romano-British
The descendants of the inhabitants of Roman Britain (also known as 'Welsh').

Vikings
A generic term applied to the peoples of Scandinavia.

Weregild
An Anglo-Saxon system of monetary payment and compensation for injury or theft.

Wessex
An Anglo-Saxon kingdom that consisted of the English western peninsula and which eventually took in most of southern England.

Ecclesiastical Terms

Abbot/Abbess
The superior of a monastery.

Acculturalization
The Christianization of pagan customs and traditions by the Church (similar to syncretism – only with Church approval!).

Acrostical Hymn
A hymn with the first letter of each line representing a letter of the alphabet, usually constructed so as to form a statement of praise.

Apostate
One who has renounced or deserted Christianity by deed, statement or implication (as opposed to a 'heretic', i.e. one who differs from the official position of the Church whilst staunchly claiming to be in conformity with its true position on doctrinal matters).

Asceticism
Intense spiritual struggle, accompanied by prayer and fasting.

Breviary
A monastic book containing the psalms and versicles for the services of the day, mainly used for the services of the 'Hours'.

Canonical
In accordance with the laws and edicts of the Church.

Catechizing
Teaching and instructing.

Continental Mission
The mission that emanated from Rome in 597 onwards, initially under the leadership of the Italian monk St Augustine and inspired by St Gregory the Great, Pope of Rome.

Demons
Legendary evil spirits who figure as the opponents of the righteous in Christian mythology.

Desert Fathers
The third- and fourth-century dwellers of the Egyptian and Judaean deserts who founded the ideals of monasticism.

Hagiography
The writing of saints' lives.

Hermit
A monastic living as a solitary, or recluse.

Hierarchy
The bishops of the Church.

Hours
Short monastic services consisting of set psalms and prayers to mark the traditional divisions of the day.

Iconography
The artistic depiction of Christ and the saints.

Incorruption
The allegedly miraculous preservation of a saint's body after death.

'Life'
A stylized account of a saint's deeds, virtues and miracles.

Litany
A long petitional prayer used liturgically in the Church.

Liturgical Calendar
A Church service book containing major festivals and saints' commemorations for each day of the year, sometimes including a brief summary of the 'Life' of a saint.

Martyrology
A collection of the 'Lives' of the saints.

Mass
The eucharistic service of the Church (Holy Communion, or the Divine Liturgy).

Monastic Reform Movement
The tenth-century movement emanating from Cluny Abbey in France which sought to restore the monasteries along strict Benedictine lines.

Mynsters
Small communities of clergy, often dependent upon a major monastery, in outlying areas and serving the needs of scattered communities.

Paschalion
The method for calculating the correct date for the celebration of Easter.

Passions
'Lives' of saints often dealing with their sufferings, witness and exemplary virtues.

Patriarchate
The exercise of jurisdiction of the most senior hierarchs of the Church, e.g. the Pope of Rome.

Prelate
A senior hierarch of the Church (e.g. an archbishop, patriarch or pope).

Psalter
The Book of Psalms used liturgically, particularly for the services of the 'Hours'.

Recension
The adaptation and re-presentation (sometimes in abbreviated form) of a Church text.

Relics
The physical remains of the saints, said to be a repository of their virtues by the grace of God.

See
The geographical territory of a bishop's jurisdiction.

Styli
Types of pens or markers used for writing on wax tablets.

Syncretism
The combination of Christianity with other belief and ritual systems (i.e. the paganization of Christianity – unlike acculturalization, it usually emanated from the pagan, or semi-pagan, laity and did *not* meet with Church approval!).

Thaumaturge
A saint claimed to be possessed of the gift of healing by the grace of God.

Theocracy
The notion of God's rule descending downwards through his divinely appointed earthly agents (usually kings anointed by the Church).

Tonsure
The shearing of the hair of clergy and monastics indicating consecration.

Translation
The exhumation of a saint's body for the purpose of verifying incorrupti-
bility and further glorification.

Bibliography

Abbreviations Used in the Bibliography and Notes

ASC *The Anglo-Saxon Chronicle*, trans. G. N. Garmonsway, London, 1975

ASS *Acta Sanctorum Bollandiana* (Acts of the Saints), 69 vols., Antwerp, 1754–

EHD *English Historical Documents vol. 1*, ed. Dorothy Whitelock, London, 1955

HE *The Ecclesiastical History of the English People*, ed. B. Colgrave and R. A. B. Mynors, Oxford, 1960

LE *Liber Eliensis* (The Book of Ely), ed. E. O. Blake, London, 1962

LG Felix, *Life of Guthlac*, ed. and trans. B. Colgrave, London, 1985

ibid. in the same place as cited in the previous note

op. cit. in the work already quoted (Where there are two or more titles by an author, the relevant title is added to the reference in the Notes; full details may be found by checking under the author and title in the Bibliography below.)

Primary Sources – Texts, Editions and Translations

Acta Sanctorum Bollandiana (Acts of the Saints), 69 vols., Antwerp, 1754
  includes: *Codex Salmanticensis*
  Folcard, *The Life of St Botolph* (in vol. 4, 1867, pp. 324–30)
  Life of St Fursey

Aelfric, *Lives of the Saints*, ed. W. W. Skeat, Early English Text Society, London, 1881–1900

Aelfric, *Three Lives of English Saints*, ed. Michael Winterbottom, Toronto, 1972

The Anglo-Saxon Chronicle, trans. G. N. Garmonsway, London, 1975

Anon, *The Life of Ceolfrith*, in *EHD* pp. 697–707

Asser, *The Life of King Alfred*, ed. W. H. Stevenson, London, 1904

Bale, Bishop John, *The Acts of English Votaryes*, London, 1546

Beda Venerabilis (Bede), *Historia Ecclesiastica Gentis Anglorum*, ed. B. Colgrave and R. A. B. Mynors, Oxford, 1960

Bede, *The Ecclesiastical History of the English People*, ed. B. Colgrave and R. A. B. Mynors, Oxford, 1960

'The Dream of the Rood', in *The Earliest English Poems*, trans. M. Alexander, Middlesex 1966

The Earliest English Poems, trans. M. Alexander, Middlesex, 1966

Eddius Stephanus, 'The Life of St Wilfred', in D. H. Farmer, ed., *The Age of Bede*, London, 1983, pp. 105–184

Eddius Stephanus, *Vita S. Wilfridi*, text, translation and notes by B. Colgrave, Cambridge, 1927

English Historical Documents vol. 1, ed. Dorothy Whitelock, London, 1955

Felix, *The Life of Guthlac*, ed. and trans. B. Colgrave, London, 1985

Gildas, *The Ruin of Britain and Other Works*, ed. and trans. Michael Winterbottom, Surrey, 1978

Gildas (Sapiens), *De Excidio et Conquestu Brittanniae*, in E. B. Graves, *A Bibliography of English History to 1485*, London, 1975

Ingulphus, *Historia Croylandis*

Keynes, S. and Lapidge, M. *Alfred the Great, Asser's 'Life of King Alfred' and Other Contemporary Sources*, London, 1983

Liber Eliensis (The Book of Ely), ed. and trans. E. O. Blake, London, 1962

The Life of St Ethelbert King and Martyr 779AD–794AD, ed. and trans. Edwin Brooks, Bury St Edmunds, 1996

'The Penitential of St Theodore', in J. T. McNeill and H. M. Gamer, ed., *Medieval Handbooks of Penance, Bk. 1, Ch. 15*, Columbia/London, 1938

The Peterborough Chronicle of Hugh Candidus, trans. W. T. Mellows and A. Bell, London, 1949

Roger of Wendover, *Flores Historium*, trans. G. A. Giles, Bohn's Antiquarian Library, 1849

Rolls Series, London, 1882–85

Symeon Dunelmis (Symeon of Durham), *Monachi Opera Omnia 2*, in

Thomas Arnold, ed., *Chronicles and Memorials of Great Britain and Ireland*, Rolls Series, no. 75, London, 1882–85

Tacitus, *The Agricola and The Germania*, ed. H. Mattingly, Middlesex, 1987

William of Malmesbury, *De Gestis Pontificum Anglorum*, ed. N. Hamilton, London, 1890

Secondary Sources

Backhouse, J. *et. al.*, *The Golden Age of Anglo-Saxon Art*, London, 1984

Bassett, Steven, ed., *The Origins of Anglo-Saxon Kingdoms*, Leicester, 1989

Blakeman, Pamela, *The Isle of Ely*, Ely, 1994

Bradley, S. A. J., *Early English Poetry*, London, 1962

Brooks, Edwin, ed. and trans., *The Life of St Ethelbert, King and Martyr, 779AD–794AD*, Bury St Edmunds, 1996

Brooks, Nicholas, *The Early History of the Church of Canterbury*, Leicester, 1984

Butler, Alban, *The Lives of the Saints*, 4 vols., London, 1956–

Campbell, James, *The Anglo-Saxons*, Middlesex, 1982

'The First Century of Christianity', *The Ampleforth Journal* 76 (1973) pp. 12–29

Carey-Evans, Margaret, 'The Contribution of Hoxne to the Cult of St Edmund, King and Martyr, in the Middle Ages and Later', *Proceedings of the Suffolk Institute of Archaeology* 36 (1987) pp. 182–93

Hoxne and St Edmund, Hoxne, 1993

Charles-Edwards, Thomas, 'The Social Background to Irish *Peregrinatio*', *Celtica* 11 (1976) pp. 43–59

Clayton, Mary, *The Cult of the Virgin Mary in Anglo-Saxon England*, Cambridge, 1990

Dales, Douglas, *Light to the Isles*, Cambridge, 1997

Darby, Henry, *The Medieval Fenland*, Newton Abbot, 1974

Deansley, Margaret, *The Pre-Conquest Church in England*, London, 1961

Duffy, Eamonn, *The Stripping of the Altars*, Yale, 1992

Dumville, David, 'Essex, Middle Anglia and the Expansion of Mercia in the South-East Midlands', in Steven Bassett, ed., *The Origins of Anglo-Saxon Kingdoms*, Leicester, 1989 pp. 123–40

Dutt, W. A., *Highways and Byways in East Anglia*, Bury St Edmunds, 1914

Ellis-Davidson, Hilda, *Gods and Myths of Northern Europe*, London, 1964

Farmer, D. H., ed., *The Age of Bede*, London, 1983

Farmer, David, *The Oxford Dictionary of Saints*, 4th edn., Oxford, 1997

Fell, Christine, *St Edward King and Martyr*, Leeds, 1978

Galbraith, V., 'The East Anglian See and the Abbey of Bury St Edmunds', *English Historical Review* 40 (1925) pp. 222–4

Godfrey, Charles, *The Church in Anglo-Saxon England*, Cambridge, 1962

Godfrey, John, 'The Double Monastery in Early English History', *The Ampleforth Journal* 79 (1974) pp. 19–32

Gransden, Antonia, 'The Alleged Incorruption of the Body of St Edmund, King and Martyr', *The Antiquaries Journal* 74 (1994) pp. 135–55

'Abbo of Fleury's *Passio Sancti Edmundi*', *Revue Bénédictine* 105 (1995) pp. 20–78

Historical Writing in England, c.550–1307, Cambridge, 1974

Green, Miranda, *Celtic Goddesses*, London, 1995

Higham, Nicholas, *The Convert Kings*, Manchester, 1997

Roman Britain and the Anglo-Saxons, London, 1996

Hill, David, *An Atlas of Anglo-Saxon England*, Oxford, 1989

Hollis, Stephanie, *Anglo-Saxon Women and the Church*, Woodbridge, 1992

Hopko, Father Thomas, *The Orthodox Faith, vol. 1 Doctrine*, New York, 1976

Houghton, Bryan, *St Edmund – King and Martyr*, Lavenham, 1970

Hughes, Kathleen, *The Modern Traveller to the Early Irish Church*, London, 1977

James, M. R., 'Lives of St Walstan', *Proceedings of the Norfolk Archaeological Society* 19 (1917) p. 250

Suffolk and Norfolk, London, 1950

Johnson, S., 'Burgh Castle: Excavations by Charles Green, 1958–1961', *East Anglian Archaeology* 20 (1980)

Jones, Trefor, 'Pilgrim's Progress', *The Norfolk Journal* (October 1997) pp. 12–13

Lapidge, Michael, *Archbishop Theodore*, Cambridge, 1995

Larken, Hubert, *The Crowland Abbey Guide Book*, Crowland, 1925

McNeill, J. T. and Gamer, H. M., ed., *Medieval Handbooks of Penance*, Columbia/London, 1938

MacNiócaill, Geároid, *Ireland before the Vikings*, Dublin, 1972

Morris, Richard, *Churches in the Landscape*, London, 1989

Owen, A. E. B., 'Herefrith of Louth, Saint and Bishop; a Problem of Identities', *Lincolnshire History and Archaeology* 15 (1980) pp. 15–19

Page, Raymond, *Runes*, London, 1987

Phillips, Andrew, *The Hallowing of England*, Thetford, 1996

Pirenne, Henri, *A History of Europe*, London, 1961

Roeder, Helen, *Saints and their Attributes*, London, 1975

Rollason, David, 'Relic Cults as an Instrument of Royal Policy *c*.900–1050', *Anglo-Saxon England* 11 (1983) pp. 91–103

Rose, Edwin, 'A Tale of Two Derehams', *The NAHRG Quarterly*, Vol. 9, Norwich, 1993.

Scarfe, Norman, 'The Place-Name Icklingham – A Preliminary Examination', *East Anglian Archaeology* 3 (1976) pp. 127–34
Suffolk in the Middle Ages, Bury St Edmunds, 1986
Suffolk in the Landscape, Bury St Edmunds, 1987

Stafford, Pauline, *The East Midlands in the Early Middle Ages*, Leicester, 1993

Stenton, F., *Anglo-Saxon England*, Oxford, 1990

Stevenson, F. S., 'St Botulph and Iken', *Proceedings of the Suffolk Institute of Archaeology* 18 (1922) pp. 29–52

Twinch, Carol, *In Search of St Walstan*, Norwich, 1995

Wade-Evans, Angela, *The Sutton Hoo Ship Burial*, London, 1986

Wallis, Heather, 'Excavations at Church Loke, Burgh Castle, 1993–94', *Norfolk Archaeology* 43, 1 (1998) pp. 62–78

Ware, Timothy, *The Orthodox Church*, London, 1972

Warner, Peter, *The Origins of Suffolk*, Manchester, 1996

West, Stanley, 'A New Site for the Martyrdom of St Edmund', *Proceedings of the Suffolk Institute of Archaeology* 31 (1969)

West, Stanley, *et al.*, 'Iken, St Botolph, and the Coming of East Anglian Christianity', *Proceedings of the Suffolk Institute of Archaeology* 35 (1984) pp. 279–301

Whitelock, Dorothy, 'The Conversion of the Eastern Danelaw', *Saga Book of the Viking Society* 12 (1943) p. 52
'Fact and Fiction in the Legend of St Edmund', *Proceedings of the Suffolk Institute of Archaeology* 31 (1969) p. 220
'The Pre-Viking Age Church in East Anglia', *Anglo-Saxon England* 1 (1972)

Williamson, Tom, *The Origins of Norfolk*, Manchester, 1997

Wormald, Patrick, *Ideal and Reality in Frankish and Early English Society*, Oxford, 1983

Journals and Their Places of Publication

The Ampleforth Journal (Ampleforth Abbey, York)
Anglo-Saxon England (Cambridge)
The Antiquaries Journal (London)
Celtica (Dublin)
East Anglian Archaeology (Norwich)
English Historical Review (London)
Lincolnshire History and Archaeology (Lincoln)
Norfolk Archaeology (Norwich)
*The Norfolk Archaeological and Historical Research Group (NAHRG)
    Quarterly* (Norwich)
The Norfolk Journal (Bury St Edmunds)
Proceedings of the Suffolk Institute of Archaeology (Ipswich)
Revue Bénédictine (Brussels, Belgium)
Saga Book of the Viking Society (London)

Notes

Introduction

1 Raymond Page, *Runes*, London, 1987, p 2.
2 Father Thomas Hopko, *The Orthodox Faith, vol 1 Doctrine*, New York, 1976, p 27.
3 David Farmer, *The Oxford Dictionary of Saints*, 4th ed, Oxford, 1997, pp xii–xiii.
4 Margaret Deansley, *The Pre-Conquest Church in England*, London, 1961, p 341.
5 Ibid.
6 Douglas Dales, *Light to the Isles*, Cambridge, 1997, p 10.
7 Antonia Gransden, *Historical Writing in England c. 550–1307*, Cambridge, 1974, pp 67–8.
8 Farmer, op cit, pp xii–xiii.
9 Nicholas Higham, *The Convert Kings*, Manchester, 1997, pp 277–8.
10 An example of this is the Fenland area, the border zone between East Anglia and Mercia.

Chapter 1

1 This whole issue is discussed by Nicholas Higham, *Roman Britain and the Anglo-Saxons*, London, 1996, pp 97–157.
2 Bede, *The Ecclesiastical History of the English People*, vol 2, ed B. Colgrave and R.A.B. Mynors, Oxford, 1960, ch 2.
3 Gildas, *The Ruin of Britain and Other Works*, ed Michael Winterbottom, Surrey, 1978, ch 24.
4 *HE* I, ch 14.
5 Charles Godfrey, *The Church in Anglo-Saxon England*, Cambridge, 1962, p 215.

6 There are possible hints of late British survival in the 'Lives' of St Botolph and St Guthlac – see chs 4 and 6.

7 See the arguments for this in James Campbell, 'The First Century of Christianity', *The Ampleforth Journal* 76 (1973) pp 12–29.

8 James Campbell, *The Anglo-Saxons*, Middlesex, 1982, pp 57 and 64.

9 Tacitus *The Agricola and The Germania*, ed H. Mattingly, Middlesex, 1987, pp 134–5.

10 Ibid.

11 Ibid, p 135.

12 Eddius Stephanus, 'The Life of St Wilfred', in D. H. Farmer, ed, *The Age of Bede*, Middlesex, 1986, p 119.

13 *HE* I, ch 30.

14 Hilda Ellis-Davidson, *Gods and Myths of Northern Europe*, London, 1964, pp 113–14.

15 'The Dream of the Rood', in *The Earliest English Poems*, trans M. Alexander, Middlesex, 1966, pp 106–9.

16 W. A. Dutt, *Highways and Byways in East Anglia*, Bury St Edmunds, 1914.

17 F. Stenton, *Anglo-Saxon England*, Oxford, 1990, pp 97–101.

18 Ibid.

19 Ibid.

20 'The Penitential of St Theodore', in J. T. McNeill and H. M. Gamer, ed, *Medieval Handbooks of Penance*, Bk. 1, ch. 15, Columbia/London, 1938, pp 182–215.

21 Ellis-Davidson, op cit, pp 113–14.

22 Ibid.

23 Ibid.

24 Stenton, op cit, pp 97–101.

25 Ibid.

Chapter 2

1 *HE* 2, ch 15.

2 *HE* 3, ch 22.

3 *HE* 2, ch 12.

4 Ibid.

5 For the East Anglian kings, see Appendices 2 and 3.

6 *HE* 2, ch 15.

7 *HE* 2, ch 5.

8 *HE* 2, ch 15.
9 Dorothy Whitelock, 'The Pre-Viking Age Church in East Anglia', *Anglo-Saxon England* 1 (1972) p 5.

    St Columbanus of Luxeuil and Bobbio (559–616), an Irish monk and missionary, travelled extensively in southern Gaul founding monasteries. His austere Irish monastic rule remained in place for a considerable time on the Continent.

10 See Thomas Charles-Edwards, 'The Social Background to Irish *Peregrinatio*', *Celtica* 11 (1976) p 59.
11 It is a misnomer to speak of the 'Celtic Church', as though it was a liturgically and jurisdictionally distinct communion. It is more correct to refer to the Church in the Celtic-speaking lands or simply, the Irish Church, Welsh Church etc.
12 *HE* 3, ch 8.
13 See C. Stancliffe, 'Kings Who Opted Out', in Patrick Wormald, *Ideal and Reality in Frankish and Early English Society*, Oxford, 1983, pp 154–76.
14 *HE* 3, ch 18.
15 Angela Wade-Evans, *The Sutton Hoo Ship Burial*, London, 1986, pp 83–5.
16 See Appendix 2.
17 *HE* 3, ch 7.
18 See ch 5, pp 87ff.
19 See ch 4, p 77.
20 *HE* 4, ch 19 and see ch 5.
21 See ch 3, p 59.
22 *HE* 3, ch 21.
23 D. Whitelock, 'The Pre-Viking Age Church in East Anglia', p 12, n 1.
24 See Appendix 2.
25 *HE* 3, ch 21.

Chapter 3

1 Richard Morris, *Churches in the Landscape*, London, 1989, ch 1.
2 Ibid, ch 3.
3 See ch 2, p 31.
4 *English Historical Documents*, vol 1, ed Dorothy Whitelock, London, 1955, p 731.

5 See ch 2, p 30.
6 Discussed by Nicholas Higham, *The Convert Kings*, Manchester, 1997.
7 Ibid.
8 Ibid.
9 'It was not because it was Christian, but because it was Roman that the Church acquired and maintained for centuries its hold over society; because it was the depository of a more ancient and more advanced civilization. Decadent though it was, the Church was the civilizing force of the period; indeed, we may say the only civilizing force.' Henri Pirenne, *A History of Europe*, London, 1961, p 57.
10 A form of monetary compensation.
11 See ch 8, pp 161–64.
12 For the question of British Christian survival, see ch 1, p 18.
13 i.e. Confirmation, Holy Communion, Marriage, and the Anointing of the Sick and Dying.
14 Morris, op cit, ch 3.
15 Roman and Irish-style monasteries may well have helped produce a distinctive native English style of monasticism in the early centuries.
16 At least two brothers are named as having been part of his community; his other companions may well have been tribal kindred.
17 Kathleen Hughes, *The Modern Traveller to the Early Irish Church*, London, 1977, p 50.
18 In accordance with the prescribed customs and traditions of the wider (Western) Church at that time.
19 They were not separated from communion with the Pope of Rome and his patriarchate but constituted an integral part of it. Such differences as there were arose from geographical and cultural isolation, combined with local particularisms.
20 This edict was issued by the Church in the fourth century.
21 In the 630s.
22 Tonsuring entailed the shaving of the head, symbolizing consecration. The prevailing Western custom was to shave the crown of the head in a circular form, representing Christ's crown of thorns. It seems that the Irish preference (and presumably the Welsh) was to shave the front of the head from ear to ear.
23 This required the participation of several bishops – the Irish used only one.
24 Whatever these differences may have been, we have no real knowledge

of them. All local churches at this time seem to have practised triple and full immersion. Perhaps the Irish administered confirmation immediately following baptism (as do the Eastern Churches to this day), as opposed to the Western custom of administering the rite some time after, and only by a bishop (the Eastern Churches permit priests to do this). This is pure speculation, though.

25 Which was why Pope St Gregory sent Italian missionaries directly to England in 597, rather than permit the work to be carried out by the Frankish Church.

26 *HE* 2, ch 15.

27 Ibid.

28 Ibid.

29 Ibid.

30 *Liber Eliensis* (The Book of Ely), ed E. O. Blake, London, 1962.

31 Ibid.

32 i.e. as part of an East Anglian consolidation there.

33 *HE* 2, ch 15.

34 Ibid.

35 Most of Dunwich has disappeared into the sea over the centuries and coastal erosion still continues.

36 William of Malmesbury, *De Gestis Pontificum Anglorum*, ed N. Hamilton, London, 1890, p 147.

37 Since the nineteenth century due to coastal erosion.

38 One of a series of Roman coastal forts dating back to the fourth century.

39 Close to the centre of royal power.

40 Usually (though not necessarily correctly) identified as Soham in the Cambridgeshire Fenland area.

41 See Map 4, pp 158–59.

42 Morris, op cit.

43 See Map 4, pp 158–59.

44 St Brendan 'the Voyager' was a notable example, and there were many others.

45 His Irish name was *Feársa* (meaning 'virtue'), its Latinized form having been '*Fursa*', usually anglicized to 'Fursey'.

46 *HE* 3, ch 19.

47 Ibid.

48 This identification and supposition having been no earlier than the sixteenth century!

49 The 'province of the English' being a loose term used by Bede to identify the origins of the Germanic peoples of East Anglia, Northumbria and Mercia.

50 *HE* 3, ch 19.

51 i.e. by the 680s, or thereabouts.

52 The source is from one of the versions of the 'Life of St Fursey' in the *Codex Salmanticensis*, printed in *ASS*, op cit.

53 Ireland, like England and Wales, was divided into several kingdoms. See Geároid MacNiócaill, *Ireland before the Vikings*, Dublin, 1972.

54 All of which seems strange as Ireland had been Christianized since the mid-fifth century.

55 'The Life of St Fursey', op cit.

56 Not to be confused with St Brendan the Voyager.

57 'The Life of St Fursey', op cit.

58 St Meldhan would later appear to Fursey in his famous visions, together with St Beoan.

59 Which means 'Fursey's Church' or 'Cell'.

60 Gobhan also appears in Bede's account, *HE* 3, ch 19.

61 They are to be found in 'The Life, Visions and Virtues of St Fursey', a version of which is in *ASS*, op cit.

62 We assume that they all accompanied Fursey to East Anglia.

63 The whole issue of exile in this context is discussed by Thomas Charles-Edwards, op cit, pp 43–59.

64 The south-eastern lowlands of Scotland were, at this time, within the Kingdom of Northumbria.

65 Probably a well-used thoroughfare between East Anglia and Northumbria.

66 Archaeological investigation, the latest having been in 1993–94, has failed to provide any confirmation as yet. See Heather Wallis, 'Excavations at Church Loke, Burgh Castle, 1993–94', *Norfolk Archaeology* 43, 1 (1998) pp 62–78.

67 See S. Johnson, 'Burgh Castle: Excavations by Charles Green, 1958–1961', *East Anglian Archaeology* 20 (1980).

68 Ibid.

69 Norman Scarfe, *Suffolk in the Landscape*, Bury St Edmunds, 1987, pp 84–5.

70 Hughes, op cit, pp 55–7.

71 Ibid.

72 Ibid.

73 Ibid, p 58.
74 Ibid, p 29.
75 'The Life of St Fursey', op cit.
76 Ibid.
77 See Map 2, p 70.
78 *HE* 2, ch 15.

Chapter 4

1 *Anglo-Saxon Chronicle*, trans G. N. Garmonsway, London, 1975, p 28.
2 Folcard, 'The Life of St Botolph' can be found in *ASS* 4, op cit, 1867, pp 324–30.
3 A monastic service book containing daily readings of the 'Lives of the Saints'.
4 The Kingdom of Northumbria at that time stretched into the lowlands of Scotland.
5 St Willibrord (658–739) preached in what are now parts of Holland and north-east Germany.
6 Probably in about 690.
7 See ch 3, p 46.
8 A rather loose and generic term used by Bede to describe the original Germanic settlers of parts of southern England; also applied to some tribes in northern Europe.
9 See ch 3, p 68.
10 *HE* 4, ch 12.
11 Perhaps as one of the 'five brethren' to whom Bede referred (*HE* 4, ch 12).
12 Folcard's 'Life of St Botolph', op cit.
13 There is no evidence of this on any of the episcopal lists of Utrecht for the period; see F. S. Stevenson, 'St Botulph and Iken', *Proceedings of the Suffolk Institute of Archaeology* 18 (1922) pp 29–52.
14 He was slain at the Battle of the Winwaed (555) – Bede portrays Aethelhere as a 'turncoat' (*HE* 3, ch 24).
15 *LE*.
16 The whole issue is discussed by Stanley West, Norman Scarfe and Rosemary Cramp, in 'Iken, St Botolph, and the Coming of East Anglian Christianity', *Proceedings of the Suffolk Institute of Archaeology* 35 (1984) pp 279–301.

17 Ibid, p 279.

18 Folcard's 'Life of St Botolph', op cit.

19 See ch 6, p 118.

20 The same possibility is suggested in the account of St Guthlac's experiences at the hands of Welsh-speaking devils in the remote Fens – see ch 6, p 118.

21 West *et al*, op cit, pp 284–92.

22 Ibid.

23 Folcard's 'Life of St Botolph', op cit.

24 For the 'Anonymous "Life of Ceolfrith"', see *EHD*, pp 697–707.

25 West *et al*, op cit, pp 294–5.

26 The sponsorship by one king of another at baptism was as often as not a form of establishing overlordship.

27 For a discussion of the Fens at this time, see ch 6 and Henry Darby, *The Medieval Fenland*, Newton Abbot, 1974, ch 1.

28 This could have been due to later popularity of the saint though.

29 *HE* 3, ch 22.

30 It was probably *c* 655.

31 Perhaps just before King Aethelhere's death (655).

32 He seems to have been back at *Icanhoe* during the 670s, so it could have been in the late 660s.

33 West *et al*, op cit, pp 294–5.

34 Aethelhere was killed in 655, though this could be a reference to the enigmatic and elusive 'King Alchmund'. The claim is more likely to have been an erroneous assumption of Folcard's!

35 West *et al*, op cit, pp 294–5.

36 Bury St Edmunds Abbey possessed what it claimed to be the arm of St Botolph, which was used for blessing the fields in times of drought.

37 For the East Anglian bishops of St Botolph's time see the episcopal list in Appendix 4.

38 This is feasible as the canonical age for bishops was thirty-five upwards. Also the Irish Church carried out episcopal consecrations by only one officiating bishop – an uncanonical practice; St Cedd could thus have consecrated Botolph as bishop, though from Archbishop Theodore's primacy, 668 onwards, he would not have been permitted to function as such unless reconsecrated.

39 Bede's master, Ceolwulf, had been with Botolph at *Icanhoe*, so presumably he gave some information about Botolph to him.

40 If indeed this was so.
41 The Kingdom of Essex was more extensive than the late twentieth-century county of that name.
42 See p 77.
43 Not to be confused with the St Jurmin said to have been the son of King Ana and slain with him in 654.
44 *HE* 3, ch 21.
45 The possible East Anglian 'proto-mission' of St Paulinus, referred to in ch 2, p 32.
46 *HE* 3, ch 22.
47 David Dumville, 'Essex, Middle Anglia and the Expansion of Mercia in the South-East Midlands', in Steven Bassett, ed, *The Origins of Anglo-Saxon Kingdoms*, Leicester, 1989, p 136.
48 There is no agreement that power-sharing involved rule over territorial or tribal blocs – see Dumville, op cit, p 138.
49 See ch 3.
50 See ch 2.

Chapter 5

1 For a description of the medieval Fenland, see Darby, op cit, ch 1.
2 Major drainage commenced in the seventeenth century; the only fen now in something approaching the earlier state is Wicken Fen, near Ely.
3 See ch 6, p 118.
4 The name means 'marsh dwellers'.
5 See ch 2, pp 40–1.
6 *HE* 4, ch 9.
7 Felix, *The Life of Guthlac*, ed and trans B. Colgrave, London, 1985.
8 Darby, op cit, pp 20–2.
9 For the concept of the 'desert', see the Introduction.
10 Roger of Wendover, *Flores Historium*, trans G. A. Giles, Bohn's Antiquarian Library, 1849.
11 See ch 2, p 39.
12 Ibid.
13 Bathildis, Queen of the Franks, was said to have originally been taken to France as an English slave-girl, and as such could have been one of Penda's victims.
14 *HE* 3, ch 8.

15 She was probably not a daughter of King Ana at all. See below, note 39.

16 At Holkham and then at East Dereham.

17 'Etheldreda' is the Latinized form of her name, which, in the later Middle Ages, became shortened and corrupted to 'Audrey'.

18 See Appendix 2.

19 *HE* 3, ch 8.

20 Ibid.

21 See Appendix 4.

22 *HE* 3, ch 8.

23 See note 13 above.

24 Ibid.

25 As a stepdaughter, she was probably more useful in this context than for a marriage alliance – Ana seems to have had rather a large number of female dependants to arrange for!

26 See ch 3, p 66.

27 See ch 2, note 14, p 231.

28 Ana's successors, her own close relatives, seem to have been pro-Mercian or, at least, willing to be compliant with them. They may well have wished to be quickly rid of Ana's offspring after AD 654.

29 Charles Godfrey, 'The Double Monastery in Early English History', *The Ampleforth Journal* 79 (1974) pp 19–32.

30 St Theodore of Tarsus, a Greek monk and cleric, who became Archbishop of Canterbury in 668. For a detailed study of his career, see 'The Career of Archbishop Theodore', in Michael Lapidge, *Archbishop Theodore*, Cambridge, 1995, pp 1–29.

31 Stephanie Hollis, *Anglo-Saxon Women and the Church*, Woodbridge, 1992, p 134.

32 Ibid.

33 *HE* 3, ch 8.

34 Ibid.

35 Ibid.

36 Ibid.

37 See the Introduction, p 8.

38 Bede actually says that there were few in England, and seems to imply that there were none at all in East Anglia, which was likely.

39 This assumes that St Witburgha was a daughter of King Ana, but see below and note 15 above.

Notes

241

40 For the career of St Chad of Lichfield, 'Apostle to Mercia', see *HE* 4, ch 3. For St Wilfred of York, see Eddius Stephanus, 'The Life of St Wilfred', in D. H. Farmer, ed, *The Age of Bede*, London, 1983, pp 105–84.

41 According to late Ely tradition, the supposed place was a stream at Exning in Suffolk (near Newmarket).

42 *LE*.

43 In the sense of using royal monasticism for the purposes of political expediency.

44 If we assume this to have been the purpose of the marriage, we might have to accept an earlier pre-654 date, when Ana was locked in struggle with Penda.

45 The name seems to be Welsh (i.e. Romano-British) and, if he originated from this territory, it raises serious questions about late British, and Christian, survival so far east in Britain.

46 A future king, and an opponent of St Wilfred of York.

47 He had succeeded Aethelhere in 655.

48 A territory stretching from the Humber to the Trent and a buffer zone between Mercia and Northumbria.

49 *HE* 4, ch 19.

50 The only information for *Cratendune* is in the *Liber Eliensis* and, due to the lateness of the source, needs to be treated with extreme caution.

51 *HE* 4, ch 19.

52 It is difficult to ascertain whether or not we should make too much of this, as both the Irish and Continental traditions seemed to have co-existed in East Anglia without too much difficulty. Northumbria may have presented a different situation, due to the heavy Irish Church influence there. This situation was further complicated by the vigorously pro-Roman attitude of St Wilfred and the power agenda of the Northumbrian kings.

53 *HE* 4, ch 19.

54 Ibid.

55 Ibid.

56 Interestingly, this is also the name recorded for the mother of 'King Aethelmund' in the 'Life of St Botolph' (see ch 4, p 74) and that of the mother of King Edmund in a 'Life of St Edmund'.

57 Needless to say, there is no reference to this in Bede, and it is probably a pious fiction of no truth.

58 See Map 3, p 131.

59 According to local tradition. A later foundation may have commemorated her having passed through the locality.

60 See Map 3, p 131.

61 *HE* 4, ch 3.

62 Ibid.

63 *HE* 4, ch 19.

64 It seems unlikely that St Augustine himself would have travelled this
   far from Kent.

65 King Ealdwulf was her uncle; her brother could have been the
   'Aethelmund' referred to in the 'Life of St Botolph' (see ch 4, p 00),
   assuming that he had survived to such a late date. The Ely source
   was probably wrong though.

66 The same pandemic of bubonic plague referred to in ch 4, p 81.

67 *HE* 4, ch 3.

68 In the south nave of Ely Cathedral.

69 Pamela Blakeman, *The Isle of Ely*, Ely, 1994, pp 14–15.

70 Ibid.

71 Hollis, op cit, p 257.

72 *HE* 4, ch 19.

73 The early morning office and praises of the monks, usually preceded
   by Matins.

74 So called, as it was considered to be the first hour of the day.

75 *HE* 4, ch 19.

76 Ibid.

77 Ibid.

78 This, if true, is surprising – they certainly plundered the tombs of
   Guthlac and his disciples at Crowland (see ch 7, p 138) in the search
   for treasure. Possibly Etheldreda's relics were moved to a place of
   safety, or what were claimed to have been her relics after the restoration of Ely were in fact a substitution.

79 If this relic was what it was claimed to have been, presumably it had
   been detached from the body at the Reformation or, alternatively, it
   had been separated at some time during the Middle Ages for the
   purpose of administering blessings; c.f. the arm of St Botolph, kept
   at Bury Abbey – see ch 4, p 79).

80 The relic can still be seen at the church upon request.

81 '*Hun*' is a form of '*Heonn*' (Latinized to 'Ana').

82 Hollis, op cit, p 67.

83 *HE* 4, ch 1.

84 *HE* 4, ch 19.
85 Ibid.
86 HE 4, ch 12.
87 See Appendix 2.
88 Her 'Life', which is mainly fictitious, was written by the Anglo-Norman Chronicler, Goscelin de Brakelond, and can be found in *ASS*, vol 1, pp 391–4.
89 The legend is worthless as an historical source (see below in the text for further discussion).
90 Dumville, op cit, pp 391–4. For the location of Middle-Anglia, see Map 1, p 12.
91 See Appendix 1.
92 Either Minthryth was another name for Wendreda (see M. R. James, *Suffolk and Norfolk*, London, 1950, p 14, or she was a local saint of whom nothing is remembered.
93 See Appendix 3.
94 See Appendix 2.
95 *HE* 3, ch 8.
96 See Map 2, p 70.
97 *HE* 3, ch 8.
98 Ibid.
99 The sources are in the *Liber Eliensis* and Bede's omission is only curious if we accept the Ely account as true.
100 See ch 2, p 41.
101 West Dereham, also in Norfolk, is a possibility: see Rose, Edwin, 'A Tale of Two Derehams', *The NAHRG Quarterly*, Vol. 9, Norwich, 1993.
102 There appear to have been two 'St Witburgha Wells' in East Dereham churchyard at one time.
103 The undoubted aim was to further enhance the growing power and prestige of Ely in the wake of the Monastic Reform Movement. Even if Witburgha had not been one of Ana's daughters, which seems likely, this would have been the reason for the furtherance of such a claim.
104 See Appendix 3.
105 *ASC*, p 31.
106 *ASC*, p 29.
107 *ASC*, p 31.

Chapter 6

1 Felix, *The Life of Guthlac*, ed and trans B. Colgrave, London, 1985, p 16. He was probably an East Anglian monk, or living in East Anglia.
2 See Appendix 3.
3 Possibly Bettelin and Ecgberht.
4 One of the few surviving heroic sagas of the early English period.
5 S. A. J. Bradley, *Early English Poetry*, London, 1962, pp 248–50.
6 *LG*, p 3.
7 Ibid.
8 Ibid.
9 Ibid.
10 Norman Scarfe, 'The Place-Name Icklingham – A Preliminary Examination', *East Anglian Archaeology* 3 (1976) pp 127–34.
11 *Ibid.*
12 *LG*, p 3.
13 Ibid.
14 Ibid.
15 *HE* 5, ch 24.
16 See Appendix 3.
17 To whom Guthlac may have been related. Bede describes him as a devout and pious man – *HE* 5, ch 13.
18 Pauline Stafford, *The East Midlands in the Early Middle Ages*, Leicester, 1993, p 107.
19 See ch 3, p 56–69.
20 Bradley, op cit, pp 248–50.
21 Literacy was largely confined to the clergy and the monks.
22 See Map 4, pp 158–9.
23 Darby, op cit, p 1.
24 *LG*, p 93.
25 *LG*, p 107.
26 *LG*, p 95.
27 *LG*, p 2. (See ch 4 in respect of St Botolph and *Icanhoe*, and ch 5 for Sts Etheldreda and Owen.)
28 *LG*, p 111.
29 Matthew Paris – see *LG*, pp 23–4.
30 See Appendix 3.
31 *LG*, p 111.
32 Ingulphus, the late eleventh-century Abbot and alleged historian of

Crowland (his 'History' is now known to have been a fourteenth-century forgery and its author is therefore referred to as 'pseudo-Ingulphus'). See *LG*, p 3.

33 *LG*, p 3.

34 Eadbeorht Praen, a Kentish king of the later eighth century, and also a priest, was spared execution though granted the alternative of blinding instead!

35 *LG*, p 117.

36 See Map 3, p 131.

37 For 'double monasteries', see ch 5, pp 88–9.

38 *LG*, p 169.

39 Ibid.

40 This may have arisen from resistance to the hereditary rule of a monastery, which was uncanonical.

41 According to Orderic Vitalis, she was buried in a church later named after her, the location of which is no longer known. Peakirk Church stands on the site of her former hermitage.

42 *LG*, pp 165–7.

43 Ibid.

44 He became Abbot of Crowland in 716.

45 This is according to the foundation charter of Crowland Abbey, which was in fact a later forgery (common practice amongst the monasteries). *LG*, p 8.

46 St Berthelm, whose relics were venerated at Fécamp in France and, apparently, at Stafford. See Alban Butler, *The Lives of the Saints*, vol 3, London, 1957, p 517.

47 The little that is recorded of her is to be found in pseudo-Ingulphus. She seems to have existed and was probably placed at Crowland in order to keep it as a royal Mercian 'spiritual' dependency.

48 See Appendix 2.

49 His 'Life' (see note 55 below) says that he was born in 779.

50 Stenton, op cit, pp 206–9.

51 Ibid, p 210.

52 She was also referred to (somewhat confusingly) by later chroniclers as 'Etheldreda of Crowland'.

53 He had undertaken a similar arrangement with Northumbria by marrying a daughter to its king – another daughter, Eadburgha, was similarly given in marriage to the King of Wessex.

54 According to the '*Life of St Ethelbert*' (see note 55 below).

55 Osbert de Clare and Geoffrey of Monmouth – both Anglo-Normans. A translation of their texts can be found in Edwin Brooks, ed and trans, *The Life of St Ethelbert, King and Martyr, 779AD–794AD*, Bury St Edmunds, 1996, pp 28–58.

56 Ibid.

57 Hollis, op cit, p 217.

58 Ibid.

59 Nicholas Brooks, *The Early History of the Church of Canterbury*, Leicester, 1984, pp 116, 131 and 184.

60 For the importance of this in terms of royal power, see David Rollason, 'Relic Cults as an Instrument of Royal Policy c. 900–1050', *Anglo-Saxon England* 11 (1983) pp 91–103.

61 Ibid.

62 Ibid.

63 Ibid.

Chapter 7

1 *ASC*, p 55.

2 Campbell, *The Anglo–Saxons*, p 147.

3 See ch 8, p 160–65.

4 *ASC*, p 62.

5 *ASC*, p 68.

6 Ibid.

7 According to Anglo-Norman sources of the twelfth century onwards.

8 A rather curious epithet which some have attributed to his having been a 'beserk' (see Glossary) – there is no evidence for this claim.

9 See ch 1, pp 14–16.

10 *ASC*, p 71.

11 In fact, it was not founded until the post-Danish recovery period.

12 *ASC*, p 71.

13 According to the late, and very dubious, account by Crowland's eleventh-century chronicler, pseudo-Ingulphus.

14 Ibid.

15 These three were also listed as the original founding hermits of the previous century. Clearly this is wrong, or else it is a confusion with the destruction of their relics.

16 Until the 1980s a skull was kept on open display at Crowland Abbey Church, said to have been that of Abbot Theodore. I am told that

it was examined by the British Museum who said that it was many centuries old and of a man over the age of forty with a prominent nose. It showed a wound coming through the eye socket and was consistent with a dagger blow inflicted from behind on a man kneeling down. Theodore was said to have been praying for his enemies when he was killed. Apparently, the skull was stolen from the church during the early 1980s.

17 Pseudo-Ingulphus; see note 13 above.

18 *ASC*, p 71.

19 Asser. *The Life of King Alfred*, ed W. H. Stevenson, Oxford, 1904, p 26.

20 *ASC*, pp 69–71.

21 This whole issue is dealt with by Antonia Gransden, 'Abbo of Fleury's *Passio Sancti Edmundi*', *Revue Bénédictine* 105 (1995) pp 20–78.

22 Ibid, pp 35–7.

23 Ibid, pp 58–9.

24 Aelfric, *Three Lives of English Saints*, ed Michael Winterbottom, Toronto, 1972, pp 67–87.

25 Ibid.

26 Ibid.

27 Ibid.

28 Ibid.

29 Gransden, 'Abbo of Fleury's . . .', p 41.

30 Perhaps power-sharing – a common feature of East Anglian kingship, it would seem.

31 Gransden, 'Abbo of Fleury's . . .', p 41.

32 Ibid, p 36.

33 Ibid, pp 36–8.

34 Ibid.

35 This whole subject is dealt with by Antonia Gransden, 'The Alleged Incorruption of the Body of St Edmund, King and Martyr', *The Antiquaries Journal* 74 (1994) pp 135–55.

See also Norman Scarfe, *Suffolk in the Middle Ages*, Bury St Edmunds, 1986, pp 57–72.

Both Gransden and Scarfe are convinced that what were claimed as the relics of St Edmund were a medieval fraud, though Scarfe is a little more cautious in his assessment, allowing for the possibility of a genuine body at the outset.

36 This whole movement was centred on the Church's successful attempt to free itself from royal control, and to establish its own temporal power, thus requiring the compliance of what it perceived and defined to be 'ideal kings'. The issue is admirably discussed by Stenton, op cit, ch 13, and Campbell, *The Anglo-Saxons*, chs 7 and 8.

37 See Christine Fell, *St Edward, King and Martyr*, Leeds, 1978, in which she assesses the propaganda aspects of the Monastic Reform Movement in terms of its encouragement of the cult of St Edward.

38 Unlike Edward, Edmund had been slain by pagans and enjoyed the posthumous advantage of having been the defender of his people, as well as of the interests of the Church.

39 These would include some of those condemned by Bede (*HE*, ch 6), together with the married clergy who were living under some sort of collective 'rule'.

40 His baptismal name.

41 *ASC*, p 77.

42 Aelfric, in Hollis, op cit.

43 Ibid.

44 V. Galbraith, 'The East Anglian See and the Abbey of Bury St Edmunds', *English Historical Review* 40 (1925) pp 222–4.

45 Bryan Houghton, *St Edmund – King and Martyr*, Lavenham, 1970, ch 5. Fresh Danish attacks probably encouraged the St Edmund cult.

46 Ibid.

47 Three are recorded – Theodred, Bishop of London (and Hoxne?), *c* 950; Theodred I of *Elmham*, *c* 974; Theodred II of *Elmham*, *c* 995.

48 Houghton, op cit, ch 5.

49 This was the monk Aylwin.

50 Gransden, 'The Alleged Incorruption of the Body of St Edmund . . .', p 143.

51 Houghton, op cit, ch 6.

52 Ibid, ch 9.

53 This whole Toulouse claim is based upon the most tenuous and flimsy of evidence and is put forward vigorously, but unconvincingly, by Houghton (op cit, chs 7 and 8).

54 As does Scarfe, *Suffolk in the Middle Ages*, p 59.

55 Ibid.

56 Ibid. (There is disagreement about this – see Gransden, note 50 above.)

57 Ibid.

58 Scarfe, *Suffolk in the Middle Ages*, p 60.

59 Gransden, 'The Alleged Incorruption of the Body of St Edmund . . .', p 144.

60 There seem to be conflicting views on this; the reverse order is another possibility!

61 Some of the wood from this tree was used for a panel screen in Hoxne parish church, where it can still be seen. The panel contains depictions of scenes from Edmund's martyrdom.

62 Margaret Carey-Evans, 'The Contribution of Hoxne to the Cult of St Edmund, King and Martyr in the Middle Ages and Later', *Proceedings of the Suffolk Institute of Archaeology* 36 (1987) pp 182–93, and *Hoxne and St Edmund*, Hoxne, 1993, pp 25–6.

63 Ibid and Carey-Evans, *Hoxne and St Edmund*, pp 21–2.

64 Gransden, 'Abbo of Fleury's . . .', pp 63–75.

65 Dorothy Whitelock, 'Fact and Fiction in the Legend of St Edmund', *Proceedings of the Suffolk Institute of Archaeology* 31 (1969) p 220.

66 Carey-Evans, *Hoxne and St Edmund*, p 12.

67 See Map 4, pp 158–9.

68 West, Stanley, 'A New Site for the Martyrdom of St Edmund', *Proceedings of the Suffolk Institute of Archaeology* 31 (1969).

69 Ibid.

70 The whole issue must be seen in the context of the propaganda of the East Anglian bishops and their struggles with Bury St Edmunds Abbey, as discussed above.

71 Symeon Dunelmis (Symeon of Durham), *Monachi Opera Omnia*, 2, in T. Arnold, ed, *Chronicles and Memorials of Great Britain and Ireland*, The Rolls Series, no 75, London, 1882–85, pp 30–66.

72 Symeon probably just assumed that it was *Hunberht* as he was the last-named bishop on the episcopal list for *Elmham* (entered for 845 – thereafter all was blank!).

Chapter 8

1 *HE* 1, Preface.

2 Dorothy Whitelock, 'The Pre-Viking Age Church in East Anglia', *Anglo-Saxon England* 1(1973), p 19.

3 Ibid.

4 Ibid, p 16.

5 Ibid.

6 Ibid.

7 Williamson, op cit, p 144.

8 Ibid.

9 Ibid.

10 Peter Warner, *The Origins of Suffolk*, Manchester, 1996, p 115.

11 Williamson, op cit, p 148.

12 Ibid, p 149.

13 See ch 1, p 17.

14 *EHD*, p 735.

15 See ch 6, p 114.

16 See Appendix 4.

17 *EHD*, p 817.

18 See ch 7, pp 146–7.

19 See Appendix 3.

20 See Appendix 4.

21 *The Peterborough Chronicle of Hugh Candidus*, trans W. T. Mellows and A. Bell, London, 1949, p 14.

22 Ibid, p 28.

23 Ibid, p 27.

24 See ch 5, p 110.

25 Butler, op cit, vol 3, pp 240–1.

26 Ibid, pp 333–4.

27 David Farmer, *The Oxford Dictionary of Saints*, 4th edn, Oxford, 1997, p 234.

28 A. E. B. Owen, 'Herefrith of Louth, Saint and Bishop; a Problem of Identities', *Lincolnshire History and Archaeology* 15 (1980) pp 15–19.

29 Ibid.

30 See ch 5, pp 108–9.

31 See Appendix 4.

32 *LE*.

33 The name given to the saint could also derive from the Old English '*Eofor*', meaning a wild boar, which figured prominently in Welsh, i.e. Romano-British, mythology. It was an Anglo-Saxon personal name.

34 Dorothy Whitelock, 'The Conversion of the Eastern Danelaw', *Saga Book of the Viking Society* 12 (1943) p 52.

35 See David Farmer, op cit, p 362.

36 Ibid.
37 Ibid, p 30.
38 Ibid, p 387.
39 Ibid.
40 M. R. James, 'Lives of St Walstan', *Norfolk Archaeology* 19 (1917) p 250.
41 Trefor Jones, 'Pilgrim's Progress', *The Norfolk Journal* (October 1997) pp 12–13.
42 Ibid.
43 Ibid.
44 M. R. James, *Suffolk and Norfolk*, p 20.
45 Helen Roeder, *Saints and their Attributes*, London, 1975, p 55.
46 Unless she was descended from the East Anglian royal house, which still seems unlikely.
47 Miranda Green, *Celtic Goddesses*, London, 1995, pp 82–3.
48 Bishop John Bale, *English Votaryes*, 1546.
49 Eamonn Duffy, in *The Stripping of the Altars*, Yale, 1992, doubts the very existence of either Walstan or Blide.
50 James, 'Lives of St Walstan', p 250.
51 Carol Twinch, *In Search of St Walstan*, Norwich, 1995, p 19.
52 Ibid, pp 19–20.
53 Ibid.
54 'The Laws of Cnut', in *EHD*, p 420.
55 The extent to which this might have been is very difficult to assess.
56 See ch 1, p 25.
57 This, of course, refers to the Danes in their homeland and not necessarily in England.
58 Bale, op cit.
59 Jones, op cit, p 13.
60 See Appendix 4.
61 Known as the *Pynson Ballad*.
62 About 200 yards away and the site of the 'Holy House'. The site is in the abbey grounds.
63 Mary Clayton, *The Cult of the Virgin Mary in Anglo-Saxon England*, Cambridge, 1990, pp 139–41.
64 Ibid.
65 The wells were contained within a chapel dedicated to St Lawrence the Martyr.
66 See Clayton, op cit.

67 The 'Holy House' of Loretto in Italy was said to have been transported through the air from the Holy Land by angels.
68 It was written by Thomas of Monmouth.
69 Written by Goscelin de Brakelond.
70 The Book of Revelation.
71 1 November.